The Human Side
of Mergers
and Acquisitions

The Human Side of Mergers and Acquisitions

Managing Collisions Between People, Cultures, and Organizations

By
Anthony F. Buono
James L. Bowditch

BeardBooks
Washington, DC

Library of Congress Cataloging-in-Publication Data

Buono, Anthony F.
    The human side of mergers and acquisitions : managing collisions between people,
cultures, and organizations / by Anthony F. Buono, James L. Bowditch.
        p. cm.
    Originally published: San Francisco : Jossey-Bass Publishers, 1989, in series: The
Jossey-Bass management series..
    Includes bibliographical references and indexes.
    ISBN 1-58798-176-9 (pbk : alk. paper)
    1. Consolidation and merger of corporations--Psychological aspects. 2. Personnel
management. 3. Corporate culture. I Bowditch, James L. II. title.

    HD2746.5.B86 2003
    658.3--dc21

                                                            2003040407

Contents

Tables and Figures

Preface

Mergers, acquisitions, and related downsizing and divestiture activities have been front-page news for so long that we take them for granted. Indeed, the net worth of corporate combinations and consolidations that reached unprecedented $100 billion levels in the early 1980s continues to set new dollar records with each passing year. From 1985 to the third quarter of 1987 alone, over nine thousand mergers and acquisitions were announced, with the estimated combined net worth of the merged organization amounting to more than $520 billion. Although this activity has stimulated numerous debates and congressional inquires into the societal ramifications of what is often called merger mania, the impacts and costs for the individuals caught up in the change – the employees and managers at all organizational levels – have largely been ignored. In fact, until the last few years, there has been little direct, substantive assessment of the human side of such large-scale organizational transformations.

The Human Side of Mergers and Acquisitions is about the impact that mergers and acquisitions have on people in the workplace: the psychological difficulties that people experience, the culture clashes that can emerge in organizations during the post-merger integration period, and the ways in which these problems can manifest themselves – such as communication breakdowns, a "we-they" mentality between the component organizations in a merger, lowered commitment, drops in productivity, organizational power struggles and office politicking, and loss of key organizational members. We adopt primarily an organization development (OD) perspective on mergers and acquisitions: given the myriad problems and difficulties mentioned above, what can be done to facilitate the post-combination integration of two previously autonomous organizations? In choosing this focus we do not mean to imply that the technical aspects of mergers – the operational, financial and strategic concerns that such organizational combinations raise – are insignificant. No merger or acquisition will be successful unless market, legal, and financial analyses are competently carried out, the accounting questions generated by the combination are settled, tax considerations are weighed, antitrust concerns and state legal guidelines are followed, and so forth. An emphasis on such concerns, however, frequently overshadows the reality that a merger of two organizations is actually a merger of individuals and groups.

Anecdotes about mergers and acquisitions underscore how narrowly many participants in organizational combinations interpret their responsibility. Consider the case of a bank president who, when entering into merger negotiations, was instructed by one of his directors that "the only position you should consider is that of the owner" (American Bankers Association and Ernst & Whinney, 1985, p. 4). In actuality, however, there are multiple stakeholders with potentially conflicting interests and values. The key for all those involved in a merger or acquisition is to be able to understand, cope with, and ultimately attempt to temper these differences.

Audience

The Human Side of Mergers and Acquisitions is intended for both academics and practitioners. Scholars researching and teaching the dynamics and processes underlying mergers and acquisitions should find it useful as a detailed account of the human dimension of such combinations. On another level, the book attempts to translate eight years of field study, interviews, organizational surveys, and archival research on mergers and acquisitions into practical prescriptions for organizational members going through a merger, with an emphasis on human resource considerations. Thus, corporate executives, human resource professionals, and consultants involved in organizational consolidations should find this book useful as well.

While we have attempted to be straightforward in our assessment of the concerns and issues inherent in organizational combinations, we have also tried to avoid oversimplifying the psychological, cultural, and human resource considerations. At the same time, it is clear from a managerial perspective that even the simplest verities need repeating if they tend to be ignored in practice. Spelling out these concerns in detail is a necessary first step toward establishing a broader view of organizational mergers, acquisitions, and related large-scale organizational transformations. Our main intent is to focus on the managerial decisions and actions that can make the difference between successful and failed efforts to merge the human resources of two previously autonomous organizations. While we cannot guarantee that any list of guidelines or recommendations can stave off post-acquisition difficulties, by sharpening managerial insight into the dynamics underlying mergers and acquisitions we can begin to explore this particular aspect of organizational change in a more fruitful manner.

Background

This book is based on eight years of field research on the impacts of mergers and acquisitions on organizational members. We initially became immersed in the subject in the way most people get caught up in a merger or acquisition – by chance. In 1976, we were hired by a medium-sized savings bank to develop a survey-based organizational development and quality of work life program. Over a four-year period, we worked extensively with the vice-president of human resources, his staff, and numerous managers and employees to gather information about how employees felt about the bank and how conditions could be improved, and to create "action teams" to address specific issues and concerns raised by the surveys. In 1980, the institution began a friendly merger with another medium-sized savings bank in the same geographical area.

While the quality of work life project ended during this period, we were fortunate to have developed sufficient rapport with many people at the bank that our request to "go along for the ride" and observe and document what took place following the merger was readily accepted. At the time, we really did not realize the uniqueness of the opportunity that lay before us. This serendipitous situation allowed us gradually to gain insight into a complex web of reactions – trust and betrayal, opportunities and restricted options, openness and deception, hope and despair, support and retaliation – dynamics that characterized the dual nature of the merger. The intrigue, culture clashes, hostilities, and tensions that emerged from this friendly merger were frankly much more striking than we had expected.

During this initial research effort, it was often hard to remain objective observers of the process. Many of the people we had worked closely with over a four- to five-year period were losing their jobs or facing severe reductions in status and responsibility and, in general, were being confronted with major questions about their careers. As a result, at times we were unsure whether our own feelings about what was happening to these individuals were biasing our interpretation of what was going on. At that time, John Lewis, one of our colleagues at Boston College, began to work on the bank project as part of an effort to keep us as impartial and objective as possible. John did not have any contact with either organization before the merger – and his assessments corroborated our findings and concerns.

The research on the bank merger ultimately led to other opportunities as the wave of mergers and acquisitions began to swell around us. In these latter situations, we did not have the same organizational and personal allegiances, so the issue of bias was more easily controlled. Although it is still difficult to be dispassionate and objective in such situations, we have attempted to be as impartial as possible in our observations of merger and acquisition processes and outcomes.

During this time, findings from other studies began to reinforce what we were witnessing in our own research. As the 1983 meeting of the Academy of Management in Dallas, Texas, we presented a paper entitled, "When Cultures Collide: The Anatomy of a Merger." Much to our surprise, Phil Mirvis and Amy Sales of Boston University were presenting an almost identically titled paper, "When Cultures Collide: The Case Study of a Corporate Culture," based on their research in an acquisition. Since then, other papers and articles with similar titles have also emphasized the need to explore and assess the sociocultural and psychological ramifications of organizational combinations.

Overview of the Contents

This book has three basic analytic focuses: the human issues presented by mergers at both an individual and cultural level, the organizational issues that these human concerns raise, and the resulting implications for managing the merger and acquisition process. In the first chapter we provide a general overview of the issues raised by combination-related change and its impact on organizational members. Based on these issues and concerns, Chapter Two provides a descriptive account of three organizational combinations we have studied over the past several years: the aforementioned merger between two savings banks of approximately equal size, a series of acquisitions and divestitures involving a large food retailer, and a joint venture with a merger stipulation between two entrepreneurial computer services companies.

The next six chapters explore these and other cases in fuller detail and depth. In Chapter Three we discuss how different types of merger and acquisition activity resemble or differ from each other in strategic intent, degree of friendliness or hostility, and level of integration desired. Chapter Four develops a model of the organizational combination process, exploring salient concerns of organizational members and the kinds of uncertainty and ambiguity they experience. In Chapter Five we explore the effects of organizational consolidation on organizational members, paying particular attention to merger-related stress and to common human reactions, breakdowns in the psychological contract (the unspoken agreement between an organization and its members, which creates a bond between them), and employee expectations during the transformation process. Chapter Six provides an in-depth look at organizational culture, focusing specifically on levels of cultural integration in mergers and acquisitions and on potential culture problems and clashes. On the basis of this assessment, we examine the process of culture change in Chapter Seven, delineating specific problems and difficulties that can occur in organizational combinations.

The final three chapters synthesize this material and detail the implications for those involved in managing such transitions. In Chapter Eight we examine interventions and techniques that can facilitate postcombination integration. In Chapter Nine we discuss the hidden costs associated with organizational combinations, focusing on both employee attitudes and behaviors during a merger or acquisition and on the financial performance of the combined firm. Finally, Chapter Ten summarizes this material and stresses the role that human resource considerations should play in large-scale organizational change. Because much of our analysis presented in this book is based on a series of longitudinal and cross-sectional studies we have conducted since 1980, a complete discussion of research methodology and study design is included in the back of the book.

Acknowledgements

As with any project of this magnitude, this book would never have been completed if it were not for the support of a number of people and organizations. Bentley College and Boston College, our respective institutions, generously provided us with sabbatical leaves, graduate assistants, travel funds to attend conferences, and computer support. Many of our colleagues working in the mergers and acquisitions area have been quite open in sharing their research and ideas with us. Among those influence we would like to acknowledge (alphabetically) are Kenneth DeMeuse, David Jemison, Gerald Ledford, Michael Lubatkin, Ali Malekzadeh, Philip Mirvis, Afsaneh Nahavandi, David Schweiger, Lawrence Stybel, James Walsh, and Gordon Walker. Other colleagues and students who participated in some of the interventions and research discussed in this book also provided invaluable assistance, particularly Peter Carbone, Philip Christiano, Michael Byrne, Timothy Finnegan, Christopher Hogan, John Horrigan, John Lewis, Scott Moy, the late Michael Murphy, John Petrosa, Jeffrey Smith, Jeffrey Shuman, and Roxanne Warniers.

During our eight years of researching this book, we have been fortunate to work closely with some of our graduate students, who assisted in various phases and aspects of the project: Patricia Campbell, Christopher Dimock, Christine Fairnney, Thomas Jenik, Douglas Lifton, T. Nicole Mauro, Dianne Proia, Marshall Sugarman, George Thompson, and Cheryl Tully. We are also indebted to many of our friends and associates who willingly listened to and critiqued our ideas and read and responded to article and chapter drafts – particularly Jean Bartunek, Joseph Byrnes, Jeffrey Cohen, L. Marcy Crary, Dalmar Fisher, Judith Gordon, Aaron Nurick, William Torbet, Nikolas Travlos, and Joseph Weiss. Our wives, Mary Alice and Felicity, have once again been highly supportive of us and more than patient during the completion of our third book together.

This book is dedicated to Christopher, a five-year-old boy who we hope will someday appreciate why "Daddy always sits in front of his computer"; and to all the students who worked with us on this research project. One final point: if it were not for the willingness and openness of the hundreds of people we interviewed, surveyed, and observed as part of our research, this book would truly never have been written. It is our greatest hope that this book will be of use to those involved in a merger or acquisition.

November 1989   Anthony F. Buono
                                              Waltham, Massachusetts

                                              James L. Bowditch
                                              Chestnut Hill, Massachusetts

The Human Side of Mergers
and Acquisitions

One

The Human Toll
of Mergers and Acquisitions

A genuinely dedicated employee, still stunned, ar-
rives home later than usual one Friday afternoon.
His children stop their play and run and greet him.
His wife meets him at the door. Today, he tells
them, the company which has provided his liveli-
hood for the past twelve years has been purchased
by a huge conglomerate. They may ask him to
move to another state; he may have to take a demotion. He could lose his job. Their lives, family ties,
planned career paths are all suddenly at risk. On
this Friday afternoon, the only certainty is that
nothing is certain [Robino and DeMeuse, 1985, p.
33].

"Don't go down the cellar," Chris Donahue's
suicide note warned his family. That's where the
thirty-eight-year-old economist hanged himself,
four days after he lost his $63,000-a-year job at
Heublein, Inc., following a takeover by R. J. Reynolds Industries. A week earlier, he thought he'd
been promised an auspicious Reynolds headquarters job. Instead, he got eleven weeks' severance

pay. "Tell someone at RJR that I loved their generosity and compassion," his note continues. "They owed me more. . . . I know you will think I failed, and maybe I did. . . . I didn't have the strength to endure the pain that was coming" [Magnet, 1984b, p. 44].

"I worked for 18 years and gave them everything I had. Look how I end up, just like a run-over flat can in the street. There is no loyalty, no commitment, no feeling. When it got tough, they bailed out and let us sink [in a hostile acquisition]" [Schweiger and Ivancevich, 1985, p. 47].

"We couldn't make a move [after the acquisition] without being told that our methods were outdated and that we'd have to adjust to the company's way of doing things. When I complained to Corporate about the situation, I was told that if I squawked too loud, my position would be in jeopardy. The net result was that company morale was destroyed and my key people began leaving. It wasn't long before I followed them" [Hayes, 1981, p. 131].

"The rumor mill was hot every single day. I'd go to work and wonder, what next? Why? I had no control over what I heard or the course of events. Then the rumors became reality. First accounting was hit, then marketing, and finally our unit. The whole series of events made me sick. I now have ulcers, migraines, and eating problems. I'm falling apart, and so are my career plans. What a mess!" [Schweiger, Ivancevich, and Power, 1987, p. 128].

As these examples amply illustrate, mergers and acquisitions can have a profound impact on organizational members and their families. Indeed, mergers and acquisitions can sufficiently transform the organizational structures, systems, processes, and cultures of one or both of the firms that people often feel stressed, disoriented, frustrated, confused, and even frightened. On a personal level, these feelings can lead to a sense of loss, psychosomatic difficulties, marital discord, and at the extreme, as one of the illustrations underscores, suicide. On an organizational level, these feelings are typically manifested in lowered commitment and productivity, increased dissatisfaction and disloyalty, high turnover among key managers, leadership and power struggles among the managers who stay, and, in general, a rise in dysfunctional work-related behaviors at all levels of the hierarchy.

While much of this human turmoil may be inevitable as organizations struggle to adapt to increasingly competitive environments, the difficulties involved in such large-scale organizational changes are frequently intensified by questionable management decisions and actions. Moreover, the tragic nature of certain individual reactions, such as Chris Donahue's suicide following his takeover-related job loss, should readily raise our awareness and concern about the potentially disastrous human consequences of corporate acquisitions. Yet, while we seem to know relatively little about the impact of mergers on organizations, groups, and individuals, we seem to know even less about the effectiveness of different approaches that might be used to manage the human side of the merger and acquisition process (Marks, 1982). Unfortunately, as a growing body of evidence strongly suggests, the human and organizational costs of the current wave of mergers, acquisitions, and related divestitures are continuing to mount and take their toll.

Merger Mania

Mergers and acquisitions have become an increasingly common reality of organizational life. It seems that almost daily one hears of corporations—some willingly, some not—involved in such transformations as part of a strategy designed to achieve corporate growth, economies of scale, vertical integration, diversification, and even provision of capital for future leveraged buyouts. The statistics are staggering. Although it is impossible to gauge the exact number of mergers, since only data on publicly held corporations involving transactions of more than $1 million are reported, it is estimated that there have been well over 70,000 mergers in the United States (Smith, 1985; "Quarterly Profile," 1987a, 1987b). According to merger and acquisition specialists W. T. Grim & Company, from 1975 to 1980 there were approximately 13,000 mergers and acquisitions, with an estimated value of $175 billion (Pear, 1981). While the rate of mergers has continued unabated during the 1980s, the estimated dollar value has risen dramatically. The year 1984 witnessed more than 2,500 deals, worth $122 billion ("Do Mergers Really Work?" 1985). In 1985, more than 3,000 mergers and acquisitions were announced, with a total value of $180 billion (Kanter and Seggerman, 1986; McLeod, 1986). According to *Mergers & Acquisitions* magazine ("Quarterly Profile," 1987a, 1987b), in 1986 there were more than 4,200 mergers among U.S. firms, involving almost $200 billion. In the first quarter of 1987 alone, 936 mergers and acquisitions were reported, involving almost $32 billion.

Even the stock market crash of October 1987, which was initially expected to put a halt to the wave of acquisition activity, has failed to slow this movement. In fact, within three months of the crash, Wall Street takeover experts and corporate American empire builders went on an acquisition rampage. Ironically, after the Dow Jones industrial average plummeted, a "marked down" sign went up at a number of firms as companies that were too expensive to take over suddenly became "affordable" (Stein, 1988, p. 25). In January 1988 alone, more than $16 billion worth of takeover attempts was put in play (Lenzner, 1988).

Perhaps even more startling than the amount of merger and acquisition activity per se is the fact that while we have come to expect small and medium-sized firms to be involved in both friendly mergers and hostile takeovers, corporate giants have increasingly gotten into the act. "Megamergers" that affect major segments of the work force are beginning to be commonplace: consider Texas Air's acquisition of Eastern Airlines, Continental Airlines, and People's Express; Chrysler and AMC's merger talks; Burroughs and Sperry's combination into UNISYS;

General Electric's acquisition of RCA; Kodak's acquisition of Sterling Drug; and Shearson Lehman's acquisition of E. F. Hutton. Threats of hostile takeovers of large corporations dominate the business news as well, as exemplified by Revlon's ongoing "courtship" of Gillette and the well-documented forays of such corporate raiders as T. Boone Pickens, Carl Icahn, Irwin Jacobs, and James Goldsmith.

The Human Toll

There is an obvious and compelling case to extend research on mergers and acquisitions to a look at mergers from a human resource point of view. *Fortune* estimates that the 10 largest mergers that took place in 1983 (out of approximately 1,500 consolidations) changed the lives of as many as 220,000 people (Magnet, 1984b, p. 44). In the more than 3,000 mergers that took place in 1985, tens of thousands of employees lost their jobs or were forced into early retirement (Kanter and Seggerman, 1986; McLeod, 1986). During the decade of the 1980s, it is estimated that over a million managers will lose their jobs (Hirsch, 1987). By 1990 in the banking industry alone, some 5,400 banks and 2,500 savings and loans are expected to be involved in mergers affecting the lives of almost 900,000 people (Wishard, 1983). A conservative estimate is that 10 percent of the U.S. work force is currently involved in either a merger, an acquisition, or a related spinoff (Kay, 1987). Assuming roughly 120 million people at work, this assessment means that 12 million individuals are directly affected by transformations of this sort. Moreover, another 36 million are closely related to those experiencing combination-related tensions and trauma.

Even if a merger or takeover fails to materialize, severe human costs and repercussions can still occur. The Revlon Group's well-publicized attempt to take over Gillette Company, for example, led to a major restructuring program to keep future raiders at bay. Gillette laid off 2,400 employees, sold off several marginal businesses, wrote off $205 million in termination costs and operating losses, and more than doubled its long-term debt to $1 billion in a "poison pill" attempt to make the firm less attractive to potential acquirers (Beam, 1987a). Unfortunately, such radical efforts may not save the independent company. Gillette continues to be a takeover target as Revlon persists in its advances and Coniston Partners, a New York–based investment firm, has also gotten into the act (Beam, 1988). Gillette's experience is not an isolated one, as reflected by Goodyear Tire & Rubber Company's attempt to fight off a raid by takeover artist James Goldsmith. Testifying before Congress, Goodyear's Dennis Rich (1987) argued that in the process the firm accumulated $4 billion in debt, cut research and development and capital expenditures, cut advertising and training budgets, closed three plants, sold three major business segments, and eliminated 1,800 salaried and 2,500 hourly employees through early retirement and other separation programs.

Even the mere fear of takeover can lead to widespread corporate restructuring, contributing to layoffs, plant and office closings, and rapid changes in business ownership (Behr and Vise, 1986b). Kroger Company, a successful supermarket chain that posted $181 million in profits in 1985, was startled by Dart Group Corporation's multibillion-dollar hostile takeover bid for Safeway Stores, Inc. Kroger management became convinced that unless it took aggressive steps to boost the company's stock price by reducing overhead, the company would be the target of a similar bid. As a result, the firm drastically cut its employee population to reduce its expenses by 25 percent (Behr and Vise, 1986a).

Beyond the human costs posed by the specter of large-scale reductions in force, merger-related organizational restructurings can traumatize and alienate people at all organizational levels. According to recent polls taken by the Opinion Research Corporation, there have been drastic declines in feelings of job security among executives and middle managers: from 1982 to 1986, the proportion of executives who reported that they felt "very secure" in their jobs dropped from 45 percent to 34 percent; among middle managers, the decline was from 43 percent to 27 percent (Behr and Vise, 1986a, p. 21). These perceptions appear to be well founded. During the first half of this decade alone, mergers and corporate cutbacks have precipitated a net reduction of approximately 500,000 managerial and professional jobs, convincing organizational members that companies will not return their loyalty. As a result, those who remain in an organization may feel betrayed by their leaders, and there is often a drastic change in their work patterns. Rising disaffection can have significant implications for organizations, from relatively minor personnel matters, such as an employee's refusal to relocate, to subtle slowdowns in work activity and lowered work goals, to increases in turnover, employee theft, and even attempts to sabotage corporate efforts (O'Boyle, 1985).

Assessing Merger and Acquisition Outcomes

As the preceding discussion strongly suggests, corporate empire builders have increasingly placed their faith in organizational growth through merger and acquisition. A basic concern, however, is that many firms appear to overestimate the potential benefits of such organizational combinations and the ease with which they can be made successful. It is often assumed, for instance, that merging companies will increase market share, reduce raw material costs and uncertainties through vertical integration, and increase productivity through consolidation and reduction of the aggregate number of employees. Yet, despite seemingly favorable strategic, financial, and operational assessments made during feasibility studies, research suggests that mergers have less than a 50-50 chance of being successful (Pritchett, 1985). Although it has been suggested that hindsight after one merger should become foresight for the next (American Bankers Association and Ernst & Whinney, 1985, p. 5), the process of postmerger integration can be sufficiently troublesome for even experienced firms that within two years many acquisitions wind up as divestitures. Research indicates that while firms can learn general lessons from acquisition activities, senior managers typically fail to draw on past merger and acquisition experiences (Haspeslagh and Jemison, 1987). During his tenure with General Instrument, General Electric, and ITT, for example, Yunker (1983), who was responsible for nine new or recent acquisitions, reports that recurring problems between people at the corporate parent headquarters and those of the acquired firms often resulted in performance outcomes that fell far short of expectations. As *Business Week* (''Do Mergers Really Work?'' 1985, p. 88) estimates, one out of every three acquisitions is later undone.

It is important to note, of course, that success has both a qualitative and a quantitative dimension, and there are disagreements as to what actually constitutes a successful merger or acquisition (Lubatkin and Shrieves, 1986; Pritchett, 1985). One basic problem concerns the diversity of groups involved. What may be beneficial for the stockholders of an acquired firm, for example, may have quite a different effect on the company's employees and the stockholders of the acquiring firm. Moreover, a merger that might initially appear to be a disaster might in fact blossom over the long run and do quite well financially, while an acquisition that looks like a success may later turn into a financial catastrophe. This situation is compounded by criticisms of accounting-based measures such as return on assets or sales growth in that they capture only one dimension of organizational performance (Dalton and others, 1980; Ford and Schellenberg, 1982), that the significance of each measure can vary widely across different industries and strategic contexts (Cameron and Whetten, 1981; Gupta and Govindarajan, 1984), and that they are fraught with measurement problems (Lev and Sundar, 1979; Rappaport, 1983). Thus, even among the financial experts there is disagreement concerning how to effectively measure merger and acquisition success.

Despite these difficulties, the evidence that is beginning to mount is startling. A growing number of studies suggest that mergers fail to lead to positive performance outcomes (Halpern, 1983; Jensen and Ruback, 1983), that acquiring firms often perform more poorly than nonacquiring firms (Bradford, 1977; Howard, 1978; Michel and Shaked, 1985), that both conglomerate mergers and horizontal acquisitions can lead to substantial losses in market share (Mueller, 1985), that mergers do not reliably yield the desired financial returns (Lubatkin, 1983), and that most firms experience significant difficulties during the post-merger integration period (''Do Mergers Really Work?'' 1985;

Louis, 1982; Yunker, 1983). Moreover, recent research using the Federal Trade Commission large merger series raises a number of questions about merger and acquisition predictions based on modern financial theory: acquisitions of unrelated companies were found to perform better than mergers of related firms (Montgomery and Wilson, 1986); and mergers tended to increase rather than decrease corporate uncertainty and risk (Lubatkin and O'Neil, 1987). A researcher for the Hay Group consulting firm argues that approximately one-third of all acquired firms are sold off within five years and that 90 percent of mergers never live up to their expectations (Lefkoe, 1987). Mitchell and Company, a consulting firm based in Cambridge, Massachusetts, found that during the first half of the 1980s, fewer than 1 percent of the U.S.-based medium- to large-sized companies made acquisitions that improved share price (Metz, 1985). A decade-long study by Louis (1982) found that only two of the ten mergers anayzed made it through the study period without experiencing significant difficulties. As a result, meaningful questions have begun to be raised concerning the rather poor showing of the high level of merger and acquisition activity. Accordingly, a 1985 *Business Week* cover story posed the question "Do Mergers Really Work?" (1985). The conclusion— "not very often."

A Financial Perspective. Historically, writings about mergers and acquisitions have been based on economic and financial assessments. Most of these studies are based on what might be termed the economic rationality assumption; that is, the assumption that individuals will do what seems to be in their best economic interests. Thus, the motives underlying mergers are typically attributed to such business performance criteria as size and growth, economies of scale, profitability, return on shares, and increases in market share and market power (Goldberg, 1983). Financial theorists argue that as long as the prospective returns of merging firms are not perfectly correlated, the merged entity will yield "an income stream for its owners" that should translate into increased shareholder wealth (Michel and Shaked, 1985, p. 109).

Given this focus, it is not surprising to find that there are a number of economic and financial explanations as to why many mergers and acquisitions fail to achieve their intended results. First, since acquiring companies often use stock of low value in the acquisition, there is an inevitable dilution of earning per share, book value per share, and return on equity (Metz, 1985). Second, the economic decision rule to determine whether a company should buy another is "buy if the value-added (that is, increase in market value) exceeds the price premium (that is, the excess to be paid above the stand-alone value of the selling company)" (Hopkins, 1983, p. 33). In highly volatile environments, however, valuation planning—establishing the proper transaction price and identifying financial and tax reporting opportunities—can be quite difficult (Keenan, 1982; Robinson, 1983). Many banks, for example, have been criticized for paying far more for interstate acquisitions than the real value they receive in return (Cates, 1985; Marshall, 1985). Thus, economic benefits to shareholders rarely accrue. Third, the acquisition may be so large that the acquirer finds it difficult to service the acquired firm's debt. At times, goodwill charges can cripple the acquiring company's earning power (LaGesse, 1984; Metz, 1985). Finally, an unfavorable economic climate can also lead to postmerger difficulties.

A Human Resource Perspective. While these economic and financial problems can contribute to the relatively low incidence of merger and acquisition success, an emerging concern deals with the individuals involved in the combination. Some mergers do fail because of financial and economic reasons. However, because of the myriad questions about merger and acquisition success, attention has begun to shift toward human resource concerns, the cultural ramifications of merger activity, management of the overall combination process, and specific efforts aimed at post-combination integration. In fact, most of the problems that adversely affect the performance of a merged firm are suggested to be internally generated by the acquirers and by dynamics in the new entity (Yunker, 1983). The reality may be that many merger- and acquisition-related difficulties are simply self-inflicted.

Each functional area within a business will have its own unique set of difficulties to deal with following a merger or acquisition (Yunker, 1983). Financial and accounting considerations, marketing and public relations issues, technology and manufacturing and service concerns, and employee benefit and compensation schedules all need to be assessed and resolved. Yet underlying these concerns are the tensions that can emerge between members of the different entities. Indeed, from a managerial perspective, there is a significant need to go beyond strategic, financial, and operational considerations per se and to examine the organizational dynamics and personal issues that emerge during the merger process.

There are numerous legitimate issues and questions that linger in people's minds in a merger period. Will my employment be terminated? Will I get a promotion? A demotion? Will I have to relocate? What will happen to my benefits? Compensation? What kind of organization will we be? What is our mission? What are the values of the new organization? What types of transitions will the firm undergo? How are we going to deal with all this change? What does all this mean for *me?* As a result, merger-related stress becomes commonplace (Schweiger and Ivancevich, 1985), psychological shock waves ripple through the organizations (Pritchett, 1985), and people experience what has been termed the "merger syndrome," a highly defensive, fear-the-worst response to the uncertainties involved (Marks and Mirvis, 1985, 1986).

Mergers and Acquisitions as Organizational Transformation. A series of questions from an organizational viewpoint also needs to be addressed. What is our obligation to the employees? What functions are necessary? How many people are needed to make the new organization effective? How do you get employees to concentrate on their jobs instead of worrying about their careers? How do you achieve essential economies of scale by retaining or attracting those people you want and dismissing those no longer needed in a way that is perceived as equitable in both appearance and fact? Can this be done without frightening and alienating the ones who remain? Should headquarters and

administrative functions be consolidated at existing or new locations? How can the company effectively maintain its operations
when so much time and attention seem to be focused on merger
discussions? (Geber, 1987; Gerard, 1986).

Since mergers and acquisitions can readily change the
nature and character of the organizations in question, they can
be usefully conceived of as a form of organizational transformation, a process of large-scale change characterized by a high
level of complexity, multiple transitions, uncertain future states,
and long-term time frames (Kilmann, Covin, and Associates,
1988; Kozmetsky, 1985). During a merger, of course, some
employees may find that little has actually changed. For a number of other organizational members, however, behaviors that
were once sanctioned by the firm may no longer be rewarded
or approved and may, in fact, be punished. Still others may
find that their services are no longer valued or needed. The result
may very well be lowered organizational commitment and satisfaction and behaviors that attempt to work against what the
organization is attempting to accomplish. Accordingly, research
has indicated that five to seven years are typically needed for
employees to feel truly assimilated in the combined entity (Stybel,
1986). Thus, managers involved in a merger or acquisition must
confront the types of problems and concerns that challenge any
major shift in organizational form, structure, or process.

Although the costs and pressures associated with such
organizational transformations increase with the level of threat
involved (for example, a hostile takeover or reduction in force),
even supposedly nonthreatening transformations (such as a
"friendly" merger) can take their toll on these individuals (Buono,
Bowditch, and Lewis, 1985). Such major organizational changes
and the uncertainties related to the transformation can precipitate high levels of stress, tension, anxiety, and resentment
on the part of many organizational members (Ackerman, 1982;
Connolly, 1977; Nadler, 1982; Kahn and others, 1964). The
stakes are quite high, the number of people that are involved
is relatively large, the emotional context is intense, and the
timing of significant changes is often unpredictable. As a result,
the potential for dysfunctional interactions and outcomes and

personal and organizational conflicts is also quite high. Yet, despite the magnitude of these changes and the outcomes involved, organizational transformations have been criticized as being generally "undermanaged," especially at the human resource level (Kimberly and Quinn, 1984; McCaskey, 1979b).

There are two basic reasons for which the human dynamics underlying organizational transformations are poorly managed (Kimberly and Quinn, 1984, p. 4). First, since technical issues generally have a "right- and wrong-way" mentality associated with them, managers often prefer to focus at that level. Errors tend to be relatively easy to find, and solutions can easily be formulated. Second, behavioral issues tend to be less concrete and easier to dismiss ante facto. Since human resource issues and their implications often cannot be effectively measured in quantitative terms, "soft" issues concerning beliefs and values, attitudes, commitment, interpersonal and organizational communication needs, and so forth are often discarded as irrelevant (American Bankers Association and Ernst & Whinney, 1985). Managers often fail to go beyond their initial reactions in order to critically examine the deeper concerns raised by such "people issues," avoiding the time and tension associated with such work. It has been suggested, however, that this type of approach is as effective in successfully bringing about large-scale organizational change as "changing the deck chairs on the Titanic" (Bice, 1986).

The basic problem, of course, is that such human resource issues are highly sensitive and often controversial at all organizational levels. The tendency, therefore, is to avoid them as much as possible, especially during preacquisition and negotiation phases. The danger is that once people make such hardnosed choices, they quickly acquire a momentum of their own and reinforce a hard-line approach to such issues (Barnes, 1981). This dynamic is especially troublesome in mergers and acquisitions, and the escalating momentum and desire to complete the acquisition process quickly often lead to premature solutions, less consideration of integration issues, and, in general, less probability of a successful outcome (Jemison and Sitkin, 1986b).

Given this reality, a number of problems pervade such large-scale organizational combinations. First, preoccupation with technical concerns hinders critical evaluation of the subtler processes involved. As a result, managers often find themselves trapped in various situations, since specific courses of action tend to set boundaries on subsequent strategies. In many instances, the consequences are poor decisions. Unfortunately, this problem is usually compounded at the human resource level, especially since the behavioral aspects of such transformations evolve more by default than by design (Kimberly and Quinn, 1984).

It is important to realize, however, that for an organizational transformation to be successful, there must be a widespread acceptance of the need for change at all levels of the hierarchy. For organizational members to develop sufficient commitment to the change, there must be a discontinuity with the past and a process of "letting go" of it. There must be a departure from old beliefs and habits. In essence, this requires a reframing process that attempts to create or discover new opportunities in and for the organization, a shift in the perceptions of organizational members, and the emergence of a new direction that is qualitatively and quantitatively different from the old (Levy, 1986).

Dilemmas and Paradoxes in Mergers and Acquisitions

There is general agreement among those researchers who have studied the merger and acquisition process that the personal, interpersonal, group, and intergroup dynamics following the actual combination of two firms are significant determinants of merger success or failure. One of the concerns that has emerged in our research, however, is that there is a paradoxical quality to many of these human and managerial interactions. These paradoxes and dilemmas are manifested in conflicting views about such issues as (1) the pace and the rate of merger-related changes; (2) the timing, type, and amount of information that should be shared with employees; (3) the manageability of organizational culture; (4) the relationship between strategic significance and successful interfirm integration; (5) prescriptions and unqualified generalizations about postacquisition tactics and strategies; and (6) the illusion of managerial control that typically exists during a merger or acquisition.

Slow Change Versus Quick Change. Mergers and acquisitions mean change. As management consultant Laurence Stybel argues, "You don't have a merger because you're happy with the status quo. You buy a company to make it more efficient, more profitable" (Kowal, 1986, p. 23B). Following a merger or acquisition, a complex set of organizational, managerial, and personal changes is inevitable (O'Boyle and Russell, 1984; Wells and Hymowitz, 1984). Typically, the questions raised by employees are focused not on whether there will be management and organizational changes but rather on how extensive those changes will be and how quickly they will take place.

While there may be a consensus that change is a reality of merger and acquisition activity, there is considerable disagreement about the rate and amount of change that should occur. Citicorp's David Franzen (1987), for example, argues that there is a "window of opportunity" of 100 days following an acquisition. During this period, people expect change; thus, his prescription is "why disappoint them?" At the same time, there is a need to fully understand systems, prepare people for the change, and carefully lay the foundation for what is to come. These activities take time. Moreover, others argue that while it may be beneficial to make changes early in the process, it is wise to hold off on "controversial" changes such as reorganizations or relocations (Smith, 1985, p. 114). On the basis of his experience in nine mergers and acquisitions, Yunker (1983) argues that firms should "go slow." Companies often "shoot themselves in the foot" by attempting to change too much, too quickly. In some areas, such as personnel and benefits, he argues that as long as five years should be allowed for complete integration.

Thus, it seems that since employees expect change, telling them that little will actually change undermines the credibility of top management. Trying to push for change too quickly, however, can generate resentment, dissatisfaction, and the loss of key personnel. The basic question that needs to be addressed is what actually constitutes "too fast" or "too much" change.

Information Sharing—How Much Is Enough. When executives are faced with a merger or acquisition, basic questions emerge in their minds concerning the nature and timing of communication to employees. Although it has been suggested that initial merger negotiations be carried out in secret to minimize uncertainty among organizational members at all levels (Graves, 1981), most research argues that the creation of formal, internal communication mechanisms as early as possible in the process may limit much of the anxiety otherwise fueled by rumors, the grapevine, or even outside news reports (Buono, Bowditch, and Lewis, 1988; Marks, 1982).

A basic problem, however, is that regardless of the openness and level of communication, members of an acquired organization will usually still maintain feelings of suspicion and never feel fully informed (Marks, 1982). In a period of stress and uncertainty, people's sensitivity is increased, and they become more attentive to the congruence and detail of organizational communications (Marks and Mirvis, 1985). Since the actual details of the merger or acquisition have to be worked out over a period of several months or even years after the combination, management rarely has accurate answers to employee questions. This situation fuels suspicions and a feeling of being kept "in the dark"—regardless of the amount and content of the communication.

The Manageability of Organizational Culture. It is increasingly being recognized that organizational culture conflicts and clashes are an underlying determinant of merger and acquisition failure. As the vice-president for human resources of a large midwestern bank argued, "A year following this past merger I told our CEO that we must not do another merger without having a cultural strategy" (American Bankers Association and Ernst & Whinney, 1985, p. 43). Good advice? Yes, but. . . . A senior vice-president for human resources, in talking about a "quadruple cultural clash" that took place when four savings institutions merged during a year and a half, described the process as incredibly chaotic: "all the cultures had to be merged," yet "we still have vestiges of the different cultures" ("Successful Mergers . . . ," 1983, p. 94). How feasible are attempts at such sweeping culture change?

Culture is a rather amorphous concept, and there are differences of opinion as to whether culture *shapes* or can be *used to shape* a given situation (Ouchi and Wilkins, 1985). One perspective, which is reflected in the popular literature, views culture as a managerial tool that can be used to create "strong" organizations. In contrast, a quite different orientation, characteristic of a growing body of empirical work, sees culture as something that *is,* an existential reality that can serve as a constraint to large-scale organizational change. This distinction is obviously important when managers are thinking about attempts to bring about culture change. True organizational culture change may be much more difficult to manage than many of us would like to believe.

The Paradox of Strategic Significance. During the past two decades, conglomerate mergers and acquisitions have come under increased scrutiny and criticism. While a number of reasons underlie this, the two primary factors are (1) the added level of complexity that top management must deal with in trying to understand the variety of industries in which the different businesses operate and (2) the virtual impossibility of imposing uniform business policies across the components of a highly unrelated company (Hall, 1987). In essence, since the lack of a central thrust in highly diversified firms would be a barrier to effective and efficient organizational operations, related and concentric diversification mergers and acquisitions were thought to result in stronger firm performance than would unrelated combinations (Lubatkin and Shrieves, 1986; Rumelt, 1974). Accordingly, managerial interventions in an acquired firm would be more effective when the parent company's managers were familiar with the product, market, and technical characteristic of the target firm (Bettis and Hall, 1982).

While such criticisms may make sense from a business strategy point of view, ironically, the more salient and significant a particular merger or acquisition is to an organization, the less likely it is that the combination will fulfill both its promise and its purpose (Jemison, 1986a; Lubatkin and O'Neil, 1987). In general, the more important a target firm becomes to an acquirer, the more the parent company will attempt to control the target firm in order to ensure that the desired results are achieved. This heightened involvement undermines much of the iterative, evolutionary nature of the postcombination integration process, raises antagonisms between the different employee groups, and reduces the chances for the two companies to effectively work together to facilitate integration. In mergers and acquisitions of related firms, organizational problems are further intensified by the ever-present threat of reductions in force that comes with consolidation of departments and units, tensions between management styles, and questions of superiority concerning different control systems (Kitching, 1967). In many combinations of unrelated companies, for example, the goal is financial diversification rather than a significant degree of operational integration. In such situations, employees tend to feel more assured that their firm will remain intact. In mergers of related firms, by contrast, the immediate perception is that the combination was undertaken to achieve greater efficiency and economies of scale (Imberman, 1985). Employees logically expect the loss of company identification, changes in reporting relationships, elimination of overlapping jobs, and geographical transfers, which exacerbate tensions and problems between the firms.

Postcombination Strategies. It has been suggested that the success of an acquisition is determined not by the acquisition choice itself but rather by the underlying development strategy that is used to guide the process (Haspeslagh and Jemison, 1987). While it is indeed important to explore and understand this facet of merger and acquisition activity, it is just as important to underscore the fact that different types of mergers and acquisitions may require different types of combination strategies. Research, for example, has indicated that the actual integration of merging firms can vary, depending on the primary link of the sought-after business function, such as finance, marketing, or manufacturing (Howell, 1970). Yet many merger prescriptions tend to be sweeping generalizations, without consideration of the potential uniqueness of each combination.

If different mergers or acquisitions unfold in quite different ways, distinctions need to be made about general tendencies or processes and more idiosyncratic dynamics. Merger-related prescriptions, therefore, should be viewed as general guidelines that may facilitate the integration of acquiring and acquired companies. The reality may be that managing the merger process will remain much more of an art than a science.

The Illusion of Managerial Control. A main concern during a merger is keeping control of a situation during an increasingly hectic and tension-laden period. While managerial work in general has been described as consisting of unrelenting, highly open-ended activities that are characterized by brevity, variety, and fragmentation (Mintzberg, 1980), this is especially the case during a merger or acquisition. Yet most managers still think that they have to be in total control, that if they feel overwhelmed by what is going on around them, they are failures. Mintzberg (1980, p. xvi), for example, reports that after his assessment of the hectic nature of managerial work was published, managers kept telling him, "You make me feel so good. All this time I thought I was doing something wrong. While *I* was constantly being interrupted, *they* were all planning, organizing, coordinating, and controlling."

Once the intention to merge with or acquire another firm is announced, change is inevitable, and normal business processes and activities begin to break down as a period of tumult sets in (Darlin and Guiles, 1984; Levin, 1984; Wells and Hymowitz, 1984). Acquisitions are often described as having "a life of their own," with shifting periods of waiting and frenzied activities, a sense of escalating momentum, cascading minor changes, rising tensions and conflicts, and stressful uncertainties (Buono, Bowditch, and Lewis, 1988; Jemison and Sitkin, 1986b; Marks and Mirvis, 1985). This view presents quite a striking contrast to the traditional depiction of mergers and acquisitions as thoughtfully planned and calculated strategic acts.

In an effort to gain control of such a frenetic situation, managers often develop what has been referred to as "merger myopia," a type of nearsightedness to merger-related problems that affects virtually all decisions (Mangum, 1984, p. 26). Especially under conditions of increasing uncertainty, problems and issues are seen in "either/or" terms. Rather than carefully assessing the situation, exploring alternative approaches, and realizing that things are not always as they seem, managers often become entrenched in a particular "solution." While this tendency obviously limits options, it is exacerbated in that people often become emotionally attached to a choice and view it as either good or bad (Barnes, 1981). As a result, a crisis-management mentality develops, which leads to premature closure of merger-related issues. While this orientation gives managers and executives the illusion that they are in control of the process, early merger strategies are usually overly simplistic, one-sided, and dysfunctional to the overall success of the combination (Jemison and Sitkin, 1986b; Marks and Mirvis, 1986).

Rather than thinking in terms of *managing* the merger and acquisition process, a more useful perspective seems to be *coping* with many of the difficulties, uncertainties, and tensions that will inevitably emerge. While this statement should not be interpreted to mean that mergers and acquisitions cannot be managed, managing something is too often viewed as exerting control. Planning and control, however, can have immense dysfunctional consequences for what the organization is attempting to accomplish. When met with tighter controls, such dysfunctions can precipitate even larger and more convoluted dysfunctions (Kelly, 1980).

Our study of the dynamics of mergers and acquisitions suggests that it is virtually impossible to prevent people's fears, uncertainties, stresses, and tensions from emerging and to stop them from disrupting organizational processes. There are simply too many things that are beyond the manager's sphere of control. At the same time, the fact that we lack complete control over the merger and acquisition process does not mean that we do not have any control. As this book will explore, the key is to understand the "controllables" and "uncontrollables" in mergers and acquisitions and to identify the areas that can be managed in the traditional sense and those that can most effectively be "managed" through coping strategies.

Important Issues to Be Addressed

Despite the significance of these human and organizational considerations, merger-related analyses are dominated by strategic, financial, and operational concerns. Much of the analysis of merger and acquisition activity still focuses on the negotiations that precede the actual combining of the firms (Mirvis, 1985). For instance, Lee and Colman's (1981) *Handbook of Mergers, Acquisitions and Buyouts,* which contains more than 700 pages on the complexities of acquiring another firm, devotes fewer than 10 pages to the personal and personnel dynamics involved. Wallner and Greve's (1982) *How to Do a Leveraged Buyout or Acquisition* does not even mention human resources as a consideration. While Smith's (1985) *Handbook of Strategic Growth Through Mergers and Acquisitions* does deal with some of the dynamics of postmerger integration, it does so in a highly sketchy manner. Finally, in his discussion of merger evaluation, Hopkins (1983, p. 87) suggests that five groups need to be considered: directors of the buying company, directors of the selling company, security analysts, buying shareholders, and selling shareholders. There is no mention of executive and managerial talent or human resource considerations at any level.

As a way of assuring merger and acquisition compatibility, most analysts have stressed the strategic fit between the merger partners (or the acquirer and its target) and the importance of ensuring overall strategic synergy (Ansoff, Bradenburg, Portner, and Radosevich, 1971; Salter and Weinhold, 1979; Jemison and Sitkin, 1986a). It seems more useful, however, to think of strategic fit as an important but not sufficient condition for acquisition success (Jemison and Sitkin, 1986b). Because of the myriad problems associated with postcombination success, attention should continue to shift toward a deeper understanding of human resource issues, the cultural implications of interfirm consolidation, and management processes during the postcombination transition period. In fact, once the idea that mergers and acquisitions are best understood as a "manifestation of the struggle for corporate control rather than merely the search for immediate profits'' (Walter, 1985a, p. 302) is acknowledged, the importance of the human side of these transformations readily becomes apparent.

Yet, although there has been a slowly growing focus on the human, organizational, and managerial aspects of mergers and acquisitions, there has been relatively little systematic study of such phenomena. Indeed, while the importance of early merger planning has been empirically documented (Ansoff, Bradenburg, Portner, and Radosevich, 1971; Kitching, 1967), it has been harder to examine the consequences of managerial actions once a merger has taken place. The difficulties of studying this aspect of the combination process are typically attributed to a lack of timely access to merging firms, problems surrounding organizational consent, and availability of research resources and appropriate methodologies for longitudinal study (Alarik and Edstrom, 1983). Moreover, much of the literature that does exist is anecdotal and oriented toward either surviving the "aftermath" (for example, "How to Survive . . . ," 1979; Hubbart, 1982; Thompson, 1982) or maintaining organizational morale and productivity (for example, Hayes, 1979; Sinetar, 1981).

What has been less fully documented is (1) the dynamics and processes underlying mergers and acquisitions; (2) the attitudes and perceptions of the merger partners regarding their old and newly formed organizations; (3) the processes through which these perceptions and attitudes are formed; (4) the types of uncertainties and ambiguities involved in the transformation; and (5) ways in which managers may facilitate the combining of different organizations. With the needs and interests of both scholars and practitioners in mind, this book attempts to delve into these concerns to (1) broaden the perspectives through which mergers and acquisitions are viewed and (2) develop a fuller understanding of the human dynamics involved in such large-scale organizational changes.

While organizations may give lip service to the idea that ''people are our most important asset,'' research indicates that human resource considerations play a relatively small role in merger and acquisition decisions (Hirsch, 1987; Robino and

DeMeuse, 1985; Schweiger and Ivancevich, 1985). It is important to emphasize, however, that efforts to minimize the pain
and suffering faced by organizational members in a merger or
acquisition should not be simply dismissed as a humanistic effort to control the harsh realities of the managerial world. What
is often overlooked is that mergers and acquisitions not only
create upheaval in the lives of individuals but inevitably disrupt
the organizations involved as well. The outcome is typically
manifested in general declines in employee performance and
a postcombination "slump" characterized by losses in productivity, revenues, and business opportunities (Buono, Bowditch,
and Nurick, 1987; Sinetar, 1981; Pritchett, 1985). Yet most
analysts involved in merger and acquisition assessments usually
disregard the human dynamics and financial ramifications of
such postcombination outcomes.

Two

The Tales of Three
Organizational Combinations

As a way of portraying some of the human dynamics, processes, and hidden costs of merger and acquisition activity, this chapter provides a descriptive account of three organizational combinations: (1) a merger between two approximately equal-sized savings banks; (2) a series of acquisitions involving a large food retailer that resulted in divestiture; and (3) a joint venture with a merger stipulation between two entrepreneurial computer services firms. In each of these consolidations, top management intended to create a more effective and efficient organization. As the outcomes suggest, however, these goals were not as simple or as straightforward as expected. The dilemmas and paradoxes outlined in Chapter One pervaded the process of combining the different firms and precipitated a number of problems and difficulties for the organizations and their management.

A large proportion of each employee population was significantly dislocated by the change efforts, which in turn had repercussions for individual and organizational performance. While the magnitude of these changes varies across the cases, in each instance there were a number of critical turning points where appropriate managerial intervention could have ameliorated the situation. Yet the top managers often appeared to have little understanding of the consequences that these changes would have for their employees or for the overall performance of their organizations.

The cases are real and, as descriptive accounts of other mergers and acquisitions throughout the book will highlight, quite representative of these types of organizational combinations. For purposes of confidentiality, however, pseudonyms are used for the companies. The research is based on a multimethod field study design involving both longitudinal and cross-sectional studies carried out between 1980 and 1987. Information on the organizations and their cultures was gathered through in-depth interviews with cross sections of organizational members, observations, and archival data. With a method based on the Bowditch and Buono (1982) survey feedback model, organizational climate profiles were obtained through a series of population and sample surveys employed across the study period. Data collection efforts were as uniform as possible across the three study sites. The analysis was guided by what Lawler (1985) has referred to as participative research, in which key organizational members assisted in interpreting the data. (A full discussion and overview of the research process are presented in the Appendix.)

A Bank Merger

In August 1981, Urban Bank and Suburban Bank, two medium-sized mutual savings banks located in the Northeast, formally began a "friendly" merger. With the instability in the thrift industry, the merger was part of a strategic effort to create a stronger, more competitive institution. Although the plan was largely supported by members of both banks, within a matter of months following the merger, employee commitment to the combination drastically declined, job satisfaction and related attitudes plummeted, and overall productivity and profitability deteriorated. What had initially seemed to be a "perfect marriage" quickly became a battleground between warring camps.

Background. Prior to the merger, Urban Bank was the fourth-largest savings bank in the state, with an asset base of $600 million. In addition to the main office, located in the heart of a major metropolitan city, the institution had a network of thirteen branches and 325 full-time employees. As a result of its urban setting and the location of its branches, the institution served a largely blue-collar clientele. It operated with a divisional structure and was rather bureaucratic in nature, with clearly defined and bounded jobs at all levels.

Suburban Bank was the fifth-largest savings bank in the state, with approximately $500 million in assets and 275 employees. In contrast to Urban Bank, the institution had its headquarters and all branches in relatively prosperous suburban areas. Its customer base was largely professional and white collar. The bank operated with a centrally controlled functional organization, but with individual jobs more loosely defined, particularly at the managerial and professional levels. For instance, there was a more complete file of job descriptions for all employees at Urban Bank, while at Suburban Bank the expressed policy was that employees should do what was needed, especially at the professional level, for the success of the bank.

As mutual savings banks, neither institution has any stockholders. Instead, the basic corporate powers of the banks are held by corporators—individuals who, in effect, have the voting power of corporate stockholders but no financial interest in or benefit from the bank. Bank trustees, who serve the role that directors do in most other corporations, are elected from among the corporators.

Although these firms were approximately equal-sized savings banks operating in the same Standard Metropolitan Statistical Area (SMSA), each employee group saw itself as quite different from the other. Members of Urban Bank perceived the institution as a very people-oriented, egalitarian, but rather bureaucratic type of organization, whose chief executive officer (CEO) and upper-level managers encouraged a participative management style. Employees of Suburban Bank, by contrast, characterized their organization as more task-oriented, an authoritarian workplace whose CEO was the key source of power and decision making. In fact, at the time of the merger the state banking commissioner described the two banks as "as different as you could possibly get—[Urban Bank] very collegial and consensual and [Suburban Bank] totally autocratic."

Although the employees described the organizational cultures of these two banks as almost extreme types, a comparison of quality-of-work-life surveys taken in the two institutions in

1979–80, prior to any merger-related discussions, indicates that both employee groups were quite accepting of their respective organizations (see the first two columns in Table 1). While there were differences in levels of premerger satisfaction on some measures (for example, training effectiveness, job challenge), similar proportions of employees reported pride in working for their bank and satisfaction with its system of compensation and advancement, the context of their work, and interpersonal relations on the job. Despite the different realities of organizational life in the two banks, the conditions had existed for an extended period of time, shaped and were shaped by quite divergent values and beliefs, and were viewed as "the way things should be."

The Merger. The idea for the merger began during an informal conversation between Urban and Suburban Banks' CEOs as they were returning from an industry association meeting in mid-1980. As mentioned above, during this period the banking industry in general and thrifts in particular were experiencing difficult times. As the CEOs left what they referred to as a "doom and gloom" meeting, they agreed that industry and general economic conditions were making it very difficult for even medium-sized savings banks to survive. They continued their discussion over the next several months and finally agreed that a merger between the two organizations was a sound idea. Since the banks were not in immediate competition with each other for either territory or clientele, and they were roughly the same size and had similar perceived goals, the CEOs reasoned that a merger would not only create a stronger, more competitive institution but in the long run could significantly expand the banks' sphere of influence as well.

In early 1981, the employees of both banks were officially informed about the merger plans at meetings held simultaneously at each institution. Although initial reaction to the announcements was generally positive, a number of employees immediately began to express reservations, doubts, and fears about the merger. Most employees of Urban Bank were initially quite favorable, since they felt that the merger would give them the opportunity to expand into the more prosperous suburban communities. Because of the volatility in the thrift industry, employ-

Table 1. Organizational Climate Comparison: Urban and Suburban Banks, Pre- and Postmerger Periods.

	Percentage Favorable									
	1979–80 *Premerger*		*1982* *Postmerger*				*1984* *Postmerger*			
			Merged Bank	*Prior Affiliation*			*Merged Bank*	*Prior Affiliation*		
Number of subjects	*Urban*	*Suburban*		*Urban*	*Suburban*	*New*		*Urban*	*Suburban*	*New*
	325	188	100	45	45	10	140	50	50	40
Organizational commitment										
Sense of pride	90%	86%	46%	34%	50%	78%	74%	68%	80%	76%
Good customer service	75	na	43	30	44	83	73	68	80	75
Job-related issues										
Overall job satisfaction	73	na	54	49	52	89	75	78	76	67
Job challenge	72	54	56	64	43	66	74	77	79	59
Satisfactory work hours	84	86	92	90	90	94	90	93	94	79
Amount of work reasonable	72	60	77	71	81	83	84	81	82	87
Job worthwhile and important	87	na	79	86	86	78	88	89	92	83
Job security and advancement										
Job secure if performed well	91	89	58	46	64	77	74	64	74	89
Say what I think without fear	58	61	54	64	36	72	57	45	66	63
Advancement opportunity	71	72	41	37	37	72	58	58	57	59
Promotions deserved	50	55	37	37	28	73	36	30	65	40
Compensation and benefits										
Paid fairly	43	39	48	53	42	50	50	49	52	44
Good benefits	86	86	88	86	90	83	82	73	98	72

Supervisor relations										
Supervisor is fair	83	90	79	79	81	56	88	86	86	91
Available when needed	75	na	82	77	85	83	87	92	84	83
Capable of doing job	na	93	84	85	82	78	91	93	90	87
Lets me know what's expected	79	76	78	79	72	72	90	90	91	87
Ensures employees are well trained	64	73	66	61	63	78	73	65	86	76
Management										
Employee oriented	72	74	38	32	36	72	40	32	46	46
Opportunity to interact with management	47	74	36	29	39	50	47	49	52	43
Training effectiveness	50	73	44	38	41	77	62	57	64	67
Organizational cooperation										
Departmental cooperation	44	48	31	27	27	67	57	52	54	66
Co-workers do their share	73	74	77	76	73	72	81	81	79	86
Good communication	36	67	27	17	29	61	46	41	47	52

ees were concerned about the long-term viability of their organization. Many of them expressed expectations that the merger would create "a chance for a stronger future," "a larger, more competitive bank," "greater service and customer convenience," and "more opportunities for advancement." In fact, when the announcement was made, a significant number of Urban Bank members spontaneously applauded it. Members of Suburban Bank, by contrast, were less enthusiastic about the proposed venture, since they felt that their organization had less to gain by it. Still, a substantial number of them felt that the merger would provide a more solid base of operation.

Employees were assured by both CEOs that as long as people did their jobs well and supported the merged entity, no one would lose their jobs. These public statements were repeated several times over the next few months to both Urban and Suburban bank employees. The consensus was that the merger would indeed be good for the banks and, as a result, good for managers and employees at all levels.

The venture was to be a "merger of equals." The CEOs made a conscious effort to use the best features of each merger partner's prior working arrangements (for example, compensation system, work hours, computer network) in the new firm. Moreover, Merged Bank's logo and headquarters were to be a hybrid of those of the two original banks. There would even be dual leadership. Urban Bank's CEO would continue as CEO of the merged organization, with primary responsibility for industry and environmental concerns. The president of Suburban Bank would assume the role of chief operating officer (COO) and would be responsible for the day-to-day operational aspects of the bank.

Prior to the formal merger, a number of joint committees were formed to resolve potential operating and procedural differences and problems between the two banks. It was clear that control systems had to be either modified or newly devised, departments had to be integrated, forms and procedures had to be assimilated, and so forth. The committees met over several months, but little was resolved. Although these groups focused on specific concerns such as which computer system, forms, and operating procedures Merged Bank would use, the discussions were largely characterized by defensiveness on the part of each group about why "our way" was better. Similarly, experimental transfers of employees between the banks prior to the merger were attempted, but employees were reluctant because of an "increase in commuting time." Thus, while a series of joint committee meetings and a transfer program were attempted as a way of preparing employees and the banks for the pending merger, nothing of substance emerged from them.

A content analysis of all memos relating to the merger during this period and interviews with organizational members indicated that despite these difficulties, no problems or potential problems were publicly anticipated. Moreover, while the initial acceptance of the merger had not waned, it was apparent that few people in either bank openly discussed the possibility of staff reductions, particularly in the headquarters group, or specific changes within departments and branches that were likely to occur. Although some concerns about job security were raised, the isue was largely diffused by the "no job loss" statements made by the CEOs.

The actual merger took place in August 1981. Almost immediately, a "storming atmosphere" began to emerge. Organizational members of both banks began to experience a growing uneasiness concerning Merged Bank and their positions in the institution. A number of uncertainties intensified with respect to structural changes ("Who do I report to?"; "What is our loan policy?"; "How do I find out about . . . ?"), the emergent culture of the new institution ("What kind of bank will this be?"; "Whose values are important?"), and the roles they would fulfill ("What will my job be like?"; "Will I still have a job?"). Although these individuals—managers and employees alike—felt initially that they had relatively clear perceptions of what would transpire during the merger, they began to discover that the images they held were quite different from those held by their co-workers. As these perceptions were shared in informal conversations, the uncertainties and uneasiness that people were experiencing rapidly eroded the initial feelings of excitement and goodwill and the potential for cooperation.

The "storming" continued through the merger aftermath period, which was characterized by a strengthening of "we-they" feelings. Soon after the merger took place, employees of each parent organization saw the other as an "invading enemy" rather than a co-equal partner. Members of both organizations reported that "they [the other bank] took us over." Responsibility for why things were not going as well as they should, why communication was so poor, or why "I" or "my boss" was not treated fairly were routinely attributed to the other bank. People also tended to become nostalgic about their prior organizational affiliation very early in the process. Frequently mentioned by both merger partners were the loss of family atmosphere, freedom, camaraderie and accessibility to management, a disruption of social ties and communication patterns, and decreased cohesion and organizational commitment.

After this "negative stereotyping" stage came what might be described as an "arm-wrestling" phase. In the functional units that had supervisors from each partner bank, there appeared to be a period when top management allowed for ambiguity as to who would be named to head a combined function. The competitors from each bank jockeyed for position to take over a particular role, but without clear signals from top management as to who was favored. As might be expected, this situation had the unintentional dysfunctonal effect of contributing to the friction at the operating level of merged departments.

Concomitant with the arm-wrestling period, members of both banks felt betrayed by their top leaders, each of whom had repeated earlier public statements that hardworking employees would be secure in their membership in Merged Bank. Subsequent management decisions to lay off organizational members— even though poor organizational performance in a dismal economy supported such action—resulted in a profound and widespread general distrust of the new leadership and the organization. The layoff, which was announced at a company meeting in mid-December, quickly became known as the "Christmas massacre." The office of the COO (the former Suburban Bank CEO) was subsequently referred to as "Murderer's Row," since most employees, especially those from Urban Bank, attributed the layoffs to his influence on the new institution. As a member of Urban Bank reported, "the massacre really destroyed any motivation. People stopped caring about the bank. When you really don't care, you're not going to put any effort into what you're doing."

Most of the employees' initially favorable expectations (for example, greater personal opportunities, a stronger bank) were not fulfilled. Organizational members reported that decisions were being made "without regard to individual circumstances," management had "withdrawn its support of employees," and there were "no positive outcomes" associated with the merger. Employees also felt that there was far less job mobility than expected, that even if they were "lucky enough" not to be laid off, they were "stuck" in their present positions. As indicated by the 1982 postmerger survey (see Table 1), these negative feelings were manifested in significantly lower levels of organizational commitment, less job satisfaction and job security, and less favorable attitudes toward management. At the same time, those variables reflecting "hard" organizational factors and characteristics, by contrast, did not significantly decline. Indeed, employee satisfaction with such tangibles as compensation, hours and amount of work, and supervision either remained the same or slightly improved. Moreover, those employees who joined the bank after the merger were generally and significantly more favorable about organizational conditions than employees of either of the merger partners.

As employees of both merger partners became increasingly antagonistic toward Merged Bank and its leadership, a significant number of dissenters—at all organizational levels— voluntarily resigned their positions. While one would predict that individuals choosing to or being asked to leave an organization would report less favorable attitudes toward their job and the company than would those remaining in the firm (whether they indicated true feelings or a rationalization of their situation), the before-and-after attitudinal comparison of organizational "leavers" indicates the powerful impact such an organizational transformation can have on individuals (see Table 2). In every instance, these people reported strikingly less positive attitudes toward management, their jobs, their compensation, and, in general, their commitment to the bank.

Table 2. Pre- and Postmerger Attitudes: Organizational "Leavers."

| | Percentage Favorable | | | | | |
| | Premerger | | | Postmerger | | |
Selected Questions	Both Banks (N = 90)	Urban (N = 69)	Suburban (N = 21)	Merged Bank (N = 90)	Urban (N = 69)	Suburban (N = 21)
Organizational commitment						
Sense of pride	88	92	76	27	27	26
Good customer service	92	94	86	36	36	33
Job-related issues						
Overall satisfaction	84	87	76	26	24	31
Job worthwhile and important	87	89	81	44	43	48
Management						
Top management paying sufficient attention to bank's future	73	74	71	44	44	43
Top management maintained credibility throughout merger	55	58	45	19	21	12
Bank hires well-qualified people	85	86	81	52	56	38
Lack of necessary information about merger	57	57	58	61	60	65

Compensation						
Paid fairly compared to others inside bank	75	73	81	56	56	55
Paid fairly compared to others outside bank	76	80	62	66	67	62
Job security and advancement						
Job was secure if performed well	92	93	88	41	37	52
I could say what I thought without fear	76	77	71	30	24	49
People were afraid to "open up" about their feelings	66	71	52	74	76	69

In the two years following the merger, numerous attitudinal and behavioral problems were reported. Organizational costs related to the merger ranged from subtle slowdowns in customer service to a whistleblowing incident that involved alleged pressure to contribute to a political action committee, an investigation by the FBI and Justice Department, and a resulting fine, and negative publicity in the local press (see Chapter Seven). Time and effort were also wasted in arguments between employees of the two banks, trying to decide "which boss really counted," and retraining employees to use new computer, accounting, and administrative systems.

During this period, the human resource department finally became more actively involved in postcombination integration efforts. Although it was resisted by Merged Bank's COO, in late 1983 a human resource–based communications committee (HRC) was formed to get employees involved in dealing with merger-related difficulties. Composed of a cross section of eleven employees and supervisors elected by organizational members, the HRC met with the vice-president of human resources every other month to discuss problems and potential solutions and to pass along information to upper-level management and the employee population. Interview data suggest that this group had a positive influence in decreasing postmerger tensions, but lingering resentment still remained.

Gradually, many of the uncertainties and hostilities became resolved, and new norms and roles began to stabilize as new routines began to be accepted. Yet, as indicated by the 1984 postmerger survey (see Table 1), although there was a steady improvement in employee satisfaction, and these attitudes were closer to the attitudes of new employees, these perceptions had still not reached premerger levels a full three years after the merger. Thus, while many employees reported that cultural issues and problems were "behind them," it is clear that the postmerger integration process was still not complete. As one employee, who reflected the attitudes of many of his co-workers, summarized, "Since the merger the entire atmosphere has changed. The 'family' feeling no longer exists. After more than two years, a 'merged' feeling has still not been achieved. We have become a more consistent organization since the merger, but we have lost the high-spirited morale that both organizations shared.''

Postscript. Ironically, despite the favorable initial reaction of Urban Bank employees to the merger, in virtually every instance these employees felt significantly more alienated and more negative about the merger than Suburban Bank employees (see Table 3). While both groups were quite negative about the consolidation and their new work situations, Urban Bank members were less committed to Merged Bank, less satisfied with their jobs, and more distrustful of top management than Suburban Bank employees.

Although the two CEOs embarked on the merger with the expressed strategic purpose of creating a stronger, more competitive institution, the bank experienced significant drops in performance during the initial years following the merger. While most related-business mergers show performance declines for a six- to eight-month period following the combination (Pritchett, 1985), Merged Bank did not make a profit until 1985, four years after the merger—in marked contrast to the industry in general. It is difficult, of course, to assess the extent to which the financial performance of the company may be attributed to the general instabilities in the thrift industry during this period, other factors beyond management's control, or the impact and instabilities of the merger. These concerns will be probed and discussed in Chapter Nine. Research has suggested, however, that especially in service-related businesses such as banking, employee attitudes and behaviors have a significant effect on performance outcomes (Schneider, 1980).

A Conglomerate Acquisition and Divestiture

Our second illustration presents a very different situation. In this case, Co-op Foods, a large food retailer, went through three changes of ownership within eighteen months. After being part of a conglomerate empire for fifteen years, the company was acquired by a larger conglomerate and then divested

Table 3. Merger Questions
by Former Bank of Employment, 1982 Postmerger Survey.

Item	Percentage Favorable Urban Bank	Suburban Bank
All things considered, the merger should not have taken place.	47%	28%[a]
My former bank's philosophy is the dominant one since the merger.	26	37[b]
There has been an improvement of policies and procedures in the new (merged) bank compared to those in my premerger bank.	20	38[a]
There is a lingering feeling of resentment between the employees of the merger partners.	78	57[b]
There is a lot of friction between former urban bank and former suburban bank employees.	64	36[a]
The atmosphere at the bank is becoming similar to that of "the good old days."	10	22[a]
My department has been strengthened by the merger.	24	53[b]
I feel that employee benefits have improved as a result of the merger.	66	83[b]
A majority of the employees have come to accept the merger as a necessary and worthwhile step.	36	58[b]
Most people are afraid to open up with their feelings about the merger.	74	37[a]

[a] $p < .01$
[b] $p < .05$

through a leveraged management buyout. Yet, despite this period of rapid and at times unstable change, employee attitudes remained relatively stable, and productivity and profitability continued to be strong. Turnover, however, especially among middle managers and employees at lower organizational levels, was a serious problem.

Background. Unlike most large supermarket chains, Co-op Foods was initially part of an agricultural cooperative in the northeastern part of the United States. Its original mission was to provide an avenue for farmers to distribute their products in a specific rural area. In 1944, the company incorporated and separated its retail stores from the cooperative. Over the next three decades, the company developed a chain of retail grocery stores, supported by a wholesale grocery distribution corporation.

In 1971, Co-op Foods was acquired by Aero Corporation, a diversified conglomerate with interests in aerospace, defense, and industrial products manufacturing that wanted to expand into food and drug retailing. According to those who were involved in this acquisition, the combination was relatively peaceful for all concerned. Essentially, the conglomerate allowed Co-op Foods to exist as it had prior to the acquisition without any disruptive internal reorganization. The parent company would benefit from the cash generated by the supermarket chain, and Co-op would have access to the corporation's finanical and computer resources.

Under the ownership of Aero Corporation, Co-op Foods became one of the largest food retail chains in the Northeast. During this period, the company had built up 90 retail stores, 68 franchise stores, and supplier relations with 220 independent markets. With more than 7,200 employees, the firm's strategy was based on a "superstore" concept: expansion through building and acquiring new stores, enlargement of all existing stores, and the addition of higher gross margin services (such as cheese, fresh fish, delicatessens) and nonfood departments (health and beauty aids, florists, general merchandise). The stores were generally located in suburban and rural areas in neighborhood shopping centers where intense price competition could be avoided through monopolization of the local market.

Overall, the general atmosphere at Co-op Foods was described as familylike. The firm's orientation was toward being a close-knit group, working together for "quality service at a quality price." Frequently mentioned by employees at all levels of the hierarchy and codified in the company's mission and belief statement were such values as the "dignity of every human being," the need for an "open, supportive atmosphere for communications," the goal of being a "community-oriented, employee-minded organization," and the importance of "honesty and integrity in all dealings." The main theme across these value statements was consultation with and the participation of employees at all levels to enable the firm to reach its goals.

The Acquisition. In October 1984, Aero Corporation was acquired by TransCo, a conglomerate involved in commercial products, consumer products, and railroad activities, with a new interest in aerospace technology. TransCo wanted to complement its growing aerospace program with Aero's well-established unit, known for its sophisticated landing-gear equipment. As part of the acquired corporation, Co-op Foods became a piece of the TransCo empire but was considered to be outside the conglomerate's strategic focus.

While most employees anticipated fairly large changes following the TransCo acquisition, Co-op Foods, as was the case with its role in the Aero Corporation, was largely left on its own. With the exception of new financial reporting requirements and procedures, there were virtually no direct changes in operating areas or in people's day-to-day lives at work. Employees in the finance function did undergo a major transition in changing Co-op's reporting systems to the "TransCo way." Many of these people reported high levels of stress and tension as they operated under tight deadlines and schedules in making these changes. However, in virtually all other organizational functions and areas, it was "business as usual." As Co-op's vice-president of finance noted, "nothing really changed with the TransCo takeover. Our top management continuum didn't change. There were no people changes. There was only a change in the ownership of the company."

Announcement of the takeover was carefully directed by Co-op's management team. Because of communication difficulties in the previous acquisition, concern was raised about potential employee reactions. When Co-op Foods was initially acquired by Aero, many employees read about it in the newspapers before they were informed about the takeover at work. To avoid a similar situation, the managers, with the support of TransCo, issued a series of well-timed memos and bulletins to keep people "officially" informed. Because of the relatively informal nature of the company, however, managers actively used the office grapevine to "keep people informed every step of the way." While the employees generally wondered how and when things were going to change and how they would be affected, most people reported that the acquisition process was "handled with care" and that they appreciated the "accurate grapevine." As suggested by the organizational climate survey, there was little, if any, real change in employee attitudes from the Aero Corporation to the TransCo eras (see Table 4). While there was a slight decline in organizational commitment and employee perceptions about upper management's desire to improve the general quality of work life at Co-op, attitudes toward the company and the job were quite stable.

Despite the relative calm surrounding the acquisition, there were still problems at both corporate and store levels. As the manager of employee relations pointed out, "there is a lot of anxiety and concern, especially among middle managers and store managers. Things have been handled fairly well, but there has still been some damage to our climate." The general feeling expressed by many low- and mid-level managers was that the TransCo takeover "shook up Co-op." As one of them argued shortly after the acquisition, "It could be real good for us, but no one really knows."

Turnover and the hiring of new employees had been a problem for the company for several years. While the human resources staff placed these difficulties in a broader industry context (for example, "many managers use us as a stepping-stone to other positions," "we've had an epidemic of maternity," "the job market for entry-level workers has been very competitive"), the takeover clearly exacerbated the problem. For example, following the acquisition, thirteen out of the thirty Co-op mid-level managers at the headquarters level left the company. While some of them were dismissed for performance reasons, a significant number left voluntarily. Interviews pointed to a

Table 4. Co-op Foods Organizational Climate Comparison:
Satisfaction During Three Ownership Periods (278 Subjects).

Selected Items	Percentage Favorable		
	Aero Era	TransCo Era	Co-op Era
Organizational commitment			
Sense of pride	96%	82%	84%
Pleasant place to work	80	74	77
Expect long career	69	64	68
Productivity high	69	70	73
Job-related issues			
Satisfied with job	77	74	78
Doing something important	84	85	88
Job Challenging	76	78	76
Amount of work reasonable	69	65	58
Advancement opportunity	51	43	44
Enough people to do job	53	48	40
High rate of turnover	43	52	51
Job security			
Say what I think without fear	55	51	55
Job secure if performed well	86	84	86
Promotions deserved	43	36	39
Compensation and benefits			
Paid fairly	55	51	42
Salary administration fair	33	33	31
Good benefits	90	84	87
Supervisor relations			
Managers are approachable	62	60	63
Know who to approach with problems	88	87	88
Supervisor listens	70	70	72
Know where I stand	79	77	75
Management aware of problems with job	45	50	37
Working conditions			
Work space okay	60	54	48
Equipment satisfactory	56	57	47
Organizational cooperation			
Employees do their share	59	57	58
Cooperation between workers	59	57	61
Cooperation between offices	60	59	62
Co-workers help when needed	60	60	62
Management keeps me informed of changes	61	55	62

Table 4. Co-op Foods Organizational Climate Comparison:
Satisfaction During Three Ownership Periods (278 Subjects), Cont'd.

| | Percentage Favorable | | |
Selected Items	Aero Era	TransCo Era	Co-op Era
Organizational transformation			
Top management improve quality of working life	54	40	53
Changes in ownership good	–	24	60
Expectations of changes accurate	66	68	62
Kept informed on ownership changes	48	47	48

number of concerns, fears, and anxieties about the implied
changes created by the acquisition. Among the questions and
issues raised by organizational members were: What would the
new managers want? What was the orientation of TransCo?
Would Co-op's values change? How would those values change?

The comments made by a number of long-term employees
echoed these sentiments: "Life here has definitely changed. The
company was very friendly, but as the organizational changes
started to take place, we see less and less of this. It is starting
to get better, though." "I've seen a lot of change in management. It does have a chain reaction, especially among other
managers, when a person who is looked up to leaves. This really
happened when TransCo took us over." "I've been here for
over fourteen years. I've been through twenty-seven supervisors
and five presidents. I can't even remember their names, they
were changing so fast."

The Leveraged Buyout. Life under TransCo seemed just to be
settling down in mid-1985 when Co-op was spun off by the conglomerate through a leveraged buyout by the supermarket's top
management team and an investment banking firm. Ironically,
although Co-op Foods would be operating as an independent
company once again after a period of almost twenty-five years,
the buyout period seemed to create more stress and difficulties
than the TransCo acquisition had. While Co-op was operating

largely as an autonomous entity under TransCo, many employees felt that, since the firm did not fit into the conglomerate's strategic plans, it was on the "option block." In fact, many people thought that Co-op's autonomy was simply a result of benign neglect ("We were TransCo's temporary cash register") until the firm could be sold off. Rumors began to emerge that another large supermarket chain would most likely acquire Co-op Foods within the next few months and dismantle what the company had accomplished over the years.

Especially considering the fears raised by the specter of another acquisition, the announcement of the buyout created a sense of relief and was well received by the employees. As soon as it was legally permissible, Co-op's president formally (through memos) and informally (through the office grapevine and hallway conversations) informed all employees about the pending change in ownership. Throughout all communication efforts, upper management was explicit in its commitment to the organization and its membership.

Yet, while the employees were generally reassured during the initial buyout period, this was a time of intense anxiety for the top management team. Literally overnight, these individuals went from being professional managers to being entrepreneurs. The debt accumulated through the buyout precipitated high levels of anxiety, tension, and stress among them. The general feeling in the top management group was "what do we do now?" For the past twenty-five years, although Co-op had operated independently, key financial decisions had been made by Aero and TransCo. Now this responsibility rested with Co-op's top management team. Management concerns about making the venture a success manifested themselves in the ways in which they dealt with employees and organizational issues. As indicated earlier, over the years, the company had developed a highly participative-consultative culture where employees were involved in most operational decisions. During both the Aero and TransCo eras, this orientation was left intact. Following the buyout, however, what many of the new owners described as "entrepreneurial stress" set in, and management shifted to an increasingly centralized, autocratic system.

During the initial buyout period, there were significant cuts in employee benefits and pay increases. As the comptroller noted, "During a leveraged buyout, there is a tremendous amount of uneasiness on the part of many key groups. Vendors that we had worked with quite well in the past were suddenly very concerned that they would not get paid. All of a sudden, the goodwill we had established over the years was gone." Without a "corporate parent," finances were much tighter, and the need for "better-tuned control systems" was translated into cutbacks and greater top management control in general. These decisions created morale problems, especially since the employees were not initially informed as to *why* these cutbacks were being made.

The following year, Co-op Foods went public in order to pay some of the debt incurred through the buyout and to support top management's expansion plans. During this period, the buyout appeared to be successful, and the management team seemed to once again gain confidence in both its ability and the expertise of its employees. Thus, within a relatively short period of time, there was an attempt to give employees more autonomy once again, to move back to a more participative structure.

Throughout the changes in ownership—from Aero to TransCo to the management buyout—most of the existing administrative procedures and personnel policies were kept in place. For instance, an "office council," which began in 1976 as a conduit for employee grievances and concerns, was continued under later owners. Similarly, there were no changes made in pension vesting or in a host of other plans and policies. Thus, while one might expect a great deal of turmoil as a result of three changes in ownership within an eighteen-month period, much of the turmoil that did exist was attributed more to the nature and pace of the business than to the change in ownership per se. While several of the upper-level managers admitted that they "probably overreacted at first" under the buyout, the relatively stable levels of employee attitudes during this period (see Table 4) suggests that the process was fairly well received by employees.

Postscript. Throughout the changes in ownership, Co-op Foods had a strong operational and financial performance record. Despite a period of relatively high inflation, interest rates, and unemployment, the company was able to consistently increase its sales and earnings. The financial and operational success of the company, of course, cannot be attributed solely to the relatively stable and favorable attitudes of its employees. As suggested earlier, however, attitudes and resultant behaviors do have a significant effect on performance outcomes in service-oriented organizations (Schneider, 1980).

Ironically, while Co-op's upper management team generally praised the way both Aero and TransCo handled their acquisitions, there seems to have been little, if any, learning from the process. Shortly after the management buyout, Co-op Foods found itself in the position of *acquirer* as the company took over five supermarket stores from Spot Company. Instead of allowing the new stores to be gradually assimilated into Co-op's structure, the firm devoured the acquired entities. All operational systems were immediately changed to the "Co-op way." As Co-op's comptroller explained, "Our mode of operation was completely different from Spot's. Much better actually, and they just couldn't cut it."

Within a matter of weeks, four of the five Spot store managers either were fired or voluntarily resigned, and scores of Spot employees left. The comments by Co-op's director of employee relations reflect much of the sentiment toward the acquired stores: "I'm not impressed with our recent acquisition of the five Spot stores, especially the attitude of the Spot people. First of all, they added a tremendous burden to our accounting effort. Second, they're not in the best neighborhoods, and I think we could have invested our money more wisely. We have brought in some of the Spot people for training. I guess a couple of them are getting better." Thus, while praising the way in which Co-op was treated by both Aero and TransCo, the company approached its first acquisition in a completely different manner.

A Computer Services Joint Venture

Our third illustration focuses on a joint venture between CompServe Corporation and NetCo, two entrepreneurial companies that are representative of many of the fast-growing high-technology service firms that have emerged in the Northeast. With the goal of adding valuable services to their firms, without expensive and time-consuming expansion efforts, in 1986 the presidents of these companies decided to enter into a joint venture agreement with a merger stipulation. Although there would not be any initial trading of stock, it was agreed that the joint venture would be a type of "dating period," after which a formal merger between the companies was likely.

Since both firms were relatively small, little, if any, difficulty was anticipated. Within a matter of months following the agreement, however, there were so many misunderstandings and conflicts between the companies that CompServe almost lost its most valued client and referral base. NetCo members complained that they were getting "nothing but headaches" from the venture. While most CompServe employees still felt that the joint venture would be a good idea once the "bugs" were worked out, the staff at NetCo became increasingly hesitant about the venture. At this point, the two presidents began to increasingly question the wisdom of their initial strategy, and all merger talks were put on indefinite hold.

Background. CompServe is a microcomputer resource company that was incorporated in 1985. Created by a twenty-one-year-old "hacker," the company literally began as a hobby. Using his bedroom as his "office," the entrepreneur worked with other college students on various consulting projects he secured while "hanging around" computer stores. Within a three-year period, he had received a sufficient number of tips and referrals that he decided that there was solid opportunity to create a computer services business. During the next year, he moved into an office condominium, hired a staff of twelve, and began formally providing microcomputer consulting and software development services to businesses in the surrounding area. CompServe's basic mission is to penetrate the computer retail market and become the largest and most highly regarded computer consulting and software development firm in the United States. The corporate philosophy is that success will come through being the best in the industry, giving businesses a name they can trust to deliver "total solutions" to their computer problems.

In many ways, NetCo is quite similar to CompServe. NetCo, which was incorporated in 1985, was started by another young (twenty-nine-year-old) entrepreneur, who had briefly worked for a large computer retailer. Similar to his counterpart at CompServe, NetCo's founder was "struck by the need for quality service and support" in the microcomputer field, especially in the emerging area of computer networks. After being laid off by the computer retailer during an industry downturn, he decided to form his own company, focused on local area network (LAN) sales and support systems. Beginning "on a shoestring" in the summer of 1985, the firm soon installed several medium-sized LANs and was doing installation and troubleshooting for a number of computer dealers in the area who lacked the technical expertise and resources to service its customers.

Within the next six months, the company developed contracts with other computer dealers to install LANs in their stores, train their sales forces in networking, and design customer service and support products for LAN users. In 1986, NetCo set up its office in a highly desirable location in a major metropolitan area with a staff of twelve "computer buffs," many of whom were long-term friends. As a "dedicated LAN organization," NetCo is focused on selling, installing, and supporting the hardware and software needs of computer networks. Like that of CompServe, the company's philosophy stresses the importance of quality service and customer satisfaction as the keys to organizational success. Its goal is to become one of the largest network sales and support companies in the United States.

The staffs at both CompServe and NetCo are relatively young, most of them in their twenties. Overall, they are intensely interested in and knowledgeable about computers and, while very casual in their approach to their work environment, quite businesslike in their orientation to their work. The expressed policy at both companies is that long hours are required to do the job well and that all organizational members bear a responsibility for project quality and completion.

Despite these similarities, there were some basic differences between the two companies. CompServe was essentially run on a "top-down" basis, with its president as the key decision maker. It operated with a hierarchical organizational structure and, in spite of its small size, gave the titles of director and vice-president to those responsible for staff and line functions. NetCo, in contrast, was described as having more of a "management by consensus" orientation, and most of its key decisions were made at weekly staff meetings. It operated with a "flat" organization structure, with overlapping responsibilities across its work activities. Moreover, NetCo's staff was described as heavily sales oriented, with a "beat the pavement" philosophy, while CompServe relied on referrals rather than aggressive sales pitches to secure its clients.

Both employee groups, however, were quite satisfied with their jobs and their roles in their respective organizations (see Table 5). A major exception, characteristic of both firms, was a rather high level of dissatisfaction with their compensation systems, which were based largely on commissions. Still, the relatively low level of satisfaction with pay and benefits did not appear to have any negative spillover effect on their commitment to the organization, satisfaction with their jobs, or interactions with management, supervisors, and co-workers.

The Joint Venture. In the fall of 1986, CompServe's founder approached NetCo's president with an idea for an alliance between the two companies. Suggesting that "collaborative possibilities" could create a "window of opportunity" for the two firms, he argued that they could both significantly benefit by working together to expand their client base and ability to service customer needs. Following a number of private meetings between the two entrepreneurs, it was decided that each company could indeed "fill a void" in the other's offerings. While

Table 5. Computer Services Firms Organizational
Climate Comparison: Before and After Joint Venture.

	Percentage Favorable			
	Pre-Joint Venture		Post-Joint Venture	
	CompServe (N = 11)	NetCo (N = 11)	CompServe (N = 11)	NetCo (N = 11)
Organizational commitment				
Sense of pride	88%	100%	82%	88%
Long-term career expectations	88	100	88	78
Job-related issues				
Overall job satisfaction	78	100	73	78
Job challenge	88	100	91	100
Amount of work reasonable	100	100	90	100
Job worthwhile and important	100	100	100	88
Participate in job decisions	88	88	82	67
Job security and advancement				
Job secure if performed well	100	88	91	78
Say what I think without fear	100	75	91	75
Career opportunity	100	100	100	78
Compensation and benefits				
Paid fairly	38	22	50	11
Good benefits	22	55	20	44
Supervisor relations				
Listens to me	88	100	88	75
Good communication	88	91	88	56
Lets me know how I'm doing	100	100	90	88
Management				
Keeps me informed	56	88	33	67
Aware of problems of my job	75	88	67	67
Training effectiveness	56	67	73	44
Makes decisions in best interest of company	88	88	91	78
Interested in quality of work life	67	88	70	78
Organizational cooperation				
Good intraorganizational co-worker support	88	67	82	67
Employees share work load	88	88	82	78

they thought that a merger was a "sound idea," the two presidents agreed that it made sense to go through a "trial phase" to see how the companies worked together. If, as anticipated, all went well, the companies would formally merge after a six- to twelve-month "dating period."

The president of NetCo immediately informed his staff of the talks and the possibility of working with CompServe. The staff members were initially favorable about the combination, since they felt that the venture would offer a significant support and service component to their existing operation, as well as increasing its marketing abilities and client base. Moreover, most employees felt quite secure in their jobs and career potential with the company (see Table 5) and felt that little would actually change in their day-to-day operations.

CompServe's president, by contrast, informed only his board of directors and executive vice-president, keeping the rest of his staff uninformed about the proceedings. When the joint venture and merger possibility were finally announced, CompServe's employees were far less enthusiastic about the agreement. Staff members were concerned that the alliance between the companies could jeopardize some of their long-term but tenuous relationships with major computer stores in the area. Since CompServe did not sell any hardware, these stores had been quite willing to pass on referrals of customers who might need further support and consultation in using the systems they purchased from them. The fear was that once CompServe, through NetCo, also began to sell hardware, these referrals and links with the stores might quickly end. Moreover, despite unanimous feelings of job security (see Table 5), these employees began raising many more merger-related questions and concerns than did their counterparts at NetCo: What would the joint venture mean for their roles in the company? How drastically would things change if the firms actually merged? Would the agreement really make them a stronger company? Why did the president undertake such a strategy without consulting them? CompServe's founder, however, dismissed these concerns outright, arguing that "there are no underlying problems in our merger plans; if any employees can't cope with the change, it's their problem."

In December 1986, the joint venture agreement was officially signed with great fanfare at a champagne ceremony at NetCo's office. One of NetCo's board members even served as a type of master of ceremonies and toasted the agreement as an "engagement" between the firms. The venture would ensure joint marketing activities, joint accounting and insurance systems, and, most significantly, a unified mission statement.

Under the agreement, NetCo changed its name to Comp-Net, and CompServe provided everything necessary for the firm's new image—from new business cards and stationery to logo design and advertising. The basic philosophy underlying the agreement was that both companies would work together to actively increase sales and their customer bases. To ensure its success, an advisory committee, composed of two members from each board of directors, the two presidents, and the two senior vice-presidents, was designated to oversee the process. Through formal and informal meetings, the committee would ensure that all strategic and operational details and concerns were satisfactorily dealt with. Formal meetings were to be held monthly, and committee members agreed to be available to deal with specific problems as they arose.

While the initial transition appeared to be well received by both groups, the perceived meanings attached to these changes differed widely. CompServe's president, for instance, characterized the process as more of a takeover than a joint venture: "At the joint venture ceremony, we stripped them of their identity and gave them a new one. I was not about to change our name. They had to change theirs. We're in charge now, but we won't invoke it at an organizational level. I think the NetCo president sees it this way, he understands that we absorbed them." NetCo's founder, however, had a quite different understanding of what the venture meant: "While I think that each of us can fill a void in the other's offerings, all we've formally agreed to is a joint marketing program. Sure we've agreed to change our name, but in return CompServe will bear all advertising and marketing costs. A merger is a probable outcome, but it's still just talk so far. Legally, we're still NetCo. A real question is who will emerge as number one. We can't take a back seat to anybody."

Despite the two presidents' different interpretations of the agreement, the first month of the joint venture proceeded smoothly. Since the accounting and billing systems of the two firms were quite similar, little difficulty was experienced in integration efforts. CompNet focused on the internal jobs-tracking procedures that CompServe had designed, while CompServe upgraded its accounting software to match CompNet's system. With a great deal of fanfare, the two companies also began to exchange customer leads—a key provision of the agreement.

Over the next month, however, CompNet personnel began to express dissatisfaction with the lack of support they were receiving from CompServe. While both companies did exchange leads, CompNet provided CompServe with many more leads than it received in return. Moreover, CompServe was far more successful in translating these customer leads into paying clients—a reality that became a point of contention between the partners. CompNet employees emphatically pointed out that CompServe's "success rate" was due largely to their own initial efforts, suggesting that they passed on solid leads while CompServe's people were not "doing the job as originally intended." CompServe, on the other hand, readily attributed its success to the firm's expertise and growing reputation. As a result, "we versus they" stereotypes began to affect much of the interaction between the employee groups.

To make matters worse, CompNet's president and senior vice-president became increasingly dissatisfied with the process through which referrals and leads were handled by Comp-Serve. While CompNet's president personally passed along all leads and referrals to his joint venture partner because of the "importance of directing leads to the appropriate specialist," CompServe used a non-technically-oriented staff member (director of communications) to process this information. This process infuriated the staff at CompNet, who viewed it as a bottleneck that prevented them from directly discussing leads with CompServe's programmers and consultants. When Comp-Net's president attempted to discuss this situation with his counterpart at CompServe, he found himself dealing with the communications director—the very person his firm wanted to avoid.

At one of CompServe's internal meetings, the vice-president for consulting suggested that the firm change its referral procedures to accommodate CompNet's concerns. She had just met with CompNet's president and senior vice-president on an unrelated matter and sensed the dissatisfaction that had emerged. After explaining the situation "as delicately as possible," she was met with adamant refusal to change any of CompServe's practices. The basic reaction was, "CompNet can conform to our system instead," further reinforcing the takeover mentality of CompServe's president.

As frustration with the lack of good leads and referrals grew, CompNet staff members began a series of sales calls to CompServe customers from a client list they had been instructed "not to use." The names of many of these customers were obtained through CompServe's main referral base, a large computer retailer in the local area that also sold networks. When CompServe's executive vice-president found out what CompNet was doing—through a phone call from one of the salespeople at the large computer retailer—"all hell broke loose." It was felt that the relationship CompServe had worked hard and long to develop with the computer retailer would be undermined by CompNet's tactics. While the situation was ultimately resolved, and the computer retailer even began to use CompNet's services as well, serious concerns about interorganizational trust further undermined interactions between the two staffs.

CompNet's employees became increasingly disgruntled about the joint venture agreement and the possibility of a merger between the companies. While the overwhelming majority of CompServe employees still thought that the agreement was a "positive decision" that would ultimately improve their effectiveness, these attitudes were not shared by CompNet's personnel (see Table 6). In fact, on every item except being kept informed as to the proceedings of the joint venture, CompNet members were far less favorable about the combined work effort. Ironically, these feelings were the opposite of pre–joint venture attitudes.

Postscript. The advisory committee that had been set up to oversee the joint venture was virtually ineffective. In fact, despite

Table 6. Joint Venture–Related Questions
by Firm of Employment, Post–Joint Venture.

Item	Percentage Favorable CompServe	NetCo
All things considered, the joint venture agreement has been a positive decision.	90%	44%[a]
My expectations about the responsibilities of my job following the joint venture were accurate.	55	44
I was kept well informed as to the proceedings of the joint venture agreement.	60	67
I think our company will become more effective because of the joint venture agreement.	100	44[a]
I have a good understanding of what services are offered by our joint venture partner.	82	67[b]
There is good communication between members of the two companies.	40	11[a]
There is good cooperation between members of the two companies.	60	44[b]

[a] $p < .01$
[b] $p < .05$

the many difficulties that emerged during the initial joint venture period, the committee never officially met after its "kickoff" meeting. Although a number of meetings were scheduled, each was canceled because of "scheduling problems" or other commitments of the group's members. It also became increasingly clear that CompServe's president and, to a lesser extent, NetCo's founder wanted to avoid much of the tension caused by the venture. Attempts to get the staffs to meet informally and to create more of a unified "team" image were all canceled because of a "heavy workload."

While the overall performance and profitability of both companies remained stable during this period, it is clear that the goals of broadening customer bases and enhancing support services have not been realized. At this point, the firms are still officially joint venture partners, but actual contact and interaction between the staffs are minimal, and merger plans have been "postponed indefinitely."

Conclusion

As each of these cases suggests, mergers and acquisitions can create a number of personal, interpersonal, group, and intergroup problems prior to, during, and after the combination. The dilemmas and paradoxes discussed in Chapter One were reflected in the reactions of and interactions between members of the different firms. Yet, in planning these transformations, strategic concerns dominated and, in many instances, overshadowed the difficult problems of integrating two different organizations and employee populations. In most instances, top management seemed not only unsympathetic to but also unprepared and unwilling to deal with the concerns, fears, and anxieties of organizational members.

A brief comparative assessment of these three cases raises six thematic issues that reflect much of the subtle and complex dynamics of the human and managerial dimensions of mergers and acquisitions. First, each case concentrates on a different *type* of merger and acquisition—from consolidations of similar businesses to conglomerate and concentric diversification strategies. Chapter Three explores the similarities and differences in these cases, with a focus on the strategic purpose of the combination, the degree of friendliness or hostility involved, the desired level of integration of the firms, and the managerial concerns and implications raised by these different types of merger and acquisition activity. Second, each of the combinations unfolded in a *sequence of events and processes*. Chapter Four develops a stage model of the organizational combination process that explores salient concerns and the different levels of uncertainty and ambiguity experienced by organizational members.

Third, each of the combinations had *psychological repercussions* for the individuals involved. While the severity of these difficulties varied across the cases, in each situation a significant number of people were dislocated by the transformation. Chapter Five examines these human problems in the context of combination-related stress and tensions, a debilitating syndrome characteristic of people going through a merger or acquisition, violations of the psychological bonds that people develop with the organizations they work for, and the feelings of loss, grief, and deprivation precipitated by such combinations.

Fourth, it is apparent that *cultural differences* across the firms contributed to combination-related difficulties. Basic organizational values and beliefs, customs, and traditions not only shape employee attitudes and behaviors but also frame expectations about what life in organizations should be like. Over time, familiar symbols and shared meanings are assimilated by organizational members and become important aspects of organizational identity. Since such cultural orientations provide the foundations for our lives, people do not readily let them go. Chapters Six and Seven take an in-depth look at organizational culture with a focus on types of cultural integration in mergers and acquisitions, interfirm cultural problems and clashes, and the dynamics and process of culture change in organizational combinations. As Chapter Eight underscores, if they are not properly attended to, such cultural tensions can work to undermine what the organization is attempting to accomplish.

Fifth, the companies involved in these transformations attempted to use a variety of *integrative mechanisms*—interorganizational advisory committees, joint task forces, employee councils, and so forth—to facilitate interfirm consolidation. As the cases illustrate, however, there were quite different levels of success associated with these interventions. Chapter Eight explores the potential of such strategies in the context of premerger processes and dynamics and employee fears, uncertainties, and expectations about the merger. Drawing on these and other cases, that chapter examines ways that managers can effectively deal with the human resource dimension of mergers and acquisitions.

Finally, the outcomes of each of these consolidations raise questions concerning the relationship between *employee attitudes and behaviors* and *organizational performance*. In each case, top management envisioned a significant strategic goal: a stronger, more competitive bank, a diversified corporation, or an expanded customer base and service ability. Yet, as the data suggest, these goals were not always attained. The process of combining two previously autonomous firms entails a number of hidden costs and difficulties that are often overlooked in premerger valuation and feasibility studies. Of course, general industry conditions and external factors beyond the control of the organizations and their management can obviously undermine even the most carefully planned and well-managed strategy. However, especially in service-oriented businesses, the role and effect of employee attitudes and behaviors cannot be easily disregarded. Chapter Nine analyzes the relationship between attitudes, behavior, and performance and assesses the implications for strategic growth and redirection through mergers and acquisitions.

Three

Assessing Different Types
of Mergers and Acquisitions

One of the basic difficulties that complicate our understanding of merger-related dynamics and outcomes is the range of merger and acquisition possibilities. There are a variety of combination types, which raise a number of different issues for the firms' employees and pose problems and possibilities for precombination planning and postconsolidation integration. From a strategic perspective, for example, a merger or acquisition can be used to diversify into different markets, expand the company's present business, vertically integrate along industry lines, or even provide capital for future leveraged buyouts. One firm may be purchased for financial reasons and another for the research and development it can bring to the parent firm or the expansion of an existing business. Each type will typically involve different dynamics and synergies. Thus, in conglomerate acquisitions where financial rather than operational integration is the goal, the processes and outcomes for the people involved may very well be different from those of mergers whose main goal is to gain operating synergies between two firms in the same business (Jemison and Sitkin, 1986b; Lubatkin, 1983).

Each of these strategic combinations can also range from overtly hostile takeovers to friendly consolidations. In hostile takeovers, of course, the potential impact on the acquired organi-

zation and its members will tend to be more severe than in more
cooperative combinations. In friendly mergers, by contrast, efforts are typically made to reduce the impact on the partner company. As Signal Companies' Forrest Shumway notes, "when
you make unfriendly deals, you have to replace management."
If the deal is handled correctly, people will not feel as if "they've
been bought" and, as a result, there "won't be any management changes" (Cole, 1982, p. 6F). As illustrated by the description of the bank merger in Chapter Two, however, even the
friendliest of mergers can result in a high degree of turmoil,
employee and management turnover, and adverse individual,
group, and organizational problems.

Conceptual Frameworks for
Assessing Mergers and Acquisitions

The growing literature on mergers and acquisitions suggests that such combinations are homogeneous in nature and
typically have the same repercussions for the firms and their
human resources (Schweiger and Ivancevich, 1987). In most
discussions of activity in this area, the terms *merger, acquisition,*
and *consolidation* are used interchangeably. The differences between such combinations, however, tend to be much more than
semantic in nature. In their study of mergers and acquisitions,
for example, Mace and Montgomery (1962) found when talking with the executives of a target firm that management representatives of the acquiring company always referred to a
"merger" of the two firms, although it was implicit that the
one firm proposed to acquire the other. When talking among
themselves and their boards of directors, in contrast, these same
people invariably described the combination as an "acquisition." As the researchers suggested, "There seemed to be an
inoffensive quality in the word 'merge' not found in the word
'acquire.' As one executive stated, 'The reasons for the difference
are unclear but managements find comfort in the merging of
mutual interests. Being acquired connotes being had!'" (Mace
and Montgomery, 1962, pp. 3-4).

Similarly, Krekel, Van der Woerd, and Wouterse (1969)
suggest that mergers and acquisitions are totally different trans-

actions, mergers involving a much higher degree of cooperation and interaction between the partners than do acquisitions,
in which one firm takes over another. While they suggest that
firm size is an important factor—mergers tend to involve equal-
sized companies, while in acquisitions one firm tends to be larger
and more powerful than the other—the key factor is the extent
to which one firm is expected unilaterally to give up its independence to the other.

For analytical purposes, mergers and acquisitions appear to
vary quite distinctly along three dimensions: (1) the dominant
strategic purpose underlying the consolidation decision, (2) the
degree of friendliness versus hostility involved in the combination, and (3) the desired level of integration between the firms
following the amalgamation. Each of these factors can have a
significant impact on the ways in which organizational members will respond to and experience the combination effort. Moreover, these factors also influence the relative salience of human
resource concerns, from explicit efforts at retaining organizational members to using a consolidation to get rid of managers
who have not created "sufficient value" for shareholders.

Strategic Purpose

The underlying strategic purpose of a merger or acquisition can significantly influence how the firms will be combined,
the likely integration strategy, and related organizational and
human resource policies and procedures (Schweiger and Ivancevich, 1987). The Federal Trade Commission (1975), for example, has classified five basic types of mergers and acquisitions
that constitute a useful base for analysis: horizontal, vertical,
product extension, market extension, and unrelated. These transaction types hold significant ramifications for organizational
members, since they are a key determinant of the probability
that a firm's top managers will have the power to effectively
negotiate. This power base is quite important in terms of such
outcomes as the degree of control of the company maintained
by management after the deal, the amount of protection afforded
employees, how compensation and benefits will be handled, and
how the combination will be communicated (Hayes, 1981).

Horizontal. A horizontal merger or acquisition occurs when the firms involved produce one or more of the same or closely related products or services in the same geographical market. While antitrust laws control horizontal mergers between large companies in concentrated industries, this strategy has been successfully followed by a number of corporations. Waste Management and Browning Ferris, for instance, each experienced significant growth and successful performance by acquiring a number of small refuse companies. Even such a corporate giant as General Motors used this approach in its initial phase by merging many small manufacturers (Hopkins, 1983). The bank merger described in Chapter Two is another example of a horizontal combination.

Vertical. A vertical merger or acquisition is one between two companies that had an actual or potential buyer-seller relationship prior to the combination. This approach tends to be popular in industries with a high promise of growth (Smith, 1985). In order to reduce the uncertainty in its environment and exert more control over its operations, an organization may choose to acquire a supplier (backward integration) or a firm that could distribute its products (forward integration). The rationale is often defensive; for instance, to stop a supplier from engaging in direct sales or going to one of your distributors, or to stop a customer from developing its own supply capability (Hopkins, 1983).

General Motors' (GM) acquisition of Electronic Data Systems (EDS) is an example of a vertical integration combination. The automotive manufacturer's strategy was to gain internal capability for the manufacturing of computer chips that it will use in its cars, eliminating the need to rely on external suppliers or create the computer chip manufacturing capacity itself, and to save money on data-processing and telecommunications activities. The acquisition was also planned as a way of entering new markets through potential and existing EDS contracts and using EDS to sell the computer systems that GM has developed or will develop to other manufacturers (Darlin and Guiles, 1984). This latter aspect of the acquisition brings us into a product-extension combination.

Product Extension. A merger or acquisition is considered to be a product extension when the acquiring and acquired companies or merger partners are functionally related in production and/or distribution but sell products that do not compete directly with one another. This type of organizational combination is often referred to as *concentric diversification.* The computer services joint venture with a merger stipulation described in Chapter Two could be classified as a product-extension merger. By bringing together CompServe's strong consulting and programming base and NetCo's networking expertise, the plan was to expand the influence and marketability of both firms. Similarly, TransCo's acquisition of Aero Corporation was an effort to extend the acquiring firm's capabilities in its aerospace unit.

At times, the distinction between product-extension combinations and horizontal mergers and acquisitions is quite fine. Chrysler's 1987 acquisition of American Motors Corporation (AMC) from Renault, for example, could be considered a product-extension strategy, since AMC's Jeep division provides Chrysler with a way of extending its product line. Since the two firms manufacture cars, however, it could also be conceived of as a horizontal acquisition.

Market Extension. A merger or acquisition is considered to be a market extension when the acquiring and acquired companies manufacture the same products but sell them in different geographical markets. There is often a fine distinction between market-extension mergers and product-extension mergers. For example, when Borden Company, which operated a dairy in New York City, acquired a dairy in another city, where it had not previously shipped any of its fluid milk products, the Federal Trade Commission (FTC) classified the combination as a market-extension acquisition. In contrast, when Procter & Gamble (P&G) acquired Clorox, which sold liquid bleach to the same grocery stores that P&G sold its soap to, it was categorized as a product-extension acquisition (Brozen, 1982).

Unrelated. Unrelated acquisitions involve the combination of two essentially unconnected companies. An example would be a high-tech manufacturer buying a food chain, such as TransCo's acquisition of Co-op Foods. Often referred to as a conglomerate diversification strategy, the rationale usually cited for such acquisitions is that the combination opens entry into an attractive business or industry and spreads out the company's risk (Hopkins, 1983).

Human Resource Implications. It is suggested that these strategic types of mergers and acquisitions lead to different kinds of synergies and postcombination outcomes: collusive, operational, and financial (Chatterjee, 1986), technical, pecuniary, and diversification (Lubatkin, 1983), and financial and operating (Rumelt, 1974). Thus, the retention of key organizational members, the importance of the acquired firm's human resources, and the extent to which people's concerns are dealt with in an open and forthright manner can vary quite considerably depending on the strategic type of merger or acquisition and the type(s) of synergies desired.

Part of the rationale underlying horizontal mergers, for example, is the achievement of significant economies of scale and operating efficiencies. With the combining of two firms, overhead can be reduced through reductions in force and integration of similar departments and functions (Hopkins, 1983). Similarly, Walsh (1988) argues that top management turnover will be higher in related mergers and acquisitions than in unrelated, conglomerate types. In related combinations, since the parent company's management is already familiar with the target firm's business, it can "afford" to lose members of the acquired company's top managers. In fact, the new parent organization may even feel that it can strengthen the target by bringing in its own management team. This same dynamic seems to hold for middle managers, supervisors, and lower-level personnel in overlapping roles.

In unrelated acquisitions, by contrast, retention of key management personnel tends to be more important, since the acquiring firm cannot afford to lose the product and market experience and expertise of the target firm's management (Pitts, 1976). Especially if the acquiring firm's management is unfamiliar with the target organization's business, it is likely that steps will be taken to retain these individuals (Walsh, 1988). When U.S. Steel acquired Marathon Oil, for example, the parent organization was reported to have "gone out of its way" to retain Marathon executives. When the corporation cut U.S. Steel management pay by 5 percent and suspended the executive compensation plan for its own executives, Marathon top managers were exempted (Ingrassia, 1982, p. 23).

It is important to note that while the FTC argues that these five categories are mutually exclusive, in reality many mergers and acquisitions are not "pure" types, but rather contain elements of two or more types (Pelster, 1981, p. 409). TransCo's acquisition of Aero Corporation, for example, could be classified as a product-extension acquisition. Since TransCo also acquired Co-op Foods as a by-product of its Aero takeover, however, it was involved in an unrelated acquisition as well. In such instances, the strategies employed by an acquiring organization to integrate the various subsidiaries of its acquisition and the ramifications for the people involved can vary quite considerably.

Degree of Friendliness or Hostility

The atmosphere surrounding a merger also exerts a significant influence on the types of problems that are most likely to occur, the severity of organizational and human resource difficulties involved, and the level of damage to "corporate health" (Pappanastos, Hillman, and Cole, 1987). While virtually any form of strategic organizational combination is likely to create problems and difficulties for the firms and their employees and managers, certain dynamics underlying the merger or acquisition can create more difficulties than others. Pritchett (1985), for example, identifies four broad categories of mergers and acquisitions based on a cooperative-adversarial continuum: organizational rescues, collaborations, contested situations, and raids. According to his framework, an organizational rescue represents the most cooperative relationship between the acquirer and its target, while a raid is hostile in nature and creates the most adversarial form of consolidation.

Organizational Rescue. A rescue combination is characterized by one firm coming to the aid of another. Pritchett (1985, pp. 20–23) identifies two basic forms of rescue: financial salvage and a friendly alternative to a hostile, unwanted takeover. In both cases, the acquired firm is looking for some form of relief. While the acquiring firm is, therefore, favorably looked upon, there still tend to be ambivalent feelings on the part of the acquired organization, which often perceives the acquiring company as the "lesser of two evils."

In a financial salvage operation, a merger is actively sought to bail the company out of financial danger. Although there is generally a feeling of relief following the acquisition agreement, since the acquired firm will be able to stay in business, the newfound security gained through the financial support of a corporate parent can be short term. In an effort to create a financial turnaround, the acquirer may close a plant, spin off a division, reduce the work force, cut a layer of management, or implement other forms of "cost-effective" decisions. Moreover, in bailout situations, since the management of the acquired firm is typically held responsible for the firm's poor performance, a significant number of the managers may be "politely asked to leave." Research has even suggested that mergers and acquisitions are useful mechanisms through which the market can replace incompetent managers in failing firms (Mandelker, 1974). As their leaders depart, however, employees—even though their jobs may not be directly affected—are no longer sure of what to expect, and organizational norms and expectations may no longer be appropriate. Financial rescues reflect the "failing firm" theory of acquisitions; that is, firms with inefficient management, slow growth, and poor performance are the most likely targets for takeover, since their low price-to-earnings ratios make them desirable candidates (Council for Community Development, 1981). Within this context, an organizational combination is viewed as an economical way of eliminating "bad" management and restructuring the acquired firm (Conn, 1976; Manne, 1975).

Rescue by a "white knight," in contrast, does not necessarily mean that the target firm is in financial difficulty. In fact, in many instances, the firm is doing quite well from both a financial and a managerial perspective. When confronted with a hostile takeover from an unwanted suitor, firms often seek a company to "save" them from the "enemy." Because time pressures rarely permit sufficient analysis of the situation, however, "white knights" often create a number of postcombination surprises (Ingrassia, 1982; Pritchett, 1985, pp. 23–24). Since important issues tend to be glossed over in the haste of "battle," these concerns have to be dealt with after rather than before the acquisition.

Unfortunately, many "white-knight" rescues turn out to be takeovers in disguise. While the possibility exists that the acquiring firm will allow the acquired firm to operate autonomously, much as it did prior to the acquisition, in many instances this does not occur. When IC Industries attempted to take over Sunbeam Corporation, for example, Allegheny International intervened and "rescued" the company from the unwanted suitor. As the comments of a long-term middle-level manager illustrate, when the Allegheny takeover was announced, most Sunbeam employees felt a sense of relief: "Right after the takeover, I had nothing but positive thoughts. I thought, 'My God, here's more of an opportunity. Thank you, Lord'" (Ingrassia, 1982, p. 23). The day the acquisition was official, however, along with a significant number of other employees—from executives to middle managers to clerical workers—he was informed that he was being fired. "I didn't even get my day in court. That's what bothers me the most. I was found guilty and executed without a trial" (p. 23).

Collaboration. According to Pritchett (1985, pp. 25–27), most mergers and acquisitions are collaborative in nature. In this situation, the two firms approach the negotiations with a sense of goodwill and diplomacy. The general emphasis in premerger bargaining is on creating a fair deal for both firms. Collaborative mergers and acquisitions tend to create an atmosphere of mutual respect and understanding, especially among those consummating the deal. These combinations, however, can still create problems and difficulties at the human resource level. Since it is usually assumed that employees will understand the importance of the agreement, the way in which the consolidation is communicated to employees and the types of statements and promises made early on are often not well thought through. As a result, many collaborative mergers and acquisitions run into problems because of poor management follow-up.

Both the bank merger and the computer services joint venture described in Chapter Two can be classified as collaborative combinations. As underscored by the description of the human processes underlying the combinations, however, there was a significant amount of resistance on the part of the members of both firms to the cultures, operating systems, and managerial orientations of the partner companies. Pritchett (1985, p. 27) refers to this dynamic as "collaboration backlash"; if not managed effectively, it can give even the friendliest consolidations a contested atmosphere.

Contested Combination. Contested mergers and acquisitions are characterized by increasing amounts of resistance on the part of the acquired firm and by aggressive negotiations and, while not as personalized and emotional as outright corporate raids, are still tension laden and anxiety provoking. In a contested combination, only one of the organizations has a strong interest in consummating the deal, or the two companies desire quite different arrangements. Contested combinations can also develop when a number of "suitors" keep upping the ante for a target firm. The result is a company characterized as a "reluctant bride," unable to successfully defend itself against being acquired (Pritchett, 1985, pp. 27-28).

Empirical evidence suggests that, contrary to the "failing firm" theory of mergers and acquisitions, favorite targets for contested acquisitions are generally well managed and profitable and frequently leaders in their primary product or service markets (Boyle, 1970; Conn, 1976; Council for Community Development, 1981). While it is relatively common for both the acquiring and acquired companies to emerge from this type of combination basically content with the deal that is negotiated, the bidding contest tends to precipitate a loss of productivity and organizational momentum during the negotiations and a measurable amount of adversity between the firms and their members (Pappanastos, Hillman, and Cole, 1987; Pritchett, 1985).

Raid. The most adversarial form of acquisition is the raid, a hostile takeover of one firm by another that produces the greatest amount of uncertainty and resistance (Pritchett, 1985, pp. 29–31; Rennert, 1979). In corporate raids, the acquiring organization typically bypasses the target's management and goes directly to its stockholders with an offer for them to tender their shares. Such strong-arm tactics attempt to shift control of the target company from the present management team to that of the raider (Fray, Down, and Gaylin, 1985; Schweiger and Ivancevich, 1987). Although the hostile takeover is the least preferred method of acquisition, raiders typically take a "blame the victim" (Ryan, 1972) posture, suggesting that characteristics of a certain group are the basic causes of their problem. For example, T. Boone Pickens (1987), head of the Mesa Limited Partnership and well known for his corporate forays, argues that the oil industry is wasteful and corrupt and its CEOs care much more about their own perquisites and power than they do about shareholder earnings. Thus, in his perspective, a raider's actions to acquire an oil company are a sound response to ineffective and entrenched management. Presumably, if the firms were well managed, corporate raiders would not engage in hostile takeover attempts.

Routine responses to raids center on the target management's attempt to create strong antagonism among its employees, shareholders, and other key stakeholders toward the raider. The target also typically engages in a variety of desperate defenses to ward off such takeovers. Polaroid Corporation, for example, has recently employed a "shark repellent" tactic to ward off raiders: the company has enacted a plan that would give all employees double severance benefits in the event of a corporate raid (Beam, 1987b). "Poison pills," a defensive issuance of any security that can be converted into cash, notes, or stock of the acquirer (Michel and Shaked, 1986), thus making a hostile takeover more costly and difficult, have also become popular

(Rosenberg, 1987). Perhaps the most intriguing of these defenses is the "Pac-Man" response, where the target turns around and attempts to swallow the raider, as played out in the 1982 fiasco involving Bendix's attempted takeover of Martin-Marietta. At one point, it appeared that each firm might actually end up owning a majority of the shares of the other, since the shareholders of each corporation took advantage of the opportunity to tender their shares to the other company at a premium price (Berg, 1984).

Raids obviously create winners and losers, but the fight and its repercussions often extend over what seems an indefinite length of time. If the target firm's management is successful in rallying its employees around the "corporate flag" but the takeover still takes place, the raider is left with an emotional, battle-scarred situation that can be almost impossible to manage. By the same token, various "kamikaze" defenses that may fend off a raider can leave the target without a significant portion of its resources ("scorched earth" tactic), with divestment of its most valuable assets ("sale of the crown jewels"), or with the acquisition of a poorly performing subsidiary ("fatman" strategy) (Michel and Shaked, 1986). As a result, management of the target can still find itself in trouble, and the company's "best and brightest" often leave in search of friendlier opportunities with greater potential for growth and advancement. Raids, therefore, pose some of the most difficult human resource issues, since any employee who stays with the company must essentially be able to quickly end one employment relationship and form another (Perry, 1986).

Human Resource Implications. The degree of friendliness or hostility involved in a merger or acquisition is a key determinant of how employees and managers will react to the combination. Pritchett (1985, pp. 32–35) suggests that the amount of resistance—the intensity of opposition to the merger and the level of resources (for example, money, time, energy) devoted to fighting the merger—increases as one moves along the continuum from a rescue to a raid. As noted above, organizational rescues and collaborations are relatively well received by the acquired firm or merger partners. At the other extreme, contested combinations and raids typically produce high levels of antagonism, adversarial interactions, and prolonged opposition during the postcombination period.

Even in relatively friendly situations, however, at the minimum there is still likely to be passive resistance to organizational changes, new policies and procedures, and what the acquiring organization or merger partner is attempting to accomplish. While raids virtually guarantee that the target firm's most talented people will leave, even collaborative mergers can precipitate conflicts and an exodus of key personnel if not managed properly. As exemplified by the Urban-Suburban bank merger discussed in Chapter Two, for organizational members, collaborative combinations can quickly become contested combinations once the merger agreement has been signed.

Level of Desired Integration

Following a merger or acquisition, some degree of interfirm integration—that is, blending of organizational components—is necessary (Schweiger and Ivancevich, 1987; Shrivastava, 1986). One of the underlying myths of postmerger integration, however, is that "sameness is next to godliness" (Cox, 1981, p. 298). Merging or acquiring companies, for example, will try to coordinate and combine organizational and human resource policies and procedures to create companywide systems of compensation, marketing, production, research and development, and so forth. Yet, while the basic idea underlying a merger or acquisition suggests that two companies are fully assimilated into each other or one company is absorbed by the other, a number of possibilities exist. Postacquisition situations for different companies, divisions, functional units, and so forth can range from total autonomy to total absorption, with a number of points in between (American Bankers Association and Ernst & Whinney, 1985; Jenster, 1987; Management Analysis Center, 1983).

Integration Continuum. In general, the strategic type of merger (horizontal, vertical, product extension, market extension, or unrelated) is a significant determinant of the desired degree of integration. In many mergers and acquisitions, the strategic goal is financial diversification, which may most effectively be achieved through the relatively autonomous operation of the acquired company. In such situations, postcombination integration efforts tend to be minimal, perhaps focusing only on financial systems and reporting requirements (Wallum, 1980). In horizontal and vertical mergers, by contrast, the goal is often to achieve significant operating efficiencies and economies of scale, which require a much greater degree of postcombination integration (Porter, 1985).

While the strategic type of merger or acquisition tends to be related to the level of desired integration, even unrelated-business acquisitions can result in significant change for the target firm. In some instances, a conglomerate pursuing an unrelated-acquisition strategy may still impose operational or strategic changes on the acquired firm if it believes that the target company can be made more effective (Morris and Johnson, 1985; Perry, 1986). By the same token, a horizontal acquisition can still result in fairly autonomous operations, with performance goals rather than outright integration as the key link between the firms (American Bankers Association and Ernst & Whinney, 1985). Thus, each of the functional areas of merging organizations needs to be assessed and evaluated to determine the appropriate level of postcombination integration.

At one end of the continuum, a *portfolio* approach can be used. Similar to maintaining a portfolio of conglomerate operations, this approach maintains the functions as totally separate entities. Acquired firms maintain their corporate identity, personnel changes are minimal, and limited control is exerted by the acquiring firm. At the other extreme, similar functions may be fully consolidated into one unit as a set of *shared activities* (Porter, 1985). This approach involves the greatest changes, typically for the acquired firm, as corporate identity is often lost, reductions in work force are usually high, and control by the acquiring firm is exerted across all operations. In a sort of "middle ground," firms can be integrated with coordinating functions and clearly stated guidelines for cooperation. Jenster (1987), for example, delineates nine different levels of integration along this continuum: (1) investment only; (2) financial control; (3) central services; (4) limited decision making; (5) retained decision making; (6) many strategic decisions; (7) all strategic decisions: (8) many operating decisions; (9) fully integrated firm.

Human Resource Implications. Analytically, the level of desired integration of different functions depends on two variables: the strategic importance of the function in question and the ease with which the integration can be achieved (Management Analysis Center, 1983). As a general rule, functions that are critical to the strategy of the firm and that are relatively easy to integrate should be consolidated; functions less important to the company's strategy and harder to integrate should be coordinated rather than consolidated; and, finally, functions that are peripheral to the firm's overall strategy and are hard to integrate should be left separate. Yet, while the normative literature advises that such decisions should be made during the preacquisition planning process (Boland, 1970; Shrallow, 1985), theoretical and empirical evidence suggests that this does not always occur (Buono, Bowditch, and Lewis, 1988; Jemison and Sitkin, 1986a, 1986b). Integration and consolidation efforts are part of a lengthy process that can unfold over the course of several years (Quinn, 1980), and it is not always clear where, when, and how integration changes should be made (Schweiger and Ivancevich, 1987).

It is important to keep in mind that organizational members are quite sensitive to postcombination integration possibilities. When a corporation interested in diversification acquires another in a different line of business, employees tend to feel reasonably assured that their firm will remain intact. In horizontal mergers, by contrast, the immediate perception is that the merger was undertaken in the interest of efficiency and economies of scale (Imberman, 1985). In these situations, organizational members logically expect the loss of their company identification, changes in reporting relationships, elimination of overlapping jobs, and transfers of employees to new locations. As suggested by the paradox of strategic significance discussed in Chapter One, such expectations can have a significant effect on how employees view the combination. However, while this dynamic tends to influence how employees initially respond and react to the merger or acquisition, the ways in which integration decisions are made, communicated to employees, and implemented have the greatest impact on how organizational members will respond in the long term.

An Integrated Typology of Mergers and Acquisitions

The three perspectives on mergers and acquisitions discussed above—strategic purpose, degree of friendliness or hostility, and level of desired integration—each help to conceptualize the dynamics underlying such organizational combinations. Individually, however, they fail to capture the true subtleties and complexities of mergers and acquisitions for organizations and their human resources. For instance, one might expect that a collaborative horizontal merger would entail different dynamics than a contested horizontal acquisition, especially if there were different levels of integration desired. Similarly, a horizontal raid might have quite different outcomes than an unrelated raid. And two rescue operations might have quite different results, especially if one acquirer chooses to allow the target to operate as it did prior to the acquisition while another desires a fully integrated operation.

Figure 1 combines these different frameworks into an integrated typology of mergers and acquisitions. In terms of the friendliness-hostility dimension, Pritchett's (1985) rescue-to-raid continuum, discussed earlier, is modified in two ways. First, collaborative mergers are seen as friendlier than rescue operations because of the potential resentment that can build up in the latter. Since this type of acquisition can also be a "false rescue," where the acquiring organization intends to make sweeping changes in the strategic direction and operational activities of the target, what initially appears to be a rescue may actually turn out to be a contested situation or even raid in disguise. Thus, the model makes a distinction between friendly-collaborative ventures and hostile-contested situations.

Figure 1. An Integrated Typology of Mergers and Acquisitions.

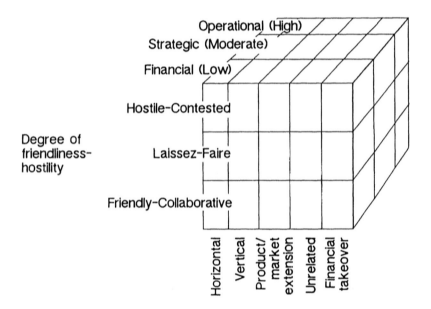

Second, a laissez-faire type of acquisition has been added. In this kind of combination, the relationship between the firms is neither friendly nor hostile but rather is neutral in nature. A company, for example, might acquire another as part of a product- or market-extension strategy. While the basic approach to the acquisition might be collaborative, with the goal of integrating many operating decisions, the acquirer might also find itself in control of a subsidiary of the target that does not fit into its plans. This is essentially what happened when TransCo acquired Aero Corporation and, as a result, Co-op Foods, one of Aero's subsidiaries (Chapter Two). While TransCo initially imposed financial control over Co-op Foods, the relationship between the two companies was much more neutral than any of the other categories would suggest. This circumstance is fairly common in mergers and acquisitions between companies that are already involved in multiple businesses (Schweiger and Ivancevich, 1987). As will be discussed below, a laissez-faire type of relationship would be a prime candidate for divestiture or spinoff.

The other two dimensions of the model are based on the preceding discussion. First, Jenster's (1987) levels of consolidation are condensed into financial (low), strategic (moderate), and operational (high) integration possibilities; second, a modified version of the FTC's merger typology (Federal Trade Commission, 1975), with the addition of a *financial takeover* category, is used for strategic purpose. While there are basic underlying processes, uncertainties, tensions, and stresses that are characteristic of all mergers and acquisitions, the model suggests that the exact nature of the process and magnitude of the ambiguities and stress involved for organizational members can vary according to the type of combination in question. These concerns will be explored in Chapters Four and Five. As will be discussed in Chapter Eight, however, once the combination process and its ambiguities are understood by the acquiring or merging companies, much of this stress and tension can be alleviated through appropriate interventions and support systems.

Before we examine the managerial implications of the model, three issues need to be briefly addressed: the nature of financial takeovers, the likelihood of occurrence of different combination types, and spinoffs.

Financial Takeovers. In what seems to be an ever-growing number of incidents, an acquisition target is pursued with the "strategic" purpose of liquidating the company. Especially if the firm is undervalued—that is, the value of its assets is greater than its market value or long-term discounted cash flow—speculators can purchase the company's stock, fire employees, and sell off its plants, equipment, and real estate for more than they paid to buy the firm (Hirsch, 1987; Magnet, 1986; Schweiger and

Ivancevich, 1987). This "buy it–divest it–fix it–sell it" philosophy, followed by many investment houses and corporate raiders, poses a harsh reality for a target's managers and employees, since there is no real desire to combine or integrate the firm with another. T. Boone Pickens's well-publicized 1984–85 takeover bids for Unocal Corporation and Phillips Petroleum Company and his threat to liquidate Phillips are examples of financial takeovers.

Although most of these financial takeover attempts have, thus far, been unsuccessful, they usually produce large stock-trading profits for the arbitragers and have precipitated extensive corporate restructuring of U.S. firms. Widespread layoffs and reductions in force seem to be more and more commonplace as firms solidify their operations, finance company stock-repurchase plans, and attempt to maximize current, short-term profits to thwart potential raids. As a result, these financial takeover attempts have become increasingly controversial. Corporate raiders and investment houses support them as a way of enhancing shareholder value and maximizing society's wealth by redistributing corporate assets to more effective and efficient managers. Critics describe the process as a type of "reverse Darwinian struggle"—rather than being part of the evolution of our business system, these financial takeovers reduce our vital corporate operations to mere fragments of what they once were (Behr and Vise, 1986b; Hennessy, 1988, p. F3).

This tension, it seems, will be with us for some time. Although a majority of states—including California, Illinois, Indiana, New Jersey, New York, and North Carolina—have passed antitakeover laws to prevent or at least contain such financial takeovers, no one is predicting the sudden demise of investment banking and arbitrage (Labaton, 1987).

Likelihood of Occurrence. While Figure 1 lays out a number of merger and acquisition possibilities, certain types of combinations are more likely to occur than others. Horizontal raids, for example, do not usually occur for financial purposes only; rather, they usually involve acquisition of a similar company with the intent of assimilating it into the parent firm's operations.

Collaborative unrelated-business acquisitions, by contrast, typically involve a level of integration far short of full operational consolidation. And true organizational rescues rarely attempt to operationally integrate unrelated companies.

Thus, given the strategic purpose of the combination and the degree of friendliness or hostility involved, there is a general pattern of likely integration efforts. For the most part, greater consolidation and integration efforts tend to be characteristic of those combinations, such as horizontal and vertical mergers and acquisitions, where various operating synergies are desired (Jemison, 1986b; Porter, 1985; Walter, 1985b). When financial synergies, such as risk reduction through diversification (Steiner, 1975) or access to more favorable financial arrangements (Lubatkin, 1983), are desired, the situation is more likely to be acquisition of an unrelated company with a relatively low level of integration of the two companies (Shrivastava, 1986). As will be discussed in later chapters, however, there is much more latitude in such decisions than is ordinarily assumed.

Spinoffs. In a merger or acquisition transaction, the decision may be made to sell off certain divisions, product lines, or assets once the deal is completed. There are a number of reasons underlying such "spinoff" strategies (Schweiger and Ivancevich, 1987). In some instances, divestment may be part of an agreement with the FTC to avoid potential antitrust problems. In others, an acquiring firm might sell off what it considers to be less important assets to help repay the debt incurred in the transaction or to pare down the size of the combined companies to reduce the scope of the business. Or, as exemplified by TransCo's divestment of Co-op Foods, a company may decide to sell off product lines or divisions that were acquired as part of a conglomerate transaction but were considered unimportant or unrelated to the parent's strategic focus.

Implications for Merger Management

As suggested by Figure 1, there are a number of possible outcomes in merger and acquisition situations—from fully in-

tegrated, collaborative horizontal mergers to financially controlled, unrelated raids to strategically integrated, contested
product-extension acquisitions, and so forth. Each merger and
acquisition type, with its own strategic focus, desired synergies,
and degree of friendliness, will require different resources, levels
of expertise, and pre- and postcombination integration efforts
to be successful. For instance, the Urban-Suburban bank merger
(Chapter Two) was a horizontal combination with an interest
in market extension. Yet, although it began as a highly collaborative venture, it quickly became a hostile contested situation
as top management pursued its goals of being a fully operationally
integrated firm. Similarly, the collaborative product- and market-
extension computer services joint venture failed to accomplish
the level of strategic integration initially envisioned by the CEOs.
What might the top management teams of each of these companies have done to ensure that their goals were fulfilled? Would
efforts comparable to those employed by TransCo's management
in its laissez-faire, unrelated acquisition of Co-op Foods be sufficient?

Researchers at the University of Southern California's
Center for Effective Organizations have begun to explore these
concerns in their assessment of combination management orientations (Siehl, Ledford, and Siehl, 1986). On the basis of the
FTC typology discussed earlier in this chapter, the Center for
Effective Organizations suggests four basic approaches that
begin to create a contingency view of postcombination integration:

1. *Pillage and plunder,* where the acquiring organization
raids a target firm and replaces all operational, strategic, and
cultural systems with its own. The main goal is to maximize corporate gains as quickly as possible. This approach is thought to
be potentially effective in horizontal and product- and market-
extension acquisitions, since the acquiring firm has relevant
market and business expertise. In vertical and unrelated acquisitions, however, the "pillage and plunder" approach would tend
to be relatively ineffective because of the acquirer's lack of expertise and the consequent need for the management and
technological skills of the target firm.

2. *One-night stand,* where a company is acquired, broken up into different parts, and divested or integrated according to need. This approach is most closely associated with conglomerate operations. Siehl and her colleagues argue that this technique is potentially effective in vertical and unrelated acquisitions, since it can provide the acquiring firm with specific resources and assets, but less effective for horizontal and product- or market-extension acquisitions, where there would presumably be a need for more complete integration.

3. *Courtship/just friends,* a friendlier combination allowing operational and cultural differences to exist across the firms. The main goal is to achieve an effective working relationship between the two companies rather than complete integration. The researchers suggest that this would tend to be ineffective for horizontal mergers but potentially effective for the other strategic orientations.

4. *Love and marriage,* the Center for Effective Organizations' last integration strategy. This focuses on full consolidation between the two firms. Integration efforts would be oriented toward a blending and assimilation of the two operations. Although quite time consuming and difficult to manage, this approach is felt to be potentially effective in horizontal and product- or market-extension mergers but less effective for vertical and unrelated ventures.

Each of these integration strategies has different implications for the way in which pre- and postmerger and acquisition techniques are handled, especially in terms of (1) the level and amount of member participation in combination decisions; (2) the speed with which the integration process is handled; (3) the extent to which the process is unilaterally as opposed to mutually directed; (4) how communication is handled; (5) the level of turnover planned and expected; (6) the amount of change that will be fostered on the acquired firm; (7) the level of integration preplanning; and (8) the overall level of concern for the people involved in the merger or acquisition (Siehl, Ledford, and Siehl, 1986). The ramifications of these approaches for an organization's human resources appear, on the surface, to be fairly obvious. The "pillage and plunder" and "one-night stand" orientations would tend to be more stressful and have more severe repercussions, especially for the acquired firm's management and employees, than either the "courtship" or "love-and-marriage" orientation. As the cases discussed in Chapter Two reflect, however, this is not always the case. The bank merger, which would be classified as a collaborative horizontal merger that attempted full operational integration, started out on a "love-and-marriage" course but quickly deteriorated into what many bank members described as a "pillage and plunder" strategy of Suburban Bank toward Urban Bank. Similarly, the "courtship/just friends" orientation of the computer services joint venture ran into many difficulties as well. Finally, the "one-night stand" approach that TransCo used in its acquisition of Co-op Foods did not appear to be dysfunctional for the supermarket or its managers and employees. As will be explored in Chapter Eight, these postcombination approaches necessitate a number of well-focused interventions that influence the way in which people react to the combination. If companies decide on either a "courtship/just friends" or a "love and marriage" strategy, a much higher and more focused level of pre- and postcombination integration efforts is required. If these efforts are not effectively carried out, the rising tensions between the firms—as exemplified by the Urban-Suburban bank merger and the CompServe-NetCo joint venture—can lead to quite hostile and contested interactions between the different employee groups.

As a way of further probing the implications of Figure 1, although speculative, it is useful to consider what might have happened in the cases described in Chapter Two if the situations had been slightly different or if they had been managed in a different way. If the bank combination had been a contested acquisition rather than a collaborative merger, for example, the outcome would probably have been much clearer from the start. The victors would have been expected to impose their control and systems on the vanquished, which would have entailed smaller costs for members of the acquiring firm but much greater costs for the managers and employees of the target. Instead, what emerged was a rather long period of ambiguity as to which institution, employee group, and orientation were going to "win." The size and financial standing of the institutions involved are important considerations here as well. In the bank merger, the two institutions were approximately the same size and had relatively equal financial performance. In contrast, when Home Owners Federal Savings and Loan Association took over Union Warren Savings Bank, described as a "marginally profitable" operation (D. M. Bailey, 1987, p. 71), it was clear from the beginning that the acquiring institution was going to dominate. Within days of the acquisition announcement, the four top officers of Union Warren were fired, ten employees in the target's mortgage servicing department were informed that their jobs would be "redundant" after the first of the year, and eighteen jobs in the mortgage origination department were threatened. As the new president flatly declared, "Home Owners dominates the area of origination. . . . We're continuing to look at the consolidation of this company [Union Warren] into Home Owners at every level" (Beam, 1987c, p. 23). In this instance, a "pillage and plunder" rather than "love and marriage" orientation dominated.

Considering the uncertainties involved in a collaborative merger of equals, a more effective integration strategy in the Urban-Suburban bank merger might have been to initially form a holding company, with the two banks as divisions, and to integrate the operations of the two firms slowly over time. Eventually, the holding company would take control over various functions, such as marketing, loans, mortgages, and so forth, to reduce any duplication of effort. In this case, each division would retain its own identity as far as customers are concerned, but strategic and mid-range decisions would be made at the holding company level. Since more rapid consolidation of operations was desired, however, top management should have been more aware of the range and level of integration strategies and techniques needed to successfully manage the "love and marriage" approach (see Chapter Eight). Given the level of operational integration desired in Merged Bank, without focused attempts to deal with employee concerns and organizational differences, the growing tensions between the two employee groups were quite predictable. According to the American Bankers

Association and Ernst & Whinney (1985, pp. 59–60), this situation is fairly commonplace, as collaborative "mergers of equals" often end in conflict and the ultimate takeover of one by the other.

The holding company approach was essentially that used in a combination between health care organizations in Maine, where a parent company currently controls a general hospital and a home for the aged as well as several other health care enterprises (Betts, 1987). After years of operating two underequipped hospitals in an area that really could support only one, a situation that was exacerbated by battles between the two institutions over resources, the parent company decided to combine the two organizations. A third, new hospital was constructed midway between the two older hospitals. Over time, the operations of the two hospitals were combined and shifted to the new medical center. The older hospital to the north of the new center was eventually changed into an expanded, modernized home for the aged, while the southern facility was sold to an organization that provided health care for the elderly. After years of highly charged battling between the two hospitals as to which facility would be in control, the new medical center and modernized home for the aged are currently working smoothly as part of a larger organization. This type of integration strategy will be explored more fully in Chapter Eight.

In many instances, however, simply slowing down the integration decision is not sufficient to ameliorate organizational differences or employee concerns. By initially operating as a joint venture rather than an outright merger, the computer services combination embarked on a different course of action than would have been the case if one had acquired the other. The effect of an outright acquisition on the two companies and their members, of course, would have been quite different if CompServe clearly dominated NetCo. While the initial effect would have been more drastic, especially on NetCo's employees, it would have eliminated the sense of "waiting around to see what would happen." Yet, even though the joint venture was initiated as a collaborative product-extension combination with strategic and many operating decisions to be eventually integrated, there was little attempt by management to bring the employee groups together and to openly confront the different orientations in the two companies. While the advisory committee (the joint unit formed to oversee the venture) was a step in the right direction, as will be explored in Chapter Eight, its membership was "top-heavy," and it failed to deal with the day-to-day realities of how the two firms actually operated.

Finally, as the TransCo–Co-op Foods case suggests, at times a minimalist integration strategy can be quite effective, especially for unrelated acquisitions. The conglomerate instituted financial controls over the supermarket and let it function as it had prior to the combination; Co-op's productivity, profitability, and member satisfaction remained stable throughout this period. TransCo, of course, had very different expectations for Co-op Foods from those of the Urban-Suburban bank merger and the CompServe-NetCo joint venture, and the supermarket chain was eventually divested. Because of the myriad differences between Co-op Foods and TransCo (and any of its subsidiaries), it was more likely that the parent would desire a lower (and less intrusive) level of integration between the firms. In this case, the significance of the combination's strategic purpose is underscored by Co-op Foods' subsequent takeover of the Spot Stores' operations. Although Co-op's management applauded the way in which TransCo handled its acquisition, rather than the one-night stand approach used by TransCo or a more friendly integration of operations, Co-op used a "pillage and plunder" strategy as it fired Spot Stores' managers, imposed its own operating and cultural systems on the company, and essentially turned the Spot Stores into Co-op outlets.

Conclusion

The American Bankers Association and Ernst & Whinney (1985) argue that the effects of a merger or acquisition on an organization's operations and performance should be assessed with two basic criteria in mind: (1) the combination must support the firm's overall strategy, and (2) combination activities should cause the least possible disruption in the company's normal operations and functioning. On the basis of these criteria, they suggest that merger- and acquisition-related activities should be fitted into ongoing management decisions and the corporate planning process. This is, of course, good advice. The specific approach and interventions that an acquiring organization and its management choose for merger and acquisition consolidation should be strategically sound and oriented toward organizationally functional rather than dysfunctional outcomes. In practice, however, there is a basic tension between these two dimensions: the more strategically related the merger or acquisition, the greater the degree of postcombination disruption.

In unrelated acquisitions, where the acquiring company is interested only in a financial investment in a target firm, acquiring companies often allow the acquired firm to operate as it did prior to the acquisition as long as specific performance goals are met. Especially in raids and contested situations, extensive efforts to integrate the two companies are usually fruitless. As discussed in Chapter Two, TransCo's acquisition of Co-op Foods had little, if any, impact on the day-to-day operating activities of the supermarket. The subsidiary had successful operations throughout the acquisition, fulfilling performance goals laid out by its acquirer and maintaining relatively stable and favorable employee attitudes. Co-op Foods, however, was not part of TransCo's strategic plan, and the acquiring firm's management did little more than ensure that financial controls and reporting requirements were in place.

In collaborative horizontal mergers, by contrast, desired operating synergies typically necessitate a more fully integrated operation. As suggested by the paradox of strategic significance discussed in Chapter One, however, this dynamic creates a dilemma for an acquiring organization. Because of the greater difficulties encountered in attempting to bring about true integration between two organizations, related mergers and acquisitions are often less successful and cause more disruption than anticipated (Jemison, 1986a; Montgomery and Wilson, 1986). The collaborative horizontal merger between Urban and Suburban banks provides a good illustration of the difficulties inherent in creating a fully integrated merger. The combination created a loss of organizational pride, as well as a strong sense of employee detachment from upper management, fractionalization between departments and branches, a loss of job security, and, in general, a feeling of helplessness among many employees. Even the collaborative product-extension joint venture between the computer services firms, which attempted a lesser degree of integration, ran into difficulties.

As the integrated typology developed in this chapter suggests, a series of questions and concerns should guide merger and acquisition management decisions and interventions. How does the strategic nature of the combination relate to the level of friendliness or hostility involved? What does this entail for postcombination integration? Are the acquiring organization and its management prepared to deal with the increasing difficulties posed by deeper levels of integration? What does the specific nature of the merger or acquisition mean in terms of employee stress, tensions, and anxiety (Chapter Five), organizational culture and culture conflict (Chapters Six and Seven), and necessary combination-related intervention strategies and activities (Chapter Eight)? Unfortunately, the strategic acquisition of a healthy company often fails to lead to the type of financial and operational synergies envisioned by precombination feasibility studies. A significant determinant of such failure appears to be misunderstanding and ineffective management of the overall process, especially during the postcombination integration period.

Depending on the strategic goals of the combination, an appropriate and satisfactory level of integration must be identified and developed before the value envisioned during preacquisition studies can be created (Jemison, 1986a). Since the transfer of different strategic capabilities is a long-term, iterative process that involves a series of substantive, administrative, and symbolic interactions between members of the two firms (Jemison, 1986b), however, there is ample opportunity for this process to break down. As will be discussed in the next two chapters, there are a number of uncertainties, ambiguities, stresses, and tensions that emerge over the merger and acquisition process that, if not dealt with effectively, can limit and constrain the achievement of organizational goals and objectives.

Four

Confronting Uncertainty During Merger and Acquisition Stages

It is generally recognized that mergers and acquisitions unfold in a sequence of stages. Researchers have even drawn an analogy between this process and peeling an onion—while each layer is quite similar to the previous one, there are distinct differences as well (Ivancevich, Schweiger, and Power, 1987). Diverse though, at times, cumulative concerns among managers, employees, and key stakeholders have been found to emerge during the precombination, negotiation, and postcombination periods (Management Analysis Center, 1983; Robino and De-Meuse, 1985; Sinetar, 1981). Yet, despite this realization, most analyses of merger and acquisition activity have focused on precombination negotiations and questions of strategic fit between the firms (Jemison and Sitkin, 1986b; Mirvis, 1985; Montgomery and Wilson, 1986; Salter and Weinhold, 1979). As the president of a management consulting firm that specializes in strategic planning and acquisitions argues, "Once the agreement is signed, the deal is done in the eyes of the investment bankers, the negotiators, the acquisition department, and the press" (Cox, 1981, p. 295).

Recent research in this area has extended our understanding of merger and acquisition dynamics by raising questions of organizational and cultural fit and postcombination integration difficulties (Buono, Bowditch, and Lewis, 1985; Sales and Mirvis, 1984; Walter, 1985a). These issues are examined in Chapters Six and Seven. As a context for a fuller exploration of these concerns, this chapter focuses on the overall dynamics— from initial conception to postconsolidation integration—that underlie such organizational combinations. Indeed, considering the complex and challenging task of combining two different organizations, an assessment of the merger and acquisition process itself can add to our understanding of why so many organizational unions fail to fulfill the expectations and projections suggested by feasibility studies (Buono, Bowditch, and Lewis, 1988; Jemison and Sitkin, 1986a, 1986b).

Combination Stages

Research has indicated that mergers and acquisitions tend to follow a fairly predictable sequence of events (Ivancevich, Schweiger, and Power, 1987; Management Analysis Center, 1983; Pritchett, 1985; Sinetar, 1981). In our own work, we have found seven distinct phases, with different ambiguities and uncertainties more salient in certain stages than in others (See Table 7). In a particular merger or acquisition, of course, each phase might not appear as distinct as the process suggests or may be only partly observable. As the discussion in Chapter Three indicates, the actual intensity and duration of these ambiguities and tensions will tend to vary according to the nature of the merger or acquisition in question. These seven stages, however, appear to capture much of the dynamics underlying mergers and acquisitions and are supported by developmental theories of conflict and group formation (Pondy, 1967; Tuchman, 1965), recent conceptualization of the acquisition process (Jemison and Sitkin, 1986a, 1986b), and descriptive accounts of other mergers and acquisitions (Darlin and Guiles, 1984; Levinson, 1970; O'Boyle and Russell, 1984; Sales and Mirvis, 1984; Sinetar, 1981).

Precombination. Although widespread organizational changes and transitions are sometimes made in response to changes in

Table 7. The Organizational Combination Process.

Stage		Characteristics
Stage 1	Precombination	Degree of environmental uncertainty (technological, market, sociopolitical) may vary, but respective organizations are relatively stable, and members are relatively satisfied with the status quo.
Stage 2	Combination planning	Environmental uncertainty increases, which precipitates discussion concerning merger/takeover possibilities; fears rise that unless the firm grows, larger companies will destroy it or the organization will become less competitive or even fail; the firm is still relatively stable, and discussion is confined to top executive level.
Stage 3	Announced combination	Environmental uncertainty continues to increase, influencing decision; the organization is still relatively stable, and while members have mixed emotions concerning the merger, expectations are raised.
Stage 4	Initial combination process	Organizational instability increases and is characterized by structural ambiguity (high) and some cultural and role ambiguity (low); although members are generally cooperative at beginning, goodwill quickly erodes.
Stage 5	Formal physical-legal combination	Organizational instability increases as structural, cultural, and role ambiguities increase; mechanistic organizations take on some organic characteristics for a period; conflict between organizational members increases.
Stage 6	Combination aftermath	High organizational instability, lack of cooperation, and "we-they" mentality exist; violated expectations lead to intra- and interunit hostility; structural ambiguity decreases, but cultural and role ambiguity remains high; dissenters leave the organization.
Stage 7	Psychological combination	Organizational stability recurs as ambiguities are clarified, expectations are revised; renewed cooperation and intra- and interunit tolerance; time-consuming process.

the internal state of the firm, most major organizational transformations take place in response to shifting environmental
demands or opportunities (Hackman, 1984; Kilmann, Covin,
and Associates, 1988; Shortell and Wickizer, 1984). When the
environment is relatively stable and predictable, organizations
tend to maintain routine and well-defined structures and processes of work (Perrow, 1970). It is usually some external crisis
or series of events that precipitates a response from the firm and
its members (see, for example, Warren, 1984) and generates
a number of questions and concerns for organizational members.

In general, such ambiguities emerge when organizational
members try to understand, make sense of, and respond to conditions in their external environment. This focus can include
concerns about influences on the organization such as technological (for example, automation, changes in work process), market
(competitive structure, consumer preference), sociopolitical (values, legal change, regulation, work force diversity), and economic (inflation, national debt, consumer spending) influences.
These uncertainties create a number of ambiguities for managers
in terms of deciding on appropriate strategic responses, how the
firm should posture itself with respect to its products, services,
and other industry players, and so forth.

The ambiguities created by changing environmental conditions are quite influential in merger and acquisition decisions
(Brenner and Shapira, 1983). Vertical mergers and acquisitions,
for example, are associated with attempts to absorb industry
interdependencies and reduce supplier-distributor uncertainties,
while horizontal combinations have been described as a strategy
to reduce competitive uncertainties. Unrelated acquisitions are
also partially explained by the motive to reduce the risks posed
by the uncertainties in a given specific industry through diversification (Pfeffer, 1972). Thus, a major determinant of merger
and acquisition activity is the attempt to reduce or avoid environmental uncertainty and the resulting ambiguities for management—the larger the degree of uncertainty, the greater the
tendency to pursue a merger or acquisition. In the Urban-
Suburban bank merger (Chapter Two), for example, the uncertainty in the larger environment—in the form of banking de-

regulation, increased competition from a growing array of financial institutions, expanding use of electronic funds transfer and
automatic teller networks, and growing financial sophistication
of customers—created a number of strategic ambiguities for the
CEOs and ultimately led to the merger decision. Internal operations at the two banks, however, were relatively stable during
this period.

Combination Planning. As the level of environmental ambiguity
increases, merger- and acquisition-related discussions start to
build. In many instances, fears arise that unless the firm grows
or gains access to additional resources, larger companies will
destroy it, it will become less competitive, or it might even fail.
In others, acquisitions are seen as a way of exploiting new opportunities, as exemplified by the rash of takeovers and friendly
acquisitions in the airline industry following deregulation. Since
such strategic discussions are usually confined to upper-level
managers and executives, however, most of the uncertainty and
ambiguity is focused at that level. The rest of the organization
tends to be relatively stable with respect to operational concerns
and issues.

A basic problem, however, is that although such planning is usually attempted in secrecy, rumors often begin to emerge
through leaks by internal negotiators or external financial experts (Ivancevich, Schweiger, and Power, 1987). While the accuracy of such rumors and informal communication processes
tends to vary quite extensively (Bastien, 1987; Bowditch and
Buono, 1987), they are usually sufficient to precipitate stressful
perceptions and appraisals of the impending event. Depending
on the extent to which these talks leak out, from an employee
perspective the planning phase can move very quickly into the
next stage. Rumors often escalate to the point where specific
departments or divisions are identified as candidates for restructuring, consolidation, and/or job layoffs (Ivancevich, Schweiger,
and Power, 1987). Especially if management fails to deal with
the rumors, the resultant fears, whether realistic or not, can
create feelings of insecurity, resentment, and depression and
lead to turnover of key people (Levin, 1984; Sansweet, 1983).

Particularly in horizontal combinations where a high level of operational integration is planned (Chapter Three, Figure 1), even the mere hint of a merger or takeover can begin to disrupt the lives of organizational members. For instance, even though Shearson Lehman and E. F. Hutton had broken off their informal merger talks, rumors that the companies would, in fact, be combined set off a high level of anxiety among the employees that persisted a year later. As one of Hutton's executives reported ("Shearson Offers . . . ," 1987, p. 63), "the lingering uncertainty over whether the deal was official, and the possibility that a merger would mean extensive layoffs, slowed work to a crawl as employees awaited the word from the top. People are extremely bitter. It's difficult to contain yourself with what's at stake, namely people's livelihoods."

Given this reality, early combination planning should focus on (1) determining the goals of the combination; (2) selecting an appropriate acquisition strategy and rationale; (3) determining appropriate acquisition criteria; and (4) devising a way to gain employee support and commitment to making the transition work. Once the decision to merge with or acquire another firm is made, top management's attention should include an integration strategy and explicit attempts to eliminate or reduce interfirm weaknesses and promote organizational strengths (Berman and Wade, 1981; Haspeslagh and Jemison, 1987; Mangum, 1984). During the planning stage, an organization's management should spend time and effort in serious self-examination to determine and understand the organization's strengths and weaknesses as well as those of its merger partner or acquisition target. As the descriptions of the three organizational combinations in Chapter Two indicate, however, this straightforward prescription is often overlooked. Especially in collaborative, horizontal mergers, the assumption typically exists that the firms will be compatible and that the combination will be successful, especially if the "numbers look good." Indeed, in related mergers and acquisitions, corporate managers, feeling that they know exactly what is being acquired, are often lulled into a false sense of security and, as a result, neglect important administrative functions and integration concerns (Kitching, 1967).

A basic difficulty that underlies these problems is that the complexity of merger and acquisition analyses leads to a segmentation of the different tasks and activities (Jemison and Sitkin, 1986b, pp. 148–149). While it is often assumed that management generalists oversee mergers and acquisitions, these people usually have a limited role. Because of the technical complexity of the different analyses and tasks that must be completed and the rather narrow roles that specialists play, most merger- and acquisition-related activities and duties are subdivided among a number of players. As a result, analyses by different experts, both inside and outside the firms, are often difficult to integrate because of the sequential and isolated nature of their work and their utilization of quite disparate perspectives and orientations. In fact, Jemison and Sitkin (1986b) argue that most often the only participants with continuity across the different merger and acquisition stages are the senior managers of the two companies.

Another problem concerns the desire to consummate the deal before news is leaked that could create any organizational disorder (Jemison and Sitkin, 1986b, pp. 151–152). As suggested above, rumors can make employees uneasy about the potential change. Moreover, if the target company's stock is publicly listed, acquisition rumors can generate a high level of trading, which can drive up the stock price and make the acquisition relatively more expensive. Thus, rather than time being taken for careful analysis of strategic and organizational fit, the combination planning stage is often characterized by frenzied activity and a perceived need to complete the process as quickly as possible.

Announced Combination. As environmental uncertainty continues to increase and the decision to merge with or acquire another firm becomes a reality, employee speculation about what the combination will mean for them personally becomes salient. What, for example, does a merger or acquisition mean for organizational strategy and structure, reporting relationships, departmental communication patterns, supervisory interactions, reward systems, organizational policies and procedures, and so forth?

Since organizational combinations can significantly alter these variables, managers and employees tend to be very wary about any changes in the degree of centralization, standardization, and integration of different functions (Evan and Klemm, 1983).

Although these concerns are initially fairly general, designing the organization structure of the combined entity is a highly sensitive and potentially controversial task. While most theorists agree with Chandler's (1962) proposition that strategy should drive structure, actual implementation of this principle in a merger or acquisition is complicated by the different levels of strategy that exist in organizations. Firms tend to have a series of strategies, both documented and undocumented, that shape their business, which is further compounded by the potential addition of new strategies for the combined firm (American Bankers Association and Ernst & Whinney, 1985). As a result, these multiple strategic concerns and their implications create a number of ambiguities for organizational members. Since strategy and structure tend to be closely related in people's minds, decisions about strategic or structural issues have a significant effect on perceptions of job security, authority and influence, organizational status, morale, and overall motivation and commitment to the combination.

While organizational members tend to have mixed emotions once their company is put "in play" (Ivancevich, Schweiger, and Power, 1987), expectations for a significant group of employees are usually raised. As a result, these employees feel fairly secure in their positions and feel that they have at least some control over the situation. Thus, although some employees will be immediately threatened by the mere mention of a merger or acquisition, many others interpret the idea of an organizational combination as a potential opportunity. Of critical importance during this stage is the nature of the merger or acquisition, which can have a significant influence on employee perceptions and rumors about the impending combination. As suggested in Chapter Three, collaborative mergers are likely to be less stressful for organizational members than contested acquisitions or outright raids. These perceptions, however, are also influenced by the strategic purpose of the combination and the level of desired integration. For instance, a collaborative horizontal merger would tend to be more stressful than a collaborative vertical combination because of the greater degree of threat to individual positions and responsibilities that the former entails. Shearson Lehman's recent acquisition of E. F. Hutton, for example, appears to have produced a high degree of employee anxiety and concern because of the high degree of planned operational integration and job overlap between the firms. The expectations are that there will be widespread job loss at Hutton ("Shearson Offers . . . ," 1987). In TransCo's acquisition of Co-op Foods (Chapter Two), by contrast, there appeared to be little threat to employees, since the unrelated takeover was not likely to result in job loss or significant organizational changes. Similarly, the joint venture with a merger stipulation between CompServe and NetCo was initially perceived as leading to opportunities rather than constraints for both the firms and their employees.

Industry conditions and management actions and interventions can also play a significant role in shaping employee expectations during this period. In the Urban-Suburban bank merger described in Chapter Two, for example, in the announced merger stage employee fears about job loss and career changes, for the most part, tended to be relatively minor. While a number of Urban and Suburban bank employees expressed reservations, doubts, and fears about the merger, most employees—especially those of Urban Bank—were quite favorable about the combination because of concerns about the viability of their institution in a highly volatile environment. Moreover, the CEOs' announcement of a "no merger-related layoff" policy further created a favorable appraisal in most employees' minds. Despite the fact that this was a horizontal merger where significant operating synergies and consolidations would ordinarily be anticipated, organizational members appeared to "buy into" the promise of job security. Once these expectations were violated through the "Christmas massacre," however, employee reaction was highly negative and, as will be explored in Chapter Seven, led to efforts to undermine what the banks were attempting to accomplish.

Initial Combination Process. During the initial combination period, organizational instability increases and is characterized by a growing number of questions about structural, cultural, and role-related changes and concerns. Although organizational members are generally cooperative at first, goodwill can quickly erode as cultural and role uncertainties increase. As a result, seemingly rational requirements for effecting organizational, procedural, and other merger-related changes may be resisted because of threats to the existing cultures and people's roles. The process of actually combining two organizations generates numerous concerns among employees about basic organizational values and beliefs and the potential disruption of social ties and relationships and creates a sense of anomie as organizational members become preoccupied with shifts in norms and expectations and threatened by potential changes in customary and traditional ways of doing things.

In most instances, organizational combinations increase the salience of culture in people's minds. Since culture is so much a part of ourselves and our lives, we are often unaware of it until it comes into conflict with or is contrasted to a different culture (Hall, 1959). Mergers and acquisitions precipitate such conflict and lead to a process of "cultural learning" that heightens organizational members' awareness of their own culture and highlights and polarizes the differences between the firms (Sales and Mirvis, 1984). As we will explore in Chapters Six and Seven, subsequent combination activity can be conceptualized in terms of the attempted shift from one level of relatively stable cultural configuration to another (Lundberg, 1984).

In the initial combination process in the Urban-Suburban bank merger, for example, a number of joint committees were formed in an attempt to resolve potential operating and procedural differences between the two organizations. Since it was clear that control systems had to be either modified or devised, departments had to be integrated, and forms and procedures had to be assimilated, representatives from each institution were assigned to work together to create operational and procedural guidelines for the merged bank. It was recognized that the merger would create a number of structural questions that had to be resolved before the two banks could operate as one. By involving employees in making these changes, top management generally felt that it could generate support for the transition. What was not recognized, however, was that these structural changes raised a number of challenges to the existing cultures of the two banks. Although the joint committees began with a cooperative spirit and goodwill between the two groups of employees, the meetings quickly deteriorated into confrontations once the cultural implications of potential changes were clarified in people's minds. While the different task groups focused on such specific concerns as which computer system, forms, and operating procedures Merged Bank would use, the discussions were largely characterized by defensiveness on the part of each employee group concerning why "our way" was better. In effect, rather than viewing these operating mechanics as impersonal aspects of the work process, employees interpreted them as reflections of each firm's "way of life."

The process used by Urban and Suburban banks is quite typical of most mergers and acquisitions. Following price bargaining by the owner-executives of the two firms, key financial, legal, and other technicians are brought together to establish operating policies and procedures (Blake and Mouton, 1981). Yet, even if these negotiations and discussions are carried out in a participative manner, there are rarely explicit attempts to deal with the cultural issues that underlie these structural concerns. The initial combination process underscores the imminence of the merger or acquisition and heightens people's reaction to the event and identification with their own firm's culture. As a consequence, the resultant personal and interpersonal fears, anxieties, conflicts, and suspicions that often characterize the interaction between two merger partners or an acquirer and its target can fester and undermine the ability of the two organizations to smoothly bring about any necessary structural changes. This dynamic and how it can be effectively managed will be explored more fully in later chapters.

Formal Combination. When two companies physically combine with each other, organizational instability increases as a cloud of uncertainty and ambiguity hovers over the firms. As managers and employees increasingly share their perceptions of what will transpire, they often discover that what they thought were relatively clear images of merger or acquisition outcomes vary considerably among people. The resulting uncertainties and tensions create stressful situations for employees, further undermining the potential for cooperation. As the combination actually unfolds, employees experience growing uncertainty regarding structural changes, the emergent culture of the new institution, and the roles that the individual employees will eventually fill in the combined firm.

The actual or potential loss of organizational identity, job responsibilities, a valued co-worker, or even a work routine can create a number of uncertainties and ambiguities that can be quite anxiety provoking and disruptive to people's lives. The impact of these concerns is reflected by a description of the "wounded list" in a corporate raid as the "executives of an acquired firm who develop health or career problems" (Hirsch and Andrews, 1983, p. 155). While it should be clear at this point that these questions and dynamics can create personal stress for individual employees, the changes can create *organizational stress* as well (Humpal, 1971). In a merger or acquisition, management must combine different organizational components that are often similar only in terms of task objective or formal structure. Informal arrangements, prevalent management style, and other cultural considerations are rarely, if ever, the same across organizations. As a result, significant tensions often occur as these different cultures clash with each other.

While virtually all mergers and acquisitions involve a high level of concern about structural, cultural, and role-related changes at this point, the actual impact of these uncertainties and related stress and strain is dependent on the strategic purpose of the merger or acquisition in question, the degree of friendliness involved, and the level of integration desired. In TransCo's unrelated, conglomerate acquisition of Co-op Foods, for instance, employee reports of tension and stress as a result of anxieties about combination-related structural, cultural, and role ambiguities were far less frequent and intense than were such reports in the Urban-Suburban bank merger. Similarly, in the CompServe-NetCo joint venture, during the initial combination process and formal combination periods, employees expressed little, if any, negative feeling toward the other firm and its members and little in the way of major personal concerns or anxieties about the agreement. Thus, while structural, cultural, and role-related questions and anxieties were raised by employees in all three cases, these concerns were far greater in the bank merger because of the higher level of integration and the resulting threat to the individual organizational members involved.

Combination Aftermath. Following the formal combination of two firms, there continues to be a high level of organizational instability, which may be compounded by a lack of cooperation between organizational members and a ''we versus they'' mentality between the groups. Although questions about organizational structure and related issues begin to decrease during this period, cultural and role ambiguities tend to remain high. Especially when employee expectations and promises about merger outcomes are violated (see Chapter Five), intra- and interunit hostility intensifies, further reinforcing the ''we-they'' orientation and precipitating an exodus, voluntary and involuntary, of organizational members.

During this stage, there is a danger of what is referred to as ''merger standstill'' or ''postmerger drift'' (Ivancevich, Schweiger, and Power, 1987; Siehl, Ledford, and Siehl, 1986; Pritchett, 1985) as management struggles with the actual integration and combination of the two firms. This process can take years to resolve and is typically manifested in decreased productivity and operating effectiveness (see Chapter Nine). Pritchett (1985, p. 101) draws an analogy to this process as comparable to the postoperative recuperation period experienced by patients who have undergone surgery. Following surgery, patients usually undergo a decline in productivity and morale until their physical and emotional strength is recovered. During this period, patients also experience difficulty in mobilizing their personal resources to deal with external difficulties posed by their environment.

While some degree of drift following a combination may be inevitable, its severity and intensity will depend on (1) the type of combination and (2) how astutely the combined firm manages the integration process (Pritchett, 1985, p. 102). Within three months of the formal merger between Urban and Suburban banks, for example, each parent bank was seen by the employees of the other firm as an "invading enemy" rather than a co-equal partner. Although one might have expected a longer "honeymoon period" between the two organizations, especially considering the initial acceptance of the merger by both employee groups, the resulting culture clashes and related ambiguities regarding culture and roles created by the push for full operational integration led to competition between the employee groups. As Schein's (1980) characterization of what happens between competing groups would predict, there were distorted perceptions about and feelings of hostility toward this "enemy." Employees from the two firms gave increased attention to negative stories regarding the merger partner that had been circulating in each bank prior to the official merger.

Merged Bank's management, however, essentially ignored these dynamics, assuming that the situation would gradually improve on its own. While employees were literally crying out for more information and discussion about the merger and related changes, management's attitude was that "we overmet" about the merger. Interviews with employees indicated that both Urban and Suburban bank members felt that communication concerning the merger was too infrequent, that the exchanges between the two groups prior to the merger raised more issues than were resolved, and that the process did not involve enough representatives from each bank. These issues and potential intervention points and mechanisms that could have facilitated the combination of the two employee groups will be explored in Chapter Eight.

Psychological Combination. Psychological combination is the final stage in the consolidation process as the transformation is completed and the organizations are appropriately integrated. Organizational stability recurs as questions and concerns about structural, cultural, and role-related issues are clarified and expectations are revised. Although this is a time-consuming process, often measured in years, psychological combination is reached when there is renewed cooperation and intra- and inter-unit acceptance between the organizations. At times, this level of true integration may not be reached until there is another "enemy" that serves as a focal point for hostility and threat. Stybel (1986), for example, discusses the case of an insurance company that was having difficulty with the hostility of the employees of another insurance company that it had acquired. All attempts that the parent firm made to bring about recon-ciliation between the two groups failed until a third insurance company was acquired. As a result, members of the first two firms rallied together against the new "common enemy."

As discussed in Chapter Five, a mourning or grief period often follows a merger or acquisition. As an indicator of the level of stress involved, Levinson (1970) compares the merger pro-cess to the forming of a new family, particularly the arrival of a stepfather or stepmother to replace the lost parent. In addi-tion to the fear associated with such life change, the child in-volved also experiences a range of negative feelings associated with the loss of part of the family and past life. Moreover, the child may also react to what is perceived as controlling behavior by the new parent with feelings of betrayal and anger and may even leave home. Levinson draws an analogy to the reactions and behaviors of organizational members when a new "parent" organization takes over their firm through a merger or acquisition.

Eventually, feelings of grief and loss give way to resigna-tion and acceptance. Along the way, however, people may ex-press their grief in a variety of ways, sometimes leading to a difficult adjustment period. In addition to longing for and idealiz-ing the past situation, people may also display a general depres-sive tone and somatic symptoms, experience a sense of helpless-ness, and express both direct and displaced anger (Fried, 1963). These repercussions appear to be a natural part of the merger and acquisition process. If not dealt with appropriately, however, such residual anger can persist for years following a merger or acquisition (Levinson, 1970). From a managerial perspective, the key is to try to resolve these feelings as effectively as possi-ble. (The dynamics underlying these individual reactions are examined in Chapter Five.)

In the Urban-Suburban bank merger, for example, only gradually over a relatively long period of time did many of the cultural and role issues and concerns become resolved as norms and roles began to stabilize and a "refreezing" into new routines began to take place. As indicated by the 1984 postmerger climate survey (see Chapter Two, Table 1), while there was a steady improvement in employee satisfaction and attitudes, these perceptions had still not reached premerger levels a full three years after the merger. In TransCo's takeover of Co-op Foods, by contrast, there appeared to be a much more stable level of employee satisfaction and commitment (Chapter Two, Table 4). As discussed in Chapter Three, the type of merger and level of desired integration are among the underlying factors that help to explain this difference; Chapter Eight assesses the different types of integrative mechanisms used by the different organizations.

Uncertainty and Ambiguity in Organizational Combinations

Ambiguity in organizations is generally conceptualized in terms of the adequacy of information available to organizational members (Kahn and others, 1964; Mueller, 1981; Pearce, 1981). In an unambiguous situation, both managers and employees would possess a high degree of knowledge about the potential outcome of their actions and a clear understanding of causal relationships between the actions and reactions of the people involved. In ambiguous settings, by contrast, there are a number of different interpretations and understandings about outcomes and causal relationships, which often conflict with each other. Especially in attempts to get people to work together on large-scale organizational changes, ambiguities about means, performance expectations, goals, outcomes, and so forth can readily decrease cooperative potential.

As part of their daily lives, of course, managers are faced with a lack of information about a number of concerns and events, so that alternatives to present strategic and operational decisions as well as their outcomes and consequences are often unpredictable (Hickson and others, 1971). Organizational members, for example, must contend with ongoing questions and uncertainties about such issues as (1) the availability, accuracy, and clarity of needed information; (2) cause-effect relationships between different personal and organizational decisions and events; (3) the motives and needs of different people at different levels of the hierarchy; (4) the time elapsing before they receive feedback on their activities; and (5) a general inability to predict events that are often beyond their control (Miles, 1980). These unknowns create much of the tension and turmoil, the "complex ambiguity" (Mintzberg, 1980, p. 191) that managers must work through as they make operational and strategic decisions. As the discussion of the different stages of the combination process indicates, however, these normal problems are intensified by the types of concerns that emerge over the various merger and acquisition phases.

Types of Ambiguity. The literature on ambiguity in the workplace has focused on role ambiguity largely in terms of two dimensions: the predictability of outcomes of an individual's behavior and the degree of information deficiency in a particular role (Kahn and others, 1964; Rizzo, House, and Lirtzman, 1970; Pearce, 1981). Environmental and structural changes and uncertainties are viewed largely as antecedents to such ambiguity. In view of the combination process discussed above and the cases described in Chapter Two, it appears that in one sense such environmental and structural changes do lead to ambiguities at the role level. However, they also seem to have differential effects in and of themselves. This finding corroborates earlier criticisms of the global nature of the role ambiguity concept and the hypothesis that different individuals may experience different types of ambiguity in the workplace (Breaugh, 1983; Connolly, 1977; Miles, 1976; Milliken, 1987).

It is often assumed, for example, that horizontal mergers minimize the level of ambiguity involved in organizational combinations. Unrelated conglomerate acquisitions are often criticized because of the ambiguities that arise from a lack of knowledge and understanding of the requirements for success in the target's business field and the differences between the organizations. In contrast, related mergers and acquisitions, based on strategic planning and a better assessment of the business "fit" between two firms, are thought to create "less ambiguous situations where the outcomes can be better predicted" (Mueller, 1981, p. 136). Yet, although this relationship may sometimes be true for certain general aspects of an acquirer's and target's operations—such as when an oil company acquires another oil company as opposed to a financial services firm—a horizontal merger will still raise a number of ambiguities with respect to the actual ways in which the two organizations "think" and "act." Especially when a significant level of operational integration is planned, this situation can create a number of ambiguities and uncertainties concerning what the structure of the new organization will look like, whose culture will dominate, and what roles employees will fulfill.

From the results of our research, it appears that four different types of ambiguity are important during mergers and acquisitions: environmental, structural, cultural, and role (Buono, Bowditch, and Lewis, 1988). *Environmental ambiguity* emerges when organizational members try to understand, make sense out of, and respond to conditions that are external to their firm. *Structural ambiguity* concerns potential changes in and questions about the formal linkages—prescribed relationships and defined patterns of interaction—in an organization. *Cultural ambiguity* focuses on the informal relationships and the dynamics and less precise patterns of interaction in organizations. Finally, *role ambiguity* emerges when individuals focus on questions and concerns about what the merger or acquisition will mean for them personally. As noted in the discussion of the combination process, these different ambiguities can create a disconcerting lack of clarity about the company and its future. Table 8 further describes the manifestations of these types of ambiguity.

The Differential Effects of Ambiguity. The fact that there are different types of uncertainty and ambiguity that organizational members experience during a merger or acquisition suggests that the *acceptance of ambiguity* is an important component of combination success. During a merger or acquisition, managers not

Table 8. Types of Organizational Ambiguity.

Level	Type	Manifestations
External (macro)	Environmental	*Technological* (for example, automation, changes in work process)
		Market (for example, competitive structure, consumer preference)
		Sociopolitical (for example, values, legal change, work force diversity, regulation/deregulation)
Organizational (meso)	Structural	*Patterned* (for example, structural considerations such as reporting relationships, communication patterns, policies, and procedures in flux)
	Cultural	*Normative* (for example, anomie, norms in flux, absence or disruption of social ties)
Individual (micro)	Role	*Positional* (for example, job and status)

only must be able to handle the ambiguities and uncertainties raised by the combination themselves but must be able to help their peers and subordinates to deal with them as well. An underlying problem, however, is that while certain ambiguities can be beneficial and relatively easy to manage at one point in a merger, those same ambiguities can be dysfunctional and much more difficult to manage at later stages.

Jemison and Sitkin (1986b) argue that ambiguity during the early phases of merger and acquisition planning is beneficial, since it provides opportunities for maneuvering during negotiations and discovering areas of compromise on seemingly unmanageable issues. Thus, ambiguity as to what structural changes will take place, which organization's cultural orientations will dominate, what specific roles people will play, and so forth allows for open discussion and negotiation. As the merger or acquisition progresses, however, these same ambiguities can create conflicts and obstacles to successful integration. In the Urban-Suburban bank merger, for example, the initial uncertainties about the merger allowed employees to "read different things into" the combination. Many Urban Bank mem-

bers, reacting to the environmental ambiguities created by being an inner-city bank during a period of rapid change and
volatility resulting from deregulation and shifting interest rates,
initially welcomed the merger. They felt that it would give their
institution an opportunity to expand its operations into the more
prosperous suburban communities and, as a result, provide them
with greater advancement and career opportunities. Moreover,
interview data suggest that during the early merger stages,
because of the collaborative, horizontal nature of the combination, people felt that they had relatively clear perceptions of what
would happen after the merger. As the banks went from early
negotiations to actual attempts to bring about a high level of
operational integration, however, organizational members began
to discover that the images they held about Merged Bank were
often quite different from the images held by their pre- and
postmerger co-workers. As these perceptions were shared, the
structural, cultural, and role ambiguities were intensified and
rapidly eroded the initial feelings of excitement and the potential for cooperation.

Conclusion

As this model of the merger and acquisition process shows,
during the different stages distinct types of uncertainties and
ambiguities are more salient than others. From a managerial
perspective, this distinction is important, since most attention
during a merger or acquisition is typically focused on the procedural and material aspects of the organizations in question.
Yet structural uncertainties such as reporting relationships and
organizational policies and procedures tend to be resolved relatively early in the process. As the three cases described in Chapter
Two suggest, however, while cultural and role-related uncertainties can create significant problems during the post combination period, these more subjective, cultural aspects of mergers
are usually overlooked in merger planning and analysis. Because
of the technical complexity of merger-related activities (for instance, industry and competitor analyses, product and market
analyses, financial valuation of the firms), combination efforts

are segmented into a series of different analyses. This segmentation leads to a disproportionate amount of attention being placed on strategic and specific operational issues at the expense of the broader dynamics and cultural ramifications of the transformation (Jemison and Sitkin, 1986b).

Obviously, mergers and acquisitions between previously autonomous organizations involve an enormous adjustment to change in a relatively compressed period of time. Even a "friendly" horizontal merger, by its very nature, can introduce a high degree of stress, conflict, and tension along a number of dimensions into the lives of organizational members. The preceding description of the different levels and types of ambiguity during the different stages of a merger or acquisition suggests that focused interventions are necessary to ensure that organizational members are able to adjust to changing organizational situations during the periods before, during, and after the actual physical combination. This book now turns to an explicit examination of the dynamics associated with these issues at both the individual (Chapter Five) and cultural (Chapters Six and Seven) levels and appropriate mechanisms and techniques (Chapter Eight) for dealing with these problems.

Five

Experiencing Merger Traumas and Handling Individual Stress

As a result of the uncertainty, ambiguity, tension, and anxiety that organizational combinations can cause, they are frequently associated with decreased organizational satisfaction and commitment, increased turnover and absenteeism, power struggles among those managers who stay, and poorer job-related attitudes and performance for a significant proportion of the new firm's work force. However, while it is clear that a hostile raid is likely to create such human resource problems in the combined company, particularly if large numbers of employees remain bitter after an acquiring organization takes control (Marks, 1982; Marks and Mirvis, 1985; Mirvis and Marks, 1985), it is not as apparent that a "friendly" merger, a popular spinoff, or a trial cooperative venture will generate similar problems among organizational members. Indeed, it could very well be that employees will "get along with" workers from their counterpart organization and that the type of synergy and level of integration hoped for will be achieved. Yet, as the cases presented thus far illustrate, even collaborative combinations—especially when a significant level of operational integration is planned—can lead to numerous conflicts and tensions.

It is important to emphasize that change in and of itself is often associated with anxiety, tension, and resistance. As highlighted in the early work by Lewin (1947, 1951), which continues to serve as the basic foundation for most organizational change models, successful change efforts occur in three basic stages: (1) the present set of relevant attitudes, values, and behaviors have to be "unfrozen" before an organization can successfully (2) implement the desired changes and (3) "refreeze" them at a new state. If an organization's management does not take the time and effort to prepare the groundwork for the change, some degree of resistance is the likely outcome. Consequently, as a way of getting people to "buy into" a transition effort and minimize resistance, change agents often suggest a combination of interactive data-collection efforts (for example, polling and sensing sessions, survey feedback), multichanneled distribution of information about why the change is necessary (for example, memos, meetings, coaching), and participation and involvement in bringing about the change (Bowditch and Buono, 1982; French and Bell, 1984; Sashkin, Burke, Lawrence, and Pasmore, 1985).

Effective management of the human dimension of mergers and acquisitions is further contingent on the extent to which organizational members are prepared for the "emotional shake-up" that accompanies this form of organizational growth (Pritchett, 1985). However, the basic problem of people's tendency to resist change is intensified by the fact that most employees whose firm has merged or been acquired do not have any say in the decision. In fact, people are often taken completely by surprise by the pending combination, which only intensifies the trauma. Consider the situation of Samuel W. Murphy, past senior vice-president and general counsel for Gulf Oil Corporation. After experiencing the trauma and strain of Gulf's proxy battle with T. Boone Pickens and its eventual takeover by Chevron Oil, Murphy moved to what he regarded a "stable situation with a company immune to the wave of merger activity— RCA." As he argued, "I was stunned when I read about the acquisition of RCA by General Electric. I was personally dismayed, but I also was upset at seeing something like that happen to a great institution. The takeover by GE was tremendously upsetting for people who had given a substantial portion of their lives to RCA. In both Gulf and RCA there were people in their late 40s who had very successful careers, who had reasonable chances to become heads of their companies, who had worked very hard for that. It was within their sights and then suddenly snatched away from them'' (Marks and Mirvis, 1986, p. 36).

Mergers, acquisitions, spinoffs, or cooperative interorganizational agreements will usually violate the expectations and/or understandings of many organizational members, at least for a short duration, even if very few internal changes are made. The very fact that the company has merged with or been acquired by another can be unsettling to many people. Once a new situation has existed for a while, however, it will be regarded as normal, much as the previous state was (Homans, 1974). Over time, bitter organizational members depart, and the employees who remain within the new organization may begin to feel better about their situation, as a new relationship with the firm is tacitly defined and internalized and the situation is ''refrozen'' at the new state. However, the costs associated with this healing process—for both the individuals involved and the organizations—can be quite high.

Accordingly, this chapter explores what might be termed the ''micro'' side of mergers and acquisitions—employee reactions, expectations, and perceptions that emerge over the course of such large-scale organizational transformations. After assessing what research in the field suggests are rather typical reactions and feelings, the discussion turns to various studies that examine the importance of employee expectations and the reasons why organizational members react the way they do when their understandings about their work arrangements change. A comparative assessment of employee expectations and reactions in the three combinations outlined in Chapter Two is used to illustrate these theories. The chapter concludes with a brief assessment of the implications raised by these dynamics for people going through a merger or acquisition.

Psychological Shock Waves and the Merger Syndrome

It has been argued that the reactions that individuals report when going through a merger or acquisition are part of a fairly predictable syndrome of merger-related stresses and tensions (Marks and Mirvis, 1985, 1986; Mirvis and Marks, 1985; Pritchett, 1985, 1987a). In many instances, the sheer timing and rapidity of combination-related events can be stressful in and of themselves. Consider the remarks of Sealy, Inc.'s Dwight Harshbarger (1987, pp. 340–341) about the events surrounding the takeover of the company: "On the Tuesday before Thanksgiving, we were shocked to learn that Sealy, Inc. had just been sold to the Ohio Mattress Company, the parent company of Ohio Sealy and one of our adversaries. . . . Happy Thanksgiving. By the end of December, the company had undergone a takeover. Merry Christmas. My senior colleagues and I greeted the New Year with foreboding, and with good reason: by mid-March, most of us were unemployed. . . . For the sake of analogy, imagine that it is France, 1940. Paris has just fallen. The occupying forces are coming and the radio daily reports their troop movements. The end of a way of life is near. We can only wait."

Combination-Related Stress

There are always stresses and tensions present in organizational life, but during the transitions and transformations that occur during a merger or acquisition, these stresses and tensions are greatly intensified. In many instances, the sheer magnitude of the structural, cultural, and role ambiguities that organizational members must endure can create highly stressful situations and experiences. Indeed, the sheer quantity of work usually involved in merging two organizations is enormous—gathering and digesting volumes of information, making rapid decisions— and can overwhelm the best prepared and most efficient executive. Moreover, since stress is cumulative in nature, individual pressures and tensions that might not ordinarily be stressful can take on new significance when compounded by other strains and ambiguities (Kahn and others, 1964; Marks and Mirvis, 1985; Miles, 1976; Schweiger and Ivancevich, 1985).

Research, however, has indicated that, while organizational combinations in general tend to be accompanied by high levels of stress and anxiety, organizational members vary significantly in their ability to handle the uncertainties and stresses involved (Brief and Atieh, 1986; Caplan and Jones, 1975; Dohrenwend and Dohrenwend, 1974). A personnel manager in an acquired bank, for example, was quite explicit in drawing out this difference when discussing two of his employees: "Bob was one of our most outstanding performers. I could count on him for anything. Yet, when the merger was announced, he fell to pieces, became totally dysfunctional. What is strange is his co-worker, who had more to lose. She's been rolling with the punches. She's had four different jobs over the last three months and has finally carved out a niche for herself in the company. Bob? I'm afraid he's not going to make it" (Wishard, 1983, p. 4). Within this context, it is important to emphasize that the degree of stress related to a particular event is influenced by a person's interpretation of the situation more than by any objective reality (Marks and Mirvis, 1985).

John Ivancevich and his associates (Ivancevich, Schweiger, and Power, 1987) have applied a stress-appraisal model (Lazarus and Folkman, 1985) to understand the ways in which organizational members react to the various tensions, strains, and uncertainties raised by a merger or acquisition, classifying the effects as irrelevant, benign-positive, and stressful.

Irrelevant. If a merger or acquisition is considered to have no effect on a particular individual, it can be classified as irrelevant. Especially for incumbents at lower organizational levels, a merger or acquisition could have relatively little effect on their lives. As a secretary of a newly merged firm reported, "It really doesn't matter who is in charge. I still have to file, type and answer telephones. As long as I'm paid on Friday, Flash Gordon could be in charge and it wouldn't matter" (Ivancevich, Schweiger, and Power, 1987, p. 20). Similarly, most of the staff employees interviewed and surveyed at Co-op Foods felt that the acquisition by TransCo posed little, if any, threat to their jobs or daily routines. When mergers and acquisitions are perceived as irrelevant, organizational members experience a low degree of stress.

It should not be assumed, however, that merger-related stress is simply a function of organizational position. A large number of Urban and Suburban tellers and clerks in the bank merger, for example, reported that the combination had created a stressful situation in the new institution. As one of Suburban Bank's clerks argued, "The merger changed the atmosphere at Suburban. You work with a person for a long time and form friendships. Then you have to work with another person from the other place and you resent it. I never realized how much this would happen. Much of the resentment is petty, and it should be left behind us as we go about our new business. But there is still a lot of tension between the banks, and it's uncomfortable to work with them."

Benign-Positive. In many instances, an upcoming merger or acquisition can be favorably perceived by organizational members. The pending combination may be viewed as a way to increase one's status in the firm, as a chance to assume new responsibilities or solidify existing ones, as an opportunity for advancement and career development, and so forth. In this instance, reactions to the combination are often quite favorable. The merger between Urban and Suburban banks, for example, was *initially* seen as a benign-positive combination by many employees, especially members of Urban Bank. As pointed out in Chapter Two, the dominant feeling was that the merger would provide the urban institution with an opportunity to expand into the more prosperous suburban communities. When the official announcement was made, a significant number of Urban Bank members even spontaneously applauded it. Because of the volatility in the thrift industry, employees were concerned about the long-term viability of their organization and felt that the merger would create "a larger, more competitive bank," "a chance for a stronger future," "greater service and customer convenience," and "more opportunities for advancement." Thus, concern for organizational survival in a highly volatile industry was an important determinant of initially favorable employee perceptions.

Organizational members can also be sufficiently secure in their positions and expertise that they do not feel threatened by the combination. This is especially likely in vertical and unrelated combinations where the skills and specialization of various target-firm employees are important to the acquiring firm (Pitts, 1976; Walsh, 1988).

Stressful. The stressful appraisal poses the greatest costs for both the individual and the organization (Ivancevich, Schweiger, and Power, 1987). Employees can be threatened by a pending combination, thinking that the merger or acquisition will result in personal harm or misfortune, such as loss of their job, organizational status, or influence in the new entity. While some people tend to view this uncertainty as a challenge rather than a loss, the potential threat and harm that are associated with the merger can readily undermine the potential for cooperation among employees. A high degree of emotional stress during a merger or acquisition has been associated with feelings of betrayal and duplicity, related employee problems of absenteeism, theft, sabotage, and other unprofessional behaviors (Buono and Bowditch, 1986; McLeod, 1986), and various psychological problems (depression, anxiety) and somatic ills (headaches, insomnia, elevated blood pressure) (Marks and Mirvis, 1985; Schweiger and Ivancevich, 1985).

Psychological Repercussions of Combination Stress

The case data presented in Chapter Two and a review of the merger and acquisition literature indicate that the psychological repercussions of combination-related stress typically show five types of manifestations by individual employees: (1) uncertainty and anxiety; (2) grief, loss, and the trauma of termination; (3) preoccupation and obsession with the combination; (4) eroded trust levels; and (5) self-centered activities. Organizationally, these psychological manifestations can be translated into a breakdown in communication, productivity, and commitment and a rise in "we versus they" tensions, power struggles, and employee "bailouts."

Uncertainty and Anxiety. As the description in Chapter Four of the different levels of ambiguity created by mergers and acquisitions indicates, such organizational combinations can create a disconcerting lack of clarity about the future of the company and its members and anxiety about further "surprises" the future may hold. This lack of information, often compounded by rumor and gossip, creates a high level of anxiety in people's lives. Ironically, in an attempt to gain control over such increasingly uncertain and anxiety-provoking situations, acquirers often escalate momentum and consolidation efforts (Jemison and Sitkin, 1986b), which serves only to heighten the anxiety of organizational members.

As the uncertainty and anxiety about the combination increase, communication among organizational members becomes even more constricted as people complain about being "kept in the dark" about organizational plans and decisions. An executive of a recently acquired company, for example, referred to the lack of information about the takeover and related changes as the "mushroom treatment" (Barmash, 1971, p. x): "Right after the acquisition we were kept in the dark. Then they covered us with manure. Then they cultivated us. After that, they let us stew awhile. And, finally, they canned us."

Grief, Loss, and Termination. Following a merger or acquisition, there is typically a mourning or grief period similar to that experienced when a family member dies (Fried, 1963; Sinetar, 1981) as the dissolution of familiar work surroundings and the slow and steady exit of friends and associates signal the "end of what was." Especially in raids and hostile takeovers, the shock and reactions of organizational members to the combination have been compared to Kubler-Ross's (1969) description of the stages of reaction to death and other types of major personal loss (Dull, 1986; Gereau, 1986; Marks and Mirvis, 1986; Schweiger, Ivancevich, and Power, 1987). Since the acquisition threatens the "old" company, people often refuse to accept the change and go through a *denial* process. There is often wishful thinking that legal maneuvers might thwart the raid, stockholders will refuse to sell, or somehow the present management team will retain its independence (Marks and Mirvis, 1986). People become *angry*, feeling that the situation is not "fair," that it should not be happening to them. There is often a high level of resistance toward the acquiring organization and what it is attempting to accomplish. People begin *bargaining* to try to keep things as they were, suggesting areas in which they could maintain present policies and procedures. Especially in horizontal acquisitions and combinations where a high level of integration is planned, organizational members eventually realize that they cannot bargain with the acquiring firm, and a sense of *depression* sets in. While such feelings are dependent on how individual employees perceive their situation and its outcomes, the result is often seen in terms of loss in a number of areas: loss of organizational identity, loss of a future, loss of attachment, loss of friends, loss of meaning, and loss of control (Bridges, 1986; Schweiger, Ivancevich, and Power, 1987).

Over time, those organizational members who remain with the firm tend to adjust to the loss and *accept* the reality of the situation. As psychological theorists (such as Janis, Mahl, Kagan, and Holt, 1969) have argued, however, the idealization of the lost entity is a typical grief reaction. Identification with a lost loved one is part of the process of "working through" the loss. The direct and displaced anger that people express (Fried, 1963) is often directed at what is felt to be the "offending" party and can result in feelings of hostility that may last for years (Levinson, 1970).

The ways in which employment terminations and staff reductions are handled are interpreted by organizational members as signals about the new management's values. Unfortunately, research indicates that most people involved in a merger or acquisition feel that termination decisions are handled arbitrarily and ineffectively (Schweiger, Ivancevich, and Power, 1987). In the bank merger described in Chapter Two, for example, the "Christmas massacre" and what employees reported as cavalier ways of dismissing organizational members fueled a high level of dissatisfaction with Merged Bank and its management and precipitated a significant rise in voluntary turnover.

Pritchett (1985, pp. 52–53) suggests that this "bailout" phenomenon, where significant numbers of people choose to leave a merged or acquired organization, has a number of causes: a desire to leave before the "axe falls"; to escape the increasing ambiguity and anxiety that the acquisition would generate; to avoid what may be perceived to be a "bleak future"; or to escape the "specter of encroaching controls." While this tendency is quite common, ironically, those who bail out are often the key people behind the success of the company. In another acquisition we investigated, for example, valued technical experts began a mass exodus following the acquisition of their chemical company (Petro) by a firm that constructed steel and nuclear power plants (SteelCo). SteelCo's acquisition of Petro was part of a diversification move, and the jobs of the technical experts were not threatened. In fact, while there was some operational consolidation of basic functional areas—human resources, accounting, and finance—SteelCo planned to leave the scientists and engineers at Petro operating as they had been prior to the acquisition. Many of these individuals, however, appeared to interpret the terminations and changes in the other sections of their company as a "sign of things to come" and opted to leave. As a result, SteelCo found itself in control of the petrochemical company, but without many of the petrochemical experts that had made the company successful in the first place.

Combination Preoccupation. Reacting to the myriad ambiguities and stresses that surround a merger or acquisition, organizational members often become so preoccupied with the combination that it distracts them from their job responsibilities (Marks and Mirvis, 1986). At the extreme, people can become obsessed with the process, continually speculating about what it means for them personally. Estimates suggest that more than two hours of potentially productive work time per employee per day are lost during a merger (Wishard, 1985), time that is spent gossiping about the combination (Cabrera, 1986). Organizational members begin imagining the worst about the consolidation as rumors and worst-case scenarios are continually passed around the organization. As noted in Chapter Four, these activities are manifested in various stress reactions, from psychological repercussions such as fear, withdrawal, and aggressiveness to somatic effects such as sleeplessness, increased smoking and drinking, and headaches.

As preoccupation with the merger or acquisition intensifies, an air of tension and chaos begins to build, and a crisis-management orientation takes over. A "combat mentality" is often adopted, and some managers even find the process to be initially exhilarating, viewing themselves as "generals and the corporate conference room as the 'war room'" (Marks and Mirvis, 1986, p. 38). As a result, managers and executives become less accessible to employees, further contributing to the communication breakdown, anxieties, and grief that permeate the organization.

Eroded Trust. One of the major human dynamics set off by a merger or acquisition is decreased trust in the organization (Pritchett, 1985, 1987b). Employees who had a low level of trust to begin with become increasingly mistrustful of the firm and its management. In many instances, they may even become overtly and covertly antagonistic toward and paranoid about the combination. Perhaps more importantly, even organizational members who were initially supportive or willing to give the company the benefit of the doubt often become skeptics or even cynics, scrutinizing and viewing with suspicion every remark or statement by management.

To a large extent, such skepticism and cynicism appear to be warranted. For example, reflecting on the turmoil and "organizational unraveling" that followed what appeared to be a friendly, strategically sound acquisition, a member of the acquired firm's board of directors (Gaddis, 1987, pp. 16, 18) commented, "First, we realized that premerger discussions bring no guarantees. The . . . managers who had discussed the merger with us did believe enthusiastically in the future they were preaching. They did not foresee any conflict arising from it. But we should have realized that the premerger statements of acquiring company managers are at best merely informed judgments. They are not commitments. They are usually not even relevant, because they are not conveyed to the senior executives who will make the implementation decisions later. Moreover, acquiring managers are rarely in a position to inform acquirees about organizational problems that could threaten a company's future." Similarly, Harshbarger's (1987, p. 342) description of the takeover of Sealy, Inc., illustrates a comparable experience and its ramifications: "in the waning days of the old company, promises were made, then broken, by people I trusted. Self-interest outweighed loyalties. I learned to fight back, not only harder but smarter, and to test the personal realities of business loyalty more carefully."

Self-Centered Activities. As the quotation above suggests, once trust begins to break down in an organization, people begin to increasingly fend for themselves, placing their self-interest well above that of the organization. As people take steps to "protect" themselves—their careers, status, prestige, and power— "hidden agendas" and political maneuvering become realities of organizational life (Pritchett, 1985; Schweiger, Ivancevich, and Power, 1987). Interactions between organizational members are often described as a "power game," and the resultant destructive competition between people at all hierarchical levels significantly detracts from organizational goals and objectives.

In the Urban-Suburban bank merger, for example, during the combination aftermath stage what was described as an "arm-wrestling" game emerged between the supervisors of the functional areas that were due to be consolidated. Instead of focusing their energies on the work process, these managers jockeyed for position with one another and attempted to enlist the support of their premerger employees. The resultant power struggles intensified the "we versus they" hostilities between the groups. Ironically, while organizational members tended to feel quite good about their premerger supervisors or managers during this period, there was a significantly decreased sense of commitment to what Merged Bank was attempting to accomplish (see Chapter Two, Table 1).

The Role of Expectations
in Mergers and Acquisitions

As a way of exploring the dynamics underlying the psychological repercussions discussed above, this section examines the perceived violation of the understandings that employees of merger and acquisition partners have about their work arrangements that is often generated by abrupt changes in the psychological contract. As part of this examination, the discussion analyzes the effect of precombination expectations and postcombination feelings of deprivation on member satisfaction and commitment.

Effects of Rapid Changes in the Psychological Contract. One of the realities of organizational life is the unwritten expectations and reactions that develop over time between organizations and their members. The basic premise of such psychological contracts is that if employees within an organization are treated as they expect to be treated, or if the organization's expectations of employees match the reciprocal expectations of its workers, then greater organizational effectiveness, work satisfaction, enthusiasm, and commitment and loyalty to the organization are likely outcomes (Argyris, 1960; Levinson, 1962; Schein, 1980). If these expectations are unilaterally changed, violated, or unfulfilled, dysfunctional attitudes and behaviors tend to emerge.

While changes in these understandings may occur gradually over time and be relatively unnoticed, organizational transformations such as a merger or acquisition can significantly and abruptly disrupt the bonds between an organization and its members. Subsequently, a sharp divergence between what workers expect and the realities they encounter can lead to higher levels of dissatisfaction and less effective work outcomes (Lawler and Porter, 1967).

Employee Expectations. From a diagnostic perspective, the expectations of organizational members are a strong indicator of an organization's readiness for change (Pond, Armenakis, and Green, 1984). Research has indicated, for example, that unrealistic expectations are a significant cause of lack of success in change programs (Pfeffer and Jones, 1978). As discussed in Chapter Eight, information on employee expectations that can be obtained through surveys and interviews is critical for alerting managers and change agents to areas of potential resistance to merger- or acquisition-related changes. These data are quite important in terms of selecting and planning appropriate interventions.

Research on mergers and acquisitions has found that the precombination expectations of a number of key stakeholders—employees, managers, shareholders—are usually unfulfilled after the combination has been implemented (Firth, 1976; Goldberg, 1983). As a result, organizational members fall into what has been referred to as a "psychological pit," characterized by performance declines, a slow learning process, and organizational dissatisfaction (Goldberg, 1983, pp. 212–213). While the depth and duration of the "pit" can be affected by different interventions, such as realistic merger previews, participative survey feedback efforts, and other merger-related integrative mechanisms (see Chapter Eight), unfulfilled expectations can undermine trust and commitment and create a high level of disenchantment and disillusionment with the organization.

What may seem unfair or unjust at one time, however, may be viewed quite differently at another. From the results of longitudinal studies such as that of the Urban-Suburban bank merger, it is clear that relationships and situations that have existed over a period of time will ultimately appear to be fair and just (Homans, 1974; Adams, 1965). With respect to organizational transformations, a sense of fairness among employees will tend to exist until a new frame of reference, such as a merger, emerges. While the particular event may create questions of fairness and equity in people's minds, once the new situation has existed for a sufficient period of time, it too will begin to appear to be fair and just.

Relative Deprivation Theory. Research on the effects on employees of mergers, acquisitions, and spinoffs is also relevant to the issues and effects of relative deprivation in organizations (Martin, 1981; Crosby, 1984). Relative deprivation theory, based on both laboratory and survey data, suggests that "feelings of deprivation depend on the joint occurrence of frustrated wants and violated entitlements" (Crosby, 1984, p. 51). Some of these feelings include perceptions of injustice and inequity that result from pay disputes, affirmative action programs, protests, turnover, drug abuse, and a general sense of alienation of employees from their organizations and from their managers. In most cases, organizational members feel a sense of deprivation when events create the perception that they are worse off than before. Especially when high expectations in the past are combined with low expectations of the future, the tension usually generates feelings of discontent.

Further research on the relative deprivation concept indicates that there are only two conditions required for individuals to experience deprivation: a discrepancy between actual and desired outcomes and a discrepancy between actual and deserved outcomes (Cook, Crosby, and Hennigan, 1977; Crosby, 1982; Davis, 1959; Gurr, 1970; Runciman, 1966). Thus, in an organizational transformation, where desired goals and the likelihood of reaching those goals change, deprivation theory provides a useful basis for understanding the discontent experienced by employees in both combination partners.

A Comparative Assessment of Expectations and Reactions in Three Combinations

As the preceding section indicates, expectations play a major role in shaping the psychological reactions of organizational members who have gone through a merger or acquisition. To further apply and illustrate these concepts, this section presents a comparative assessment of the expectations and reactions of the individuals involved in the three cases presented in Chapter Two. In two of these situations—the bank merger and the joint venture—many employees initially had relatively favorable expectations about the combination. Yet, in both instances, actions by key players violated these expectations, which resulted in antagonistic feelings toward the combination and a sense of warfare between the different groups. In the case of Co-op Foods, in contrast, while employees initially had negative expectations about the TransCo acquisition, the takeover and the way it was managed turned out more positive than anticipated. The result was a relatively stable level of job and organizational satisfaction and commitment.

Combination-Related Expectations. During the precombination period in the case of the bank merger, the two CEOs played a major role in shaping employee expectations about what was going to happen. Employees in both banks were promised by their CEOs that there would be little, if any, real change following the merger. Moreover, they were assured that there would be no merger-related layoffs ''as long as people did their jobs well.'' Some people, especially among Suburban Bank members, doubted these promises. As a Suburban Bank escrow clerk, whose remarks are representative of many of her co-workers, argued, ''When we were told that there would not be any changes, I knew it was ridiculous. They [the CEOs] should have been much more up-front. Of course there would be changes. People should have been made more aware, aware of the possibility of what could happen, not just what won't happen.'' Because of the high degree of faith that Urban Bank's members had in its CEO, however, most of that institution's employees took him at his word that they were secure in their positions.

Despite these initial assurances, within four months after the merger formally took place, a significant number of people were laid off, and it became painfully clear that organizational changes would be far more widespread than anticipated. The layoffs that were announced in mid-December 1981, referred to by employees as the ''Christmas massacre,'' clearly violated the expectations of many organizational members and spread the new expectation and fear among most employees that others too would soon lose their jobs. Members of Urban Bank had formed quite high expectations about what the merger would do for both their bank and their individual careers. Despite the fact that this was to be a horizontal combination where significant operational integration would occur, there were few expectations of wide-scale changes or reductions in force. As the escrow clerk's remarks indicate, employees of Suburban Bank, who seemed to have more realistic expectations about merger outcomes despite the assurances from their CEO, were more favorable about the merger. This difference, which will be analyzed more fully in Chapter Six, appears to be based on the distinct organizational and managerial cultures that existed in the two banks. However, while the 1982 postmerger survey data support the conclusion that former Urban Bank personnel felt significantly more deprived than former Suburban Bank members, it is just as important to note that the percentages of favorable attitudes in both banks are quite low.

Ironically, the gradually evolving expectations in the psychological contract during the premerger period might well have included the possibility of layoff as a result of the widely recognized competitive and economic problems in the thrift industry. Yet, in spite of the adverse industry conditions, no mention was made of possible downsizing in the merged entity. The perception of security in one's job is a fundamental dimension of the psychological contract, and this perception was reinforced by the public assurances of job security given by the two CEOs. As suggested by the imagery used by the banks' employees—the "Christmas massacre"—the layoffs obviously violated this basic expectation.

A similar dynamic of unfulfilled favorable expectations occurred in the computer services joint venture between CompServe and NetCo. As discussed in Chapter Two, even though the venture was initiated by CompServe's founder and CEO, the firm's employees were highly cautious about the agreement, since they felt it could jeopardize their long-term but rather tenuous relationship with major computer stores in the area. Since CompServe did not sell any hardware, the stores had been more than willing to pass on referrals of clients who might need further support and consultation for the computer systems they had purchased. The fear was that once CompServe, through NetCo, also began to sell hardware, these referrals and links with the stores might be terminated. Moreover, people questioned what NetCo could "really do for us."

NetCo's employees, by contrast, were initially quite favorable about the proposed venture. The general perception was that the combination would provide an important support and service component to their existing operation, as well as increasing its marketing abilities and client base. Thus, NetCo's employees initially had much more positive expectations about the joint venture than did CompServe's employees. It is also important to note that in contrast to the other two cases, virtually all of CompServe's and NetCo's employees felt secure in their positions and perceived good career opportunities in their firms both before *and* after the joint venture.

Within three months after the agreement was formally signed, however, NetCo's employees became disenchanted with the venture and the level of support they were receiving from CompServe. Since their expectations for a number of "hot" customer leads and a high level of support from CompServe were not met, they became increasingly negative about the inter-organizational agreement. Yet every one of CompServe's members, who as a group initially had much lower expectations about the combination, felt that their firm would "become more effective because of the joint venture agreement." In fact, in every area except feeling more informed about the proceedings of the combination, NetCo members were far less favorable about the venture than CompServe employees. As with the attitudes of Urban and Suburban Bank members, these feelings were the exact opposite of precombination outlooks.

In contrast to the above two cases, the initial reaction of Co-op Foods' employees to the TransCo acquisition was largely unfavorable. Three-quarters of those surveyed, for example, reported that they did not think that the change in ownership would be good for their company. Most people expected that there would be dramatic changes following the acquisition and that the "protected status" they enjoyed under Aero would be in jeopardy. As the acquisition unfolded, however, employees found that life under TransCo would not be very different from their situation as part of the Aero Corporation. Aside from basic changes in accounting and financial reporting procedures to bring Co-op Foods into line with the rest of TransCo, the supermarket chain was left pretty much on its own. Although Co-op's managers and employees continued to have a number of reservations, it seemed that TransCo would allow the retail food company to operate largely as it had done prior to the acquisition.

As a result, there was much more stability in employee attitudes and perceptions at Co-op Foods than among employees involved in the bank merger and the computer services joint venture. It is important to note, however, that the same ambiguities, tensions, and concerns that characterized the other two combinations were present there as well. People in the finance area, for example, reported high levels of stress and tension as they operated under tight deadlines and schedules in getting reporting procedures in line with each other. There had also been a number of changes in management personnel over the years that served to make people anxious. One employee noted that she had been there for fourteen years, had worked through twenty-seven supervisors and five presidents, and "couldn't remember many of their names, they changed so fast."

During the TransCo takeover, a number of middle managers were dismissed for poor performance. Although TransCo made no promises concerning managerial job security, these terminations initially fueled apprehension and anxiety on the part of many employees. It was also clear to most people, however, that the termination decisions were based on performance factors rather than arbitrary standards or cultural differences, and they were largely accepted. Still, especially in contrast to the bank merger, the unrelated nature of the takeover, its low level of planned integration, and the eventual spinoff and management buyout created a very different set of circumstances for Co-op's members.

Feelings of Deprivation. The sudden violation of perceived entitlements can precipitate feelings of organizational deprivation, especially when people's needs and desires are frustrated by expectations that are higher than actual outcomes (Crosby, 1984). As the bank merger and the computer services joint venture suggest, there is a "danger" of creating overly optimistic or unrealistic expectations about an organizational combination. As research indicates (for example, Stouffer and others, 1949), even in favorable situations unfulfilled high expectations can generate feelings of deprivation.

In the bank merger, open-ended comments confirmed that employees perceived that there was far less job mobility after the merger and that even if they were "lucky enough" not to be laid off, they were "stuck" in their present positions. As indicated by the 1982 postmerger survey, while employee satisfaction with pay, benefits, quality of supervision, work hours, and amount of work either remained the same or improved slightly, the merger created a loss of pride in the institution, a strong sense of detachment from upper management, a loss of a sense of job security, and a general decline in overall job satisfaction.

As a result, many organizational members—especially among Urban Bank personnel—talked about the sense of loss and the grief they experienced as a result of the merger. People became quite nostalgic about their prior bank affiliations during the initial combination aftermath period. Interview and survey data indicate that employees displayed an active dislike of their merger partner counterparts, the "other bank's" managers, and its policies and orientations.

Virtually all of the negative comments by organizational members during the postmerger period reflected a sense of deprivation and disenchantment as their expectations of merger outcomes were violated. Employees reported that decisions were being made "without regard to individual circumstance," management had "withdrawn its support of employees," and there were "no positive outcomes" associated with the merger. While Urban Bank members tended to be more vocal about their discontent, people from both merger partners complained about the layoffs, especially since they felt that "they [the CEOs] lied to us." Organizational members further complained about declines in morale and the quality of customer service and the general lack of communication and a sense of "what really is going on around here."

The significant decline in employee satisfaction and acceptance of organizational systems and processes did not occur because one merger partner's system was objectively "better" than the other—both employee groups reported similar levels of satisfaction during the premerger period. In spite of the different realities of organizational life in the two banks, the conditions had existed for a long time and had shaped the psychological contracts in each organization, and, as a result, the two sets of working relationships were regarded as fair and equitable by each employee group (Homans, 1974). Rather, it seems that employees' understandings and expectations of what their new employment relationship would be differed from the emerging reality. Ironically, while these expectations proved to be false, they were reinforced by public assurances and statements made by the two CEOs.

The perception of relative deprivation is further reflected in a comparison of merger-related attitudes of Urban and Suburban Bank employees. For both groups, there was a significant decrease in satisfaction after the merger; the perception of each merger partner's employees in 1982 was that the other group was faring better. Interview data during this period suggest that respondents from one merger partner regarded their new reference group or comparison group after the combination as the employees of the other merger partner and their executives. This assessment further contributed to feelings of being deprived *relative to* their comparison group. Even though employees of one merger partner may feel this discontent more acutely than the other, as these data illustrate, members of both employee groups can feel deprived by a merger.

A similar dynamic was found in the joint venture between CompServe and NetCo. As hostility between members of the two firms grew, each group emphasized the benefits that the other was gaining through the venture—often at their own expense. While many of these comparative assessments were often exaggerated—from the difficulty of working with the people at the "other" firm to the extent to which the companies were generating new business as a result of the interfirm agreement—the joint venture was increasingly being evaluated in terms of what "we" were getting compared to "their" gains.

Resolution. Such unfulfilled expectations and violated psychological contracts, of course, do not necessarily last forever. In many instances, employees who are especially discontented will choose to deal with these perceived inequities by "bailing out" of the organization. As the bank merger study shows, organizational leavers often report significantly more negative attitudes than those who choose to stay. Still, a substantial number of people, many of whom were initially disenchanted, did remain with the bank. As the 1984 postmerger "stayer" data and the 1985–86 interviews suggest, although employee satisfaction and attitudes had still not reached premerger levels a full three years after the merger, there had been a marked improvement in these perceptions. Many of the feelings of deprivation had begun to subside. Thus, in this friendly, collaborative merger, while it took over three years for the inequities to begin to be resolved in people's minds, norms and roles did begin to stabilize, and a "refreezing" into new routines began to take place.

Homans (1974, p. 263) might have accurately predicted this outcome when he noted that "any distribution of reward, however unjust it may have appeared at one time, that does in fact persist long enough . . . to become the expected thing will also become the just thing and cease to arouse resentment." It is clear from the bank merger data, particularly with respect to the responses to the more global, perceptual questions, that positive feelings were returning. The frequency of positive responses from the open-ended questions increased from an average of less than one response per respondent in 1982 to almost two per respondent in 1984. Moreover, positive comments regarding personal issues such as "challenging work," "personal growth," "work conditions," and "the work itself" began to emerge. Employees once again began to emphasize their coworkers and their interactions with customers as major sources of satisfaction. Thus, as both the quantitative survey data and the responses to interviews and open-ended survey questions demonstrate, the feelings of discouragement and pessimism that had followed the merger were beginning to dissipate by 1984. Psychological merger, as described in Chapter Four, had begun to take place. This could occur, however, only once the feelings of violation of the psychological contract and organizational deprivation began to decline.

This dynamic should not be interpreted to mean that the dissatisfaction and disenchantment that organizational members feel about a particular combination will necessarily be resolved favorably. As will be discussed in Chapter Seven, for example, a significant group of Urban Bank members continued to work against the merger well after the initial aftermath period. Similarly, the computer services joint venture, while still intact at the present, appears to be gradually "fading out of existence." Over the past few months, there has been less and less interaction between the companies, either formal or informal. Thus, the "resolution" in this particular case appears to be a return to the initial situation—the autonomous operation of two independent companies. In fact, one of the few remnants of the joint venture is that NetCo is still using the CompNet name and logo.

It is too soon to reach firm conclusions about the resolution of the leveraged management buyout of Co-op Foods, especially in terms of its long-term viability as an independent company. It does seem, however, that there was much less of a sense of violated expectations and organizational deprivation than in the other two combinations. Although one might expect that the changes accompanying another transformation (the spinoff and leveraged buyout) within such a short period of time could create disillusionment, despair, and large-scale departures, these did not occur.

While some middle-level managers did "bail out" of the system, largely because of their expectations of reduced opportunities and rising work loads, most survey questions about the post-buyout era reflected a slight increase in satisfaction from the Aero and TransCo eras. These findings suggest that employees' expectations were essentially being met by the new owners and the accompanying organizational arrangements. Areas where there were decreases in satisfaction from the TransCo era concerned operating tensions, such as having sufficient people to do the job, the amount of work expected, and the extent to which top management was aware of job-related problems. Attitudes toward compensation and advancement also declined from the TransCo era. The general sentiment was that the new owners were running a "tight ship," because of both a sense of caution and the debt incurred in the buyout. At the same time, there was a fairly sharp rise in the feeling that the changes in ownership would be good for the company, and a strong majority of organizational members reported commitment to the company.

Conclusion

As illustrated by the assessment of individual reactions to the horizontal bank merger, the unrelated conglomerate acquisition, and the computer services product-extension joint venture, significant problems can result from violated expectations and feelings of deprivation and frustration that often occur in organizational combinations. It is important to emphasize that despite the fact that each of these combinations was collaborative in nature, many difficulties still emerged. Considering these dynamics, it is fairly easy to imagine how these problems are typically intensified and compounded in more hostile situations.

Managers involved in a merger or acquisition should be aware of the impact that sudden changes in the psychological contract can have on employee satisfaction and commitment. Especially in the bank merger, each merger partner's members felt that their psychological contract had been violated. Employees from both Urban and Suburban banks were accustomed to particular organizational procedures and reward systems and expected to be treated much as they had been in the past. The merger, however, created a situation in which each group's expectations as to how they would be treated and regarded were unmet.

The CEOs of the two banks compounded this problem by their public assurances that there would be job security and few, if any, merger-related changes. In a postmerger interview with the CEO of Suburban Bank, however, he admitted that he knew from the start that the merger would require substantial changes. His rationale for the "no change" announcement was that he needed to gain early support for the merger. In reflecting on his decision and the turmoil that followed, the CEO told the researchers, "In retrospect, the 'no layoff' and 'no change' announcement might have been a big mistake. We [the Urban Bank CEO and I] should have said that 'inadequate' people will be let go. But it did make things easier at first." He continued, "I'm still not sure that it isn't better to have a charade at first to get people involved. Perhaps we should have been more candid, but you have to keep the morale of the troops up, even if only for the short term." Since these comments appear to be representative of the way in which merger- and acquisition-related decisions are made (for example, Gaddis, 1987; Harshbarger, 1987), it is easy to understand why trust breaks down during the combination of two firms.

As the data from the acquisition and joint venture cases indicate, rather than creating an initial "charade" to win the support of organizational members, it seems more effective to provide employees with a realistic view of what the combination will mean for the companies and the employees. An interesting illustration contrasts the attitudes of Urban and Suburban bank members with those of employees who joined Merged Bank after the consolidation. In virtually every instance in the 1982 postmerger survey, those employees who joined the bank following the merger reported more favorable attitudes about the bank, its management, and its work systems. Interview data suggest that the "new" employees were provided with quite realistic previews about what life would be like in Merged Bank. As a result, many of the decisions that violated the expectations of Urban and Suburban bank members were accepted by the new employees.

It is difficult, of course, to totally prepare organizational members to accept and deal with all the transitions that can accompany a merger or acquisition. As an executive whose company was involved in a takeover attempt aptly points out, "You can't prepare people to be hit by a truck" (Marks and Mirvis, 1986, p. 41). As will be explored in more detail in Chapter Eight, however, research has indicated that employees provided with *realistic merger previews* maintain much more stable levels of commitment, satisfaction, trust, and performance than do those who receive less open information about the combination (Schweiger and DeNisi, 1987). Similar to the idea of realistic job previews (Wanous, 1980) is the idea that accurate and honest information about what is likely to transpire during an organizational combination can begin to build the foundation for the emergent psychological contract of the combined entity.

It is clear that mergers and acquisitions involve an enormous adjustment to change in a relatively short period of time. Given the myriad issues and tensions raised by such transformations, regardless of how thoughtfully or carefully employee-related concerns are handled, some turmoil and displacement are inevitable. Managers should realize, however, that over time, people's frames of reference will change. While some people will refuse to accept the change and "bail out" of the system, to others, after a sufficient amount of time has elapsed, the transformation will appear to be fair and just. After the dissipation of the feeling that one's psychological contract has been violated, mutual understandings will stabilize as the organization takes on a new identity.

To simply assume, however, that the transformation will succeed or the myriad issues and concerns associated with it will work themselves out in the long run is naive. A merger or acquisition is ultimately a human process. Focused efforts on and sensitivity to what people are experiencing are necessary if managers hope to decrease the costs involved for both individual employees and the organization.

Six

Integrating Different Cultures and Managing Conflicts

One of the underlying reasons why mergers and acquisitions often fail to achieve the level of operational and financial performance predicted by precombination feasibility studies is the conflicts and tensions that emerge when companies try to combine disparate and frequently dramatically different cultures. A perceived threat to one (or both) of the cultures of merging firms can heighten the polarization between employee groups and increase the tendency to be highly evaluative with respect to what "our" company and "their" firm are attempting to accomplish (Sales and Mirvis, 1984). As a result, efforts to impose seemingly rational requirements for effecting organizational, procedural, and other merger-related changes may be resisted because of threats to the existing cultures.

The basic proposition that organizations have cultural properties, that they breed meanings, values, and beliefs, that they nurture stories, myths, and legends, and that they abound with rites, rituals, and ceremonies has experienced rapid acceptance and popularity (Allaire and Firsirotu, 1984). Within anthropology and sociology, of course, culture has long been recognized as a significant determinant of beliefs, attitudes, and behaviors. As such, it has been a central variable in the study of different societies and their "natural" spheres of action. The importance of culture for organizational research, however, has only recently been emphasized through the explicit recognition of the potency of culture at the organizational as well as societal levels. Scholars have used the concept to gain fuller understanding of the subtle dynamics and forces at work in organizations and in organizational change efforts (see Ouchi and Wilkins, 1985, for an extensive review). Strategy formulation, preferred leadership styles, and accepted ways of accomplishing tasks, among other central facets of organizational life, are felt to be reflections of a particular organization's culture (Deal and Kennedy, 1982; Ouchi, 1981; Peters and Waterman, 1982; Sathe, 1985; Schein, 1983, 1985; Smircich, 1983). With respect to the specific case of mergers and acquisitions, the process of combining two firms is often conceptualized as the assimilation and/or accommodation of the companies' cultures (Buono, Bowditch, and Lewis, 1985; Sales and Mirvis, 1984; Walter, 1985a). Some experts have gone as far as to suggest that it is the "most fundamental issue" that must be addressed in such transformations (American Bankers Association and Ernst & Whinney, 1985, p. 43).

Toward a General Understanding of Culture

Most definitions of culture currently used in the social sciences are modifications of E. B. Tylor's (1871, p. 1) definition of the concept as "that complex whole which includes knowledge, belief, art, morals, law, custom, and any other capabilities and habits acquired by man as a member of society." In its broadest sense, culture can be thought of as that part of the entire repertoire of human action and its products that is socially as opposed to genetically transmitted. The term, however, has been criticized as being conceptually weak, since it has been defined in a number of different ways, and no clear consensus has emerged (Child, 1981; Bhagat and McQuaid, 1982). These problems are underscored by Kroeber and Kluckhohn's (1952) assessment of 164 different definitions of culture.

Despite the broad usage and range of definitions, part of this conceptual confusion can be clarified by examining the differences between sociological and anthropological uses of the term. Sociologists, for the most part, use the term *culture* to describe the *ideational aspects* of social life, as distinguished from society or social structure. The anthropological approach, by contrast, more often takes its entire subject matter as culture. Thus, the sociological orientation stresses the process through which behavior is learned (Linton, 1936, 1945), the patterns of meaning that develop over time (Parsons, 1960), the symbolic and evaluative aspects of tradition, ideas, or beliefs (Parsons, 1951), and the set of rules governing behavior (Radcliffe-Brown, 1957). In contrast, while anthropologists such as Kroeber and Kluckhohn (1952) focus on the ideational aspects of "social heredity" (that is, patterns of behavior acquired and transmitted by symbols), they also see culture as constituting the "distinctive achievement" of people, including various artifacts. This orientation thus adds a material dimension to the concept.

On the basis of this brief comparison, two basic aspects of culture can be delineated (Barnouw, 1975, 1979; Buono, Bowditch, and Lewis, 1985; Mitchell, 1973; Morey and Luthans, 1985). First, central to both the anthropological and sociological uses of the term is the integrative theme of *custom,* traditional and regular ways of doing things. Thus, culture can be thought of as being *learned* rather than genetic or biological in nature. It is *shared* by people as members of social groups rather than being an idiosyncratic attribute. Culture is also *transgenerational* and *cumulative* in that it is passed from one generation to the next. Finally, it is *symbolic* in nature and *patterned* (that is, organized and integrated) in our lives. Second, a distinction can be made between material, or objective, culture and ideational, or subjective, culture. *Objective culture* refers to the artifacts and material products of a society (Barnouw, 1979; Mitchell, 1973). *Subjective culture,* by contrast, is a group's "characteristic way of perceiving the man-made part of its environment," the rules and the group's norms, roles, and values (Triandis and others, 1972, p. 4).

Organizational Culture

Just as culture is a central factor that influences the ways in which people act and interact in a given society, indigenous cultures evolve over time in organizations that affect individual and group behavior in predictable though subtle ways. Indeed, many conceptual similarities can be drawn between societal and organizational culture. While organizational culture is also implicitly diffused, it is, as is societal culture, a pervasive and powerful force in shaping behavior. Moreover, although there are multiple definitions and uses of the concept at the organizational level as well (Harris and Moran, 1979; Miles, 1980; Ouchi and Wilkins, 1985; Pettigrew, 1979; Sathe, 1985; Schwartz and Davis, 1981; Schein, 1983, 1985; Siehl, 1982), there is still the integrative theme of custom. This "normative glue" holds an organization together through traditional ways of carrying out organizational responsibilities, unique patterns of beliefs and expectations that emerge over time, and the resultant shared understandings of reality at given points in time.

Before we create a framework for assessing organizational culture, for analytical purposes and a fuller understanding of the subtleties of the concept, four conceptual issues need to be briefly examined: (1) the difference between objective and subjective organizational culture; (2) the difference between subjective culture and organizational climate; (3) the uniqueness of organizational cultures; and (4) the multifaceted nature of organizational culture.

Objective and Subjective Organizational Culture. Organizations have both subjective and objective cultures. *Subjective organizational culture* refers to the pattern of beliefs, assumptions, and expectations shared by organizational members and the group's characteristic way of perceiving the organization's environment and its values, norms, and roles as they exist outside the individual (Buono, Bowditch, and Lewis, 1985; Schwartz and Davis, 1981; Triandis, 1977; Triandis and others, 1972). This includes such things as organizational heroes (that is, those people who personify the culture's values and provide role models for others), myths and stories about the organization and its leadership, organizational taboos, rites, and rituals, and perceptions of "Mecca" (that is, important symbolic locations and prideful extensions of the organization) (Buono, Bowditch, and Lewis, 1985; Deal and Kennedy, 1982; Pettigrew, 1979; Smircich, 1983; Wilkins, 1984).

Subjective organizational culture also encompasses what may be termed a *managerial culture,* the leadership styles and orientations, mental frameworks, and ways of behaving and solving problems that are influenced by the values supported by the organization (Peters, 1980). Although some aspects of managerial culture may be shared across organizations, as evidenced by Peters and Waterman's (1982) "search for excellence," crucial though subtle facets tend to be indigenous to particular organizations. Thus, while two organizations may assert that "quality customer service" is the key to their success, there may be significant differences in managerial ideas of how to best achieve that end.

Objective organizational culture refers to the artifacts created by an organization. For instance, Digital Equipment Corporation's modular, open-office configuration, the comfortable rest-break areas on the assembly line of British Leyland's Solihull plant during the mid-1970s, and the chassis assembly team bays complete with saunas, coffee rooms, and separate entrances at Volvo's Kalmar plant are objective (material) reflections of each organization's culture. Such physical settings, office locations and decor, and even the fleet of cars an organization leases for its executives can reflect the values of the organization. In BankAmerica Corporation, for example, well known for its bureaucratic nature, the corporate hierarchy rigidly determined who received what kind of car: the president used a Lincoln Continental, executive vice-presidents used Buick LeSabres, while lower-level executives used Pontiac Phoenixes and Chevrolet Citations. When the corporation acquired the discount broker Charles Schwab & Company, known for its innovative, entrepreneurial style, a clash emerged over Schwab's fleet, which included Porsches, Saabs, BMWs, Mercedeses, and Jaguars. The norm at Schwab was "You go out and pick a car, and the company leases it for you." While those at Schwab did not want to change their fleet, arguing that they did not want to "squelch individuals' initiative," many of BankAmerica's executives expressed extreme displeasure and frustration with the situation, since it did not follow the parent corporation's hierarchical norms (Zonana, 1983, p. 27). BankAmerica Corporation eventually divested Schwab ("Schwab to Buy Back Brokerage," 1987).

Both aspects of culture are important for a full understanding of a particular organization. Subjective organizational culture, however, typically provides a more distinctive basis for characterizing and interpreting similarities and differences among people in different firms. While objective culture may show similarities across organizations, subjective organizational culture is more specific to a particular enterprise. At times, however, something that is part of the objective culture of an organization can begin to take on a life of its own. When this occurs, there is a distorted magnification of both the reality and the importance of the artifact, which then becomes part of the subjective culture of the organization. As will be illustrated later in this chapter, this is part of the process by which myths and stories concerning organizational life are created.

Subjective Organizational Culture and Organizational Climate.
Although the terms *subjective organizational culture* and *organizational climate* are often used interchangeably, there are basic differences between these two concepts. *Organizational climate* is defined as a "measure of whether people's expectations about what it should be like to work in an organization are being met" (Schwartz and Davis, 1981, p. 33). As defined above, subjective organizational culture, by contrast, is concerned with the *nature* of beliefs and expectations about organizational life. Climate, which is typically measured by organizational surveys, is an indicator of the extent to which these employee beliefs and expectations are being fulfilled. Organizational culture, characterized by values and expectations, is more deep-rooted and has a long-term time perspective; organizational climate, characterized more by work requirements, feelings, and interpersonal relationships, has a comparatively shorter time perspective (Burke, 1985).

Organizations with widely different cultures can have rather similar climate profiles. Organizational members perceive themselves as satisfied or dissatisfied with their corporate situations on the basis of their perceptions of what organizational life "should be." These expectations are based on the type of psychological contract formed at entry (see Chapter Five) and early socialization experiences, in addition to the individual's own prior experiences and perceptions of the larger environment. To illustrate, one organization may have a relatively autocratic managerial culture where management style is perceived as autocratic, while another may be more democratic in nature and perceived as such. Yet responses to the survey statement "My manager involves me in decisions that affect me whenever appropriate" can produce a similar favorability rating in the two organizations. Even though the actual situations may be quite different, if they are congruent with the nature of employee expectations about what life in the organization should be like, climate profiles can be similar.

Uniqueness of Organizational Cultures. Although popular use of the concept of culture suggests that differences between organizational cultures exist primarily across industries rather than between organizations in the same industry, this focus seems too restrictive. Deal and Kennedy (1982), for example, formulate four general corporate culture types based on two main dimensions—the degree of risk and the speed of feedback characteristic of a given industry. They suggest that in industries where daily decisions involve major stakes and fast results (for instance, in advertising, entertainment, and construction), a "tough guy/macho" culture dominates. In this world, success is defined by the ability to take risks and succeed. In contrast, insurance and utility companies, characterized by low risks and slow feedback, develop "process" cultures in which the ability to manage details is the key to success. According to Deal and Kennedy, "bet-your-company" cultures tend to evolve in high-risk, slow-feedback industries, as when aircraft manufacturers literally bet the success of the firm on a new plane design. In contrast to the other cultures, success is dependent on an attention to detail and the ability to cope with uncertainty for long periods of time. Finally, those industries with relatively low risks and quick feedback, such as sales organizations, develop "work hard–play hard" cultures where success depends on an action orientation and a highly motivated employee population.

While they suggest that intrafirm variations might result from functional differences (such as cultural differences between sales, research and development, operations) and locale (regional or international), their basic position is that "general cultural patterns evolve to meet the demands of the workplace" (Deal and Kennedy, 1983, p. 503). The broader tendencies in the social and business environment on which Deal and Kennedy focus *are* an important influence on the development of an organization's culture. However, while such global differences do exist, and they are useful for initial empirical investigation, cultural differences between organizations in the same industry can be just as great as cultural differences across industries.

In terms of mergers and acquisitions, even though over the long term it may be easier to accommodate intraindustry differences than interindustry differences, divergent cultures between organizations in the same industry do exist and can present many difficulties. The merger between oil company giants Gulf Corporation and Chevron Corporation, for example, was initially touted as a near-perfect match, since the two firms had approximately equal assets and complementary resources. The merger, however, was described as more of a "forced marriage," laden with fears, anxieties, and frustrations, since the companies approached the same business with widely different styles and strategies (Wells and Hymowitz, 1984). Virtually identical dynamics were characteristic of the merger that created LTV Steel, the second-largest steelmaker in the United States. While the combination and "all the numbers look[ed] good on paper," Republic Steel and Jones & Laughlin Steel, the merger partners, had sufficiently different philosophies, styles, and orientations that the simplest disagreements between employee groups often flared into "major conflicts" (O'Boyle and Russell, 1984).

The Multifaceted Nature of Organizational Culture. Thus far, the discussion has treated organizational culture as if it were a monolithic phenomenon; that is, one culture to a setting. It is important to realize, however, that a multiplicity of cultures often exists in organizations. While in a given firm there is typically a dominant culture (that is, the core values and norms that are shared by the majority of organizational members), divisions, plants, departments, and so forth may have cultures that are distinct from that of the larger group (Buono and Nichols, 1985; Martin and Siehl, 1983; Wilkins, 1983).

In culture change efforts, it is also important to realize that not all elements of a given culture will change at the same rate. Because of the resultant "culture lag" (Ogburn, 1922), full cultural integration may be far from perfect. Thus, in merger scenarios where markedly different cultures are in existence, there is a very real possibility that people, in refusing to give up certain beliefs, values, traditions, and priorities, will purposefully lag behind the rest of the organization in accepting the culture change (see Mills, 1964).

Summary. Organizational culture tends to be unique to a particular organization, composed of an objective and a subjective dimension and concerned with tradition and the nature of shared beliefs and expectations about organizational life. It is a powerful determinant of individual and group behavior. Organizational culture affects practically every aspect of organizational life, from the way in which people interact with each other, perform their work, and dress to the types of decisions made in a firm, its organizational policies and procedures, and its strategy considerations.

In order to develop a fuller understanding of the nature and implications of organizational culture in mergers and acquisitions, the remainder of this chapter focuses on issues surrounding cultural integration and the similarities and differences between the dominant organizational cultures of the merger and acquisition partners described in Chapter Two. The difficulties and complexities that are posed by a multitude of different cultures in change efforts and the possibility of countercultural backlash are explored more fully in Chapter Seven.

The Influence of Culture in Mergers and Acquisitions

The full potency of organizational culture can be seen during a merger or acquisition when two disparate cultures are forced to become one. As the cases presented in Chapter Two illustrate, oganizations that may appear to be highly compatible on the surface and that seemingly should be able to achieve valuable merger synergies can have underlying cultural differences that seriously threaten their integration. Organizational members are usually so embedded in their own culture prior to major organizational changes that they rarely fully realize its influence on their behavior. During the process of combining two organizations, however, the cultural "collision" and resultant shock for organizational members created by living in a different organizational world can disrupt the entire workings of the newly formed firm.

Types of Cultural Integration in Organizational Combinations

A common misconception about cultural integration in a merger or acquisition is that there must be a total assimilation of the different cultures for the combination to be successful. As suggested by Chapters Two and Three, however, just as there are different types of mergers and acquisitions, there are different levels of cultural integration that are possible. According to recent research and field study, for example, there appear to be four main types of cultural merger or acquisition outcomes that reflect typical organizational and operational merger implementation strategies (American Bankers Association and Ernst & Whinney, 1985, pp. 59–68): (1) cultural pluralism; (2) cultural blending; (3) cultural takeover; and (4) cultural resistance.

Cultural Pluralism. Cultural pluralism in mergers is largely based on an appreciation for the potential benefits that can result from sustaining the creative and motivational elements of an independent company. Merger implementation, therefore, allows the maximum flexibility for acquired organizations to operate autonomously. In this type of combination, cultural diversity and cultural subgroups are allowed to exist within the context of a shared strategy for growth and organizational success. The basic assumption underlying this approach is that "strength comes from diversity," that in facing organizational problems, a variety of perspectives and inputs are better than one (Falvey, 1987, p. 28).

Gould, Inc., a midwestern automotive supplier that gradually transformed itself into a high-technology company, is an example of a firm that has followed a cultural pluralism strategy in its acquisitions. In the early 1980s, the company spent over $400 million acquiring firms ranging from a small microcomputer manufacturer to a maker of electronic parts. According to the corporation's chief financial officer (CFO), Gould, Inc., looks for companies that are market leaders and then spends a considerable amount of time talking to the firms' management: "we've got to satisfy ourselves that their management team really wants to be part of Gould." Once it acquires a company, the CFO reports that it leaves the management teams alone: "It would be silly for us to impose a different management style on them and run the risk of screwing up their success" (Cohen, 1984, p. 18).

Critics of the cultural pluralism strategy point out that the approach is little more than a reflection of the conglomerate diversification movement of the 1950s and 1960s. By having a number of companies operating autonomously under the same corporate structure, firms may be able to spread out their risk but do little to achieve true organizational synergies and economies of scale and scope in their operations. As a banking executive commented, "The dictionary says autonomous means 'self-rule,' but in the original Greek it means 'self-legislating,' and in practice it often means that groups become laws unto themselves" (American Bankers Association and Ernst & Whinney, 1985, p. 62).

Cultural Blending. This particular approach attempts to create a blending or assimilation of two previously distinct cultures into a new, unified culture. This strategy is often seen in "mergers of equals," where no company officially dominates. Integration planning is usually focused on assessing the strengths of each firm's culture and merging them into one. Success is contingent on a high level of goodwill between the firms, flexibility in merger negotiations, a lack of "ego trips" between top managers, and ongoing, effective communication and interaction between the merger partners.

While this strategy appears to be egalitarian, suggesting that the best parts of each merger partner will be integrated into one, the Urban-Suburban bank merger illustrates the fact that the outcomes are often quite unpredictable. A recent merger between two Chicago law firms further illustrates some of the difficulties involved (J. Bailey, 1987, p. 29). As a result of soaring legal costs and increased competition from industry giants, mid-sized legal firms appear to be choosing between two survival strategies: remain small but become highly specialized or "join the big leagues" through a merger. In selecting the latter strategy, the two firms appeared initially to be a model for law-firm combinations. The union was friendly, a managing partner was assigned as a mediator to help resolve internal disputes, and each firm's partners admitted that the time had come to "inculcate some new values." Within a year after the merger, however, instead of "blending together," postcombination interactions were described as tension laden and confrontational. As a result, the billing system broke down, the managing partner who was supposed to resolve internal disputes quit, a number of other partners left the firm, taking millions of dollars' worth of clients with them, and long-term clients began using other law firms. Ironically, it seems that many of the problems were related to the cultural blending strategy: since neither firm emerged as dominant after the merger, virtually everything— from pay scales and whose clerks and secretaries would be dismissed to which associates would be asked to leave—had to be negotiated. Instead of exchanging values and selecting the best features of each firm, the process broke down as the cultures repeatedly clashed with each other. The difficulties are perhaps best exemplified by the actions of the founder of one of the firms after a key partner left. The founder called an emergency partners' meeting—but invited only the partners from his old firm.

Cultural Takeover. In cultural takeovers, merger implementation requires replacing the culture of the acquired firm with the dominant culture of the acquiring firm. This process involves strong, decisive leadership and skillful management of the resultant short- and moderate-term cultural crises in order to achieve the planned-for longer-term strategic success. Much of the over-all effectiveness of this approach, however, appears to be based on the acquiring organization's reputation for fairness, credibility, and success in prior mergers and acquisitions.

North Carolina National Bank (NCNB), for example, has developed a reputation for taking over small banks "the way the troops took over Iwo Jima" (Heylar, 1986, p. 1). The bank was nicknamed "No Care National Bank" after "heads rolled" following an interstate acquisition—within one year, only one of the acquisition target's department heads was still employed. With the next acquisition, about one-half of the institution's top 300 officers left NCNB within eighteen months. As a result, the bank has lost not only a number of good employees and cus-tomers but other merger possibilities as well. The word passed along among bankers is that "You wouldn't want to merge with those guys, those vicious Huns who'll slaughter, rape and pil-lage" (Heylar, 1986, p. 10).

Cultural takeover attempts, however, are not necessar-ily strife laden. A major bank holding company, for example, stages its takeovers like the "founding of a new bank" (Amer-ican Bankers Association and Ernst & Whinney, 1985, p. 67). Focusing on financially weak institutions, all acquisitions are accompanied by an immediate media blitz. Merger and human resource specialists meet individually with all organizational members to discuss openly and honestly what is going to be done. Within one week of the takeover, the corporation puts on a major event for the employees, including cocktails and dinner, a video show, and a presentation by the CEO. Every attempt is made to respond to employee concerns and discuss issues raised by the takeover.

Cultural Resistance. In many organizational combinations, merger implementation results in severe cultural conflict, charac-terized by a high level of management turnover, market-share shrinkage, and difficulty in achieving or even failure to achieve the desired operational synergy and strategic objectives sought after. In most instances, cultural resistance emerges when there is a lack of understanding of or attention to the cultures of the

merger partners. As strategic, financial, and operational concerns dominate acquisition integration efforts, cultural differences between the firms undermine much of what the acquiring firm is attempting to accomplish.

It is important to emphasize that unanticipated cultural
conflicts can readily alter intended merger strategies and plans.
In their assessment of mergers in the financial services industry,
for example, the American Bankers Association and Ernst &
Whinney (1985, pp. 59–60) found that cultural blending strategies involving mergers of "equals" often precipitated severe
cultural conflicts between the merger partners. The resulting
cultural resistance eventually led to cultural takeover by the more
dominant of the firms. Similarly, other mergers and acquisitions that are initially designed to ensure the flexibility and
autonomy suggested by cultural pluralism often result in blending or even takeover.

Moderating Factors in Cultural Integration Strategies

As this chapter has shown, culture has a powerful influence on organizational behaviors. The beliefs, values, and expectations about organizational life that develop over time and
are shared among organizational members guide employee attitudes, interactions, and decisions. This dynamic has obvious
implications for combining different organizations, especially
ones with distinctly disparate cultures. Not all organizational
cultures, however, are equally strong. There are, in fact, three
basic factors that make a significant difference in how influential a culture will be in shaping the attitudes and behaviors of
its members (Sathe, 1983, pp. 12–13). First, cultural strength
is based on the *extent* of shared beliefs and values that exist in
an organization: the greater the degree of shared beliefs and
values, the stronger the culture's influence, since there are more
basic assumptions that guide behavior. Urban and Suburban
banks, Co-op Foods, CompServe, and NetCo (Chapter Two),
as well as such companies as IBM, Procter & Gamble, and
Morgan Guaranty, are described as having "thick" cultures,
since they have a high level of shared beliefs and values that

organizational members are socialized to accept as their own. "Thin" cultures, or "pseudocultures," by contrast, have few shared assumptions and, as a result, have a much weaker influence on organizational life (Deal and Kennedy, 1983; Pascale, 1985; Sathe, 1985).

Second, organizational cultures whose beliefs and values are *more widely shared* across organizational members tend to have a more powerful effect because a greater number of personnel are guided by them. Finally, in cultures where beliefs and values are *clearly ordered*—that is, where the relative significance of different assumptions is widely known—the effect on member behavior will be more pervasive, since there is less ambiguity about which beliefs and values should prevail in conflict situations. For instance, in "thick" cultures, the distinction between central and pivotal values is clear, and people respond accordingly, while in "thin" cultures, there tends to be greater disagreement and ambiguity.

The potential problems with and differences between merging "thick" and "thin" cultures should be fairly obvious. In organizations with strong cultures, the behavior of members is significantly constrained by mutual accord rather than by organizational rules or policies. In this sense, the shared values act as a type of informal control system that tells people what is expected of them (Deal and Kennedy, 1982, 1983). In "culture-thin" organizations, by contrast, bureaucratic norms and rules provide the basis for organizational action (Wilkins and Ouchi, 1983). Thus, while the attempted consolidation between two "thick" cultures would tend to lead to a higher level of cultural resistance, a "thin" culture could more easily be taken over. Similarly, true cultural blending might be relatively more easily managed between two "thin" cultures than between two "thick" ones. Such distinctions can have a powerful impact on the ability of one organization to assimilate the culture of another. Unfortunately, before selecting a culture integration strategy, few organizations undertake any efforts to diagnose and decipher the culture of their intended merger partner or acquisition target.

Such diagnosis is important, since it is difficult on the surface to predict whether a company will have a strong or weak culture. As a general rule, smaller organizations that operate on a localized basis tend to have strong cultures, since it is easier for beliefs and values to become more widely shared between members (Sathe, 1983). However, significantly larger organizations with worldwide operations, such as IBM, can have very strong cultures. Especially if there have been a continuity of strong leadership, an ongoing emphasis on the same values and beliefs through socialization practices, and a relatively stable work force, a consistent set of beliefs and values can take hold and become widely known and shared (Pascale, 1985; Sathe, 1983, 1985).

Diagnosing Culture in Mergers and Acquisitions

To understand the full implications that culture poses for a merger or acquisition, it is important to be able to assess the degree of cultural similarity between the two firms. Deciphering a particular organization's culture, however, is a highly interpretive, subjective process that requires insights into historical as well as current activities. One cannot simply rely on what people verbally report about their culture. While such self-reports are important, the ways in which people act and interact with each other, how top management deals with various situations, how people actually spend their time, what the company says about itself in annual reports, house organs, and other documents, and the organization's physical setting contribute to a fuller understanding of a particular firm's culture (Deal and Kennedy, 1982; Jelinek, Smircich, and Hirsch, 1983; Pettigrew, 1979; Sathe, 1983).

While a number of different "interpretive frameworks" are proposed in the literature, several dimensions appear to be fairly universal:

Organizational Values. A firm's underlying values and beliefs are the essence of the organization's philosophy for achieving success. They reflect the basic view of "the way things should be" in a company that is shared by organizational members. A firm's philosophy provides a sense of common direction for its members and guidelines as to acceptable behaviors in their daily operations (Deal and Kennedy, 1982; Schein, 1985; Smircich, 1983).

Managerial Culture. A reflection of the organization's philosophy, this dimension concerns the basic concept of authority in organizations in terms of dominant leadership styles and orientations, mental frameworks, and ways of behaving and solving problems that are influenced by the values supported by the organization (American Bankers Association and Ernst & Whinney, 1985; Buono, Bowditch, and Lewis, 1985; Litterer, 1978; Peters, 1980).

Organizational Heroes. Organizations tend to have role models who personify the cultural value system and define the organization's concept of success in a tangible way. Although such heroes are frequently part of upper management, they may be identified throughout the organization. The key is that these individuals represent what the company stands for and reinforce the values of the culture by illustrating that success is attainable, acting as a role model for others, providing a symbol to the external world, setting a standard of performance, and motivating organizational members (Buono, Bowditch, and Lewis, 1985; American Bankers Association and Ernst & Whinney, 1985; Deal and Kennedy, 1982, 1983).

Organizational Myths and Stories. In many instances, employees do not speak directly of values, beliefs, and assumptions but instead imply them through a diverse set of concrete examples and stories. These narratives organize beliefs about the organization and its value system by acting as a "map" that facilitates a person's understanding of how things are done (Wilkins, 1984). Such stories and myths are often filtered through a "cultural network" (Deal and Kennedy, 1983, p. 502) that continues to reinforce and remind people of "why we do things that way." Organizational storytellers spread the corporate folklore and dramatize the exploits of the firm's heroes and heroines.

It is important to note that widely known stories do not necessarily support organizational needs. "Negative stories" can teach people which aspects or individuals of an organization to be wary of or how to "beat the system" (Wilkins, 1984, pp. 49–50). Myths and stories, therefore, can be either functional or dysfunctional for the organization. The important point is that they provide a strong indicator of how employees view the company, its culture, and its management.

Organizational Taboos, Rites, and Rituals. Organizations also have activities that are social manifestations of the dominant values and beliefs of the culture. Social rituals, referred to as the "dance of culture" (Deal and Kennedy, 1983, p. 501), define everyday interaction and reinforce the basic orientations of the organization. Special ceremonies, such as awards or honors dinners and annual parties and gatherings, and daily rites and rituals, such as departmental and committee meetings, symbolically convey the relative importance of organizational values, functions, and activities to employees (Deal and Kennedy, 1982; Shrivastava, 1986). However, just as "negative stories" inform organizational members about activities or individuals to avoid, organizational taboos convey boundaries concerning acceptable behaviors and interactions.

Cultural Symbols (Objective Culture). The material artifacts created by an organization can also reflect its values and orientations (American Bankers Association and Ernst & Whinney, 1985; Deal and Kennedy, 1982; Buono, Bowditch, and Lewis, 1985; Schein, 1985). These can range from icons such as luxury executive automobiles and designer furniture to images (logo, corporate dress styles) and building structure (open versus closed offices, assigned parking). Organizations try to create settings and images that make a statement about their company. Employee perceptions of "Mecca," those important symbolic locations and "prideful extensions" of the organization (Buono, Bowditch, and Lewis, 1985), also signal important values and orientations. Employees are usually quite explicit about where the office power base is located, where people can establish their reputation, and so forth. Similarly, specific job assignments and locations typically signify to employees longer-term intentions and plans, from advancement potential to a "dead-end" career.

Cultural Impacts in Three Combinations

An understanding of cultural similarities and differences between merger partners should be a significant component in selecting an appropriate integration strategy. It is important to determine whether there are irreconcilable mismatches between the beliefs and values across the two cultures, or whether differences are more peripheral (Sathe, 1983). While significant differences between companies do not necessarily mean that the two firms should avoid merging, they may suggest that a cultural pluralism rather than a blending strategy or a combination of the two might be more effective. At the very least, it could better prepare managers to deal with the cultural resistance that is bound to emerge when ''thick'' cultures collide.

The Bank Merger. In the bank combination presented in Chapter Two, the two CEOs initially embarked on a cultural blending strategy. Since the horizontal merger was to be a collaborative ''merger of equals'' involving a high degree of operational integration, the CEOs made a conscious effort to use the best features of each merger partner's working arrangements (for instance, compensation system, work hours, computer network) in the new institution. As a symbol of the new firm, the logo and headquarters were hybrids of those of the two original banks. Unfortunately, the two cultures, which were relatively ''thick,'' were polar extremes of each other. Virtually every effort to blend the two systems into one resulted in heated and at times quite adversarial cultural resistance. For instance, the premerger joint committees, with representatives from each partner, that were formed to resolve potential operating and procedural differences were characterized by intergroup fighting based on perceived threats to the existing cultures. Yet cultural differences between the firms were simply overlooked by the CEOs, who focused all of their attention on strategic and operational considerations.

A premerger *culture audit,* however, would have revealed significant differences between the firms. Although the two institutions were equal-sized savings banks, for example, their basic philosophies of how a bank should be run were distinctly different. Urban Bank's basic philosophy, supported by a highly activist human resource department, was that by creating a good work environment and meeting employee needs, the firm would create a more committed, motivated work force. This commitment would translate into high-quality customer service, which was thought to be an important component of organizational success. Suburban Bank, by contrast, focused much more fully on the work itself and placed relatively little importance on employee satisfaction. Thus, in terms of the relative orientation toward people versus task, Urban Bank had a much stronger emphasis on the interpersonal aspect of business than did Suburban Bank. When they were asked about life in their organization, for example, social events such as the Christmas party, the annual summer picnic, and retirement ceremonies were spontaneously mentioned by Urban Bank employees. There was a strong consensus among managers that employee job and organizational satisfaction was important and that the bank should do all it could to ensure that employee needs were met. The relative emphasis in Suburban Bank, in contrast, was more strongly task focused, with employees, especially officers, expected to continue working beyond quitting time until the job was finished. A postmerger story told by Suburban Bank's CEO recalled an incident when he returned from a trip late in the day to find a number of former Urban Bank officers leaving "on time" (a Suburban Bank taboo), which angered him. His postscript to the researchers was that "old habits die hard." There were virtually no stories spontaneously mentioned about social events in interviews with Suburban Bank personnel, and the consensus among its managers was that organizational needs and responsibilities "came first."

As suggested above, since leaders are often perceived as embodying the core values and beliefs of a group and exemplifying the group's pivotal norms, the way in which organizational members characterize their leaders can reveal much about how they see themselves as a group. In Urban Bank, the CEO's style was reported by senior officers and other administrators as highly participative and concerned with creating an egalitarian atmosphere. Employees referred to him as a "good guy" and a "Buddha," a person who delegated many internal decisions and focused his attention more on the external environment than on the internal workings of the bank. In sharp contrast, the CEO of Suburban Bank, who even referred to himself as a "Calvinist," was seen by his employees as a "bad guy" and an "elitist." His style was regarded as authoritarian, and he paid such close attention to internal bank affairs even at the detail level that he was continually referred to as "Dennis the Menace." Within this context, the locus of power was seen as more bureaucratically dispersed in Urban Bank and consolidated in the hands of Suburban Bank's CEO. These basic philosophical differences, while fully supported in the individual premerger organizations, became significant points of contention after the merger.

The orientation at the "top" of the organization was a significant factor in the way in which individual managers behaved in each bank. The *managerial culture* in Suburban Bank was characterized by its members as "management by crisis," while Urban Bank members perceived its actions and decisions as more planned and deliberate and based on widely gathered and shared information. An Urban Bank manager, for example, said that a common way to propose something was to "run it up the flagpole and see if anyone salutes it." Other organizational members added, however, that decisions from the president's office were often slow in coming. In Suburban Bank, employees remarked about the unambiguous way in which decisions came from their CEO.

A number of organizational *myths and stories*, narratives that organize beliefs about the organization and its value system, further contributed to the mosaic of life in the two banks. Both groups of employees perceived Urban Bank personnel as "fat cats," specialists to the degree that when new job duties evolved, it was not uncommon for a new person to be hired. Sharply in contrast was the image of Suburban Bank as a "hellhole," where new duties were generally distributed to existing organizational members, many of whom saw themselves as "jacks of all trades." While these perceptions did not reflect the actual policies for hiring and work delegation in the two firms, Urban Bank did have a larger employee population than Suburban

Bank, despite the relatively equal size of other aspects of the organizations. More importantly, however, this myth was a reflection of the overall philosophy of the two banks—the high people orientation of Urban Bank and the greater focus on task in Suburban Bank.

Another story about the two organizations focused on institutional commitment to the Community Reinvestment Act (CRA). The CRA, which was passed in 1977, calls for banks to play a central role in the community renewal process by working toward the revitalization of declining neighborhoods through an affirmative action program of local housing and small business lending. Since success of these efforts is thought to depend primarily on improved communication between banks and their surrounding low- and moderate-income communities, the CRA requires financial institutions to take the initiative to ensure that the bank serves the "legitimate credit needs" and "convenience" of its community (Buono and Nichols, 1985).

On the basis of CRA guidelines and the discussion sessions Urban Bank initiated with local groups, it appeared that that organization was more concerned with meeting community needs than was Suburban Bank. Urban Bank, moreover, received a considerable amount of favorable press for the rehabilitation of an urban three-decker structure that was sold (with mortgage assistance) as condominiums to three moderate-income families in the local community. Over time, the highly favorable perception of Urban Bank and the relatively unfavorable image that developed concerning Suburban Bank's community reinvestment activities exceeded the actual performance differences between the two organizations. A favorite story told by numerous employees, at all organizational levels, was that when a community group would approach the banks with a request, Urban Bank's CEO would respond, "Let's sit down and talk about it," while Suburban Bank's CEO would simply say, "[expletive deleted] them!" While the actual CRA performance between the two banks did not differ that significantly, the image of each institution and the beliefs that that image represents in the story reflect the values of each culture. Especially when such stories are about the actions of influential people or organizationally important programs, they provide ample clues about how things are "supposed to be done" in the firm. The clearer and more concrete the story, the more powerful it is as both a symbol and a guide for action (Wilkins, 1984).

Interviews with members of both institutions provided further insight into what was viewed as important in each organization. *Heroes* in Urban Bank were the vice-president for human resources and the first woman bank officer. In contrast, Suburban Bank employees identified a former CEO and the treasurer as two heroes in their organization. Similarly, "Mecca" in Urban Bank was the branches, since that was where one "established a reputation" in order to move up in the bank. In Suburban Bank, "Mecca" was unquestionably the CEO's office. Thus, the CEO's office and two top line officers were of central importance in Suburban Bank, while a "people specialist," a woman, and work locations removed from the main office were pointed to in Urban Bank.

As suggested above, various material products or artifacts created by organizations are *symbols* of their cultural traditions, beliefs, and value patterns. In Urban Bank, many of its artifacts reflected its strong commitment to its personnel, while similar types of artifacts in Suburban Bank reflected quite different values. In Urban Bank, for example, the employee eating facility in the main office was quite plush and decorated like a nice restaurant, with expensive wood paneling, numerous plants throughout the room, cushioned booths, and so forth. In Suburban Bank, by contrast, the same type of facility in the main office was much more like a traditional cafeteria, relatively spartan in nature, with simple chairs and tables and a small refrigerator in one of the corners. This distinction is a reflection of the values and orientations of each bank, the importance of a comfortable physical setting for Urban Bank (people orientation) compared to the "lean and mean," competitive aura of Suburban Bank (task orientation).

The differences in physical setting were further reflected in the branches. Urban Bank was so particular about the quality of the physical settings in the branches that it established its own subsidiary corporation to oversee and control any construction or upgrading of facilities. Suburban Bank's policy was that its branches should avoid expensive embellishments and take on a simple, functional appearance. Ironically, these policies were in direct contrast to the populations served by these institutions, the largely blue-collar population of Urban Bank and the professional, white-collar clientele served by Suburban Bank.

Another material symbol of the different cultures is the location and nature of the offices of the two CEOs. The office of Urban Bank's CEO was located in a prime corner of the third floor of the main office building, isolated from the day-to-day workings of the organization. Richly decorated, the office was framed by a panoramic window looking out over the city. The office of Suburban Bank's CEO was much simpler in nature, with two glass walls facing inside the bank, overlooking the teller cages and officer's platform. The offices, in effect, were physical symbols of the style of each CEO (McCaskey, 1979a), the external focus and preference for delegation of Urban Bank's CEO and the more internally focused concern for detail characteristic of the Suburban Bank president.

While the preceding "cultural audit" of the two banks suggests significant cultural differences, organizational climate data gathered through premerger surveys indicate that members of both banks readily accepted their cultures. Even though there were definite differences between the managerial and organizational cultures in the two banks prior to the merger, similar proportions of employees reported pride in working for their respective organizations and satisfaction with their systems of compensation and advancement, the context of their work, and interpersonal relations. Moreover, each employee group took pride in its organizational image, Urban Bank as a "good place" to work with a "happy" atmosphere and Suburban Bank as "lean and mean" and a "hellhole," while at the same time deriding the image of the other. Given the employee acceptance of and satisfaction with these highly disparate cultures and the attachments that organizational members develop to their own traditions, heroes, and other symbols of the workplace, a premerger culture audit would have revealed the potential for and probability of significant cultural resistance. Yet the two CEOs em-

barked on a cultural blending strategy with virtually no realization of the difficulties they would encounter in postmerger
integration.

The Computer Services Joint Venture. A situation quite similar to
the bank merger existed in the computer services joint venture.
Although the companies pursued a cultural pluralism strategy,
which appeared to make sense given the product- and market-
extension purpose of the venture and the goal of strategic rather
than operational integration, in each firm there was a basic lack of
understanding of and appreciation for the culture of the other.
The dominant feeling was that because of the size of the companies, little, if any, difficulty would be experienced. Yet, while
both firms were small, entrepreneurial companies, the founders of
the two institutions had very different ideas about how a successful company should be run. As Schein (1983) has argued, founders often start with a theory on how to succeed, an implicit set of
cultural assumptions about how to create and run a company.
The two organizations shared the basic *philosophy* that long-term
success would result from "being the best in the industry" and
placing a high value on quality customer service. They differed,
however, with respect to how they could accomplish those goals.
The basic styles and orientations of the two CEOs, for instance,
much as was the case with the two savings bank presidents, were
polar extremes. CompServe's founder had a strong top-down
orientation, while NetCo's CEO believed in and extensively prac-
ticed a management-by-consensus orientation.

    These disparate conceptions of authority, which created
quite different *managerial cultures,* were reflected in the ways in
which the two companies were set up. Although CompServe
had only twelve members, its structure was based on that of
the American Express Corporation. As the company's founder
explained, "I wanted to set up a company structure that we
could grow into. I believe in the 'puffer fish theory' of organizations. Even though the puffer fish may be small, when threatened
it swells up and looks big. I want to make the company look
bigger than it really is. That's the way to initially attract top
clients." CompServe's "division vice-presidents," for example,

each had a "staff" of one person (an assistant vice-president) under them. The work process was also highly structured. Staff members had to request proposals, contracts, and invoices for the various projects they were working on through an operations "department" (staff of one). Formal policy guidelines and procedures documented the appropriate way work assignments were to be carried out and communicated through the organization. The founder described his style as "management by persuasion," and while he made most of the company's decisions, he would change his position "if the point can be proved."

NetCo, by contrast, was structured on a more informal, "interactive" basis. The company operated in a highly decentralized manner, and while all staff members had formal titles and organizational responsibilities, structure and processes were far less explicitly defined than at CompServe. Most strategic decisions were "hashed out" at weekly staff meetings, and monthly "Back to Jesus" meetings (company *ritual*), usually held at a nearby bar and restaurant, emphasized the company's basic values and "why we got into business in the first place."

While both founders were identified as cultural *heroes* in their respective organizations, the *stories* that emerged reflected significant differences in how each firm operated. As discussed in Chapter Two, CompServe relied heavily on referrals from large computer stores in the surrounding areas for its customers. NetCo, by contrast, had an aggressive sales strategy, its staff priding themselves on their "intense, beat-the-pavement" orientation. Favorite stories at the company's "Back to Jesus" meetings recounted the extremes that organizational members would go to to secure a new client—the more excessive the effort, the greater the relish in telling the story.

Although most organizational members appeared to recognize that the nature of the services provided by the two firms influenced the different marketing strategies, there was little appreciation for the values and assumptions underlying these differences. NetCo employees derided CompServe's staff as "lazy" and "inept" in their sales efforts. Since the two companies had agreed to share business leads, NetCo's employees expected CompServe to be just as aggressive in its sales as they were.

When it turned out that NetCo was passing along many more "hot leads" than it was receiving from CompServe, its staff complained that their venture partner was "not doing the job as originally intended." CompServe's members, on the other hand, criticized NetCo for "not understanding computer consulting" and "seeing things only in terms of simple solutions."

As with the bank merger, these basic differences in managerial culture, conceptions of authority, and subjective organizational culture were overlooked in precombination planning and discussions. In this instance, such "cultural neglect" is ironic in that both founders emphasized the importance of creating strong cultures in their organizations. Referring to the importance of "handpicking" employees and developing a strong "team spirit," both CEOs emphasized how they had personally created their organizations. Yet, even though they had essentially agreed to allow basic differences across the organizations to exist, they made little effort to understand those differences, their implications for the ways in which the companies operated, and what it would take to work effectively together.

The Conglomerate Acquisition. Although TransCo essentially followed a cultural pluralism strategy in its acquisition of Co-op Foods, closer scrutiny of the combination reveals an integration strategy based more on indecision than on thoughtful diagnosis and assessment. In stark contrast to the close-knit, familylike culture of Co-op Foods, TransCo is a highly political, competitive conglomerate. The corporation's *philosophy* is based on aggressive growth through acquisition, integrating "winners" into the conglomerate's growing "empire" while spinning off "underperforming assets." The conglomerate, which has been averaging an acquisition every two years, many of them hostile, generally follows a cultural takeover strategy with respect to its acquisitions.

TransCo's takeover of Aero Corporation, which was described as a "sporadic courtship," was a product-extension acquisition designed to assimilate the target's aerospace division into one of TransCo's faltering subsidiaries. The conglomerate viewed the aerospace industry as a high-growth market but felt that it did not have sufficient expertise to effectively compete. Aero was subsequently acquired because of its identified strengths in research and development and its overall "technological leadership." Co-op Foods, however, was considered to be outside the conglomerate's strategic focus (unrelated acquisition), and rather than attempt to integrate the retail company into its operations, the corporation decided to initially let the company operate autonomously with financial (integration) controls.

When TransCo first acquired Aero, the conglomerate publicly announced that it did not know what it was going to do with Aero's supermarket operation. From a cultural integration perspective, the company opted to do what it virtually had never done in the past—leave one of its acquisitions alone. On the basis of an assessment of the two cultures and the disparate nature of each firm's expertise, the cultural pluralism strategy appears to be quite appropriate. In contrast to the high-growth, political nature of TransCo's culture, Co-op Foods was viewed as a "friendly place to work." Employees continually used such terms as "family," "community-oriented," and "open in its dealing with employees" to describe the company. When they were asked about the firm, several *stories* were told about community-based events and the philanthropic posture assumed by the company in aiding local charities and causes.

As a reflection of these basic orientations, a significant cultural *hero* for TransCo was its president and CEO, a person described as an "empire builder" who took what was a modest railroad operation in the mid-1960s and transformed it into a multibillion-dollar conglomerate. Co-op Foods' heroes were long-term members of the firm who had literally started at the bottom. One of the retail company's main heroes was also its president, but in contrast to TransCo's CEO, he was revered partly because "he knows who we are." Stories that began to assume mythic proportions were told about his beginnings at the store as a grocery bagger and how he worked his way up to the top. He was described as a "folksy" individual, a "great people person" who "roamed the halls in his shirtsleeves" and "talked to people on their level." All employees referred to him by first name.

Ironically, despite the autonomy that TransCo granted Co-op Foods, Co-op's top management team criticized the conglomerate for its indecisive integration efforts. Although Co-op Foods continued to prosper under TransCo's ownership, and the supermarket's management team greatly appreciated "being left to our own devices" during the acquisition, the public announcement that the conglomerate did not know what to do with the supermarket chain was unsettling to its management. Fears began to spread that the firm would be sold off to another supermarket chain. As Co-op Foods' president explained, "we were just sitting there [after the acquisition]. There's not a lot you can do when the company sits there and doesn't make up its mind."

The uneasiness created by TransCo's indecisive integration efforts was resolved approximately six months later when the conglomerate decided to divest the supermarket chain. The result was the leveraged management buyout, which, according to the president, "enabled us to go back to our original philosophy of running local stores in rural areas and to stay solely in the food business." As discussed in Chapter Two, the firm then undertook a swift, decisive cultural takeover of five of a rival chain's supermarket stores. In light of its experience with the TransCo acquisition and divestiture, Co-op Foods' management desired to act in a clear, decisive manner in its own acquisition. The supermarket chain's leaders, however, appeared to have learned very little about the role and influence of an organization's culture in the change process.

Conclusion

The task of coordinating and integrating different organizational cultures is one of the most demanding, complex, and problematic aspects of mergers and acquisitions. As this chapter has shown, culture conflicts and clashes are often a significant determinant of merger- and acquisition-related difficulties. Familiar symbols of objective culture and the shared meanings and understandings of subjective culture are important components of organizational identity as they are internalized over time by organizational members. Especially in what we have termed "strong" or "thick" cultures, these cultural orientations can significantly limit what organizational members are willing to accept and do in a merger or acquisition.

The first step in dealing with the influences and potential constraints of culture on organizations is to acknowledge their presence (Sathe, 1985; Shrivastava, 1985, 1986). Unfortunately, as the cases discussed above illustrate, most organizations planning to undertake a merger or acquisition fail to make any explicit effort to identify and assess their own culture, let alone the culture of their merger partner or acquisition target. As we have shown, however, it is important to study and understand these characteristics prior to the combination. By uncovering and critically examining the beliefs, values, and assumptions on which the cultures are based, organizations can more effectively plan and implement an appropriate cultural integration strategy. Such analysis is important if the strategic direction and desired level of integration outlined in Chapter Three are to be effectively achieved.

The importance of understanding cultural differences in a merger or acquisition is underscored by the cases discussed above. If cultural considerations are left unattended, the repercussions can create significant barriers and problems for the merged entity and its management. As the dilemma of cultural manageability outlined in Chapter One illustrates, however, there may very well be limitations as to what managers can accomplish with respect to cultural change and integration. Although the management literature suggests that most people will support organizational change if they can understand the need for it and can participate in bringing about the change, there are limits to the amount and rate of change people are able to assimilate. Cultural change is among the most difficult types of change for human beings, since culture provides the foundation for one's life. Indeed, while we may like to think of culture as a managerial tool that can be used to create "strong" organizations, culture may manage us much more than we can manage it.

Seven

Changing Organizational Cultures During the Merger

In one sense, merger and acquisition integration can be thought of as a process where two groups attempt to assimilate through an adaptation of cultural traits. Depending on the desired cultural integration strategy—pluralism, blending, or takeover—of course, employees of different combination partners may experience varying degrees of culture conflict. Yet in any merger, while some organizational members may find that little has actually changed, other employees will discover that attitudes and behaviors that were once sanctioned by the firm are no longer rewarded or approved and may, in fact, be punished. These latter role incumbents are then put on the defensive as they anticipate a threat to their values and accustomed organizational life-styles. Especially in cultural takeover situations, the result is typically manifested in frustration, anxiety, ambiguity, resentment, and conflict.

As the previous chapter noted, cultural tensions and clashes between merging organizations are often the root cause of combination-related difficulties. Indeed, organizations that appear to be compatible and that seemingly should be able to achieve valuable economies of scale and combination-related synergies can have underlying cultural differences that seriously threaten their integration. Yet popular prescriptions to ''change the culture'' rarely provide explicit advice on how this can be accomplished.

Organizational cultures, of course, do change. Since culture is an integral part of a group's learning process and experience, changes occur over time as people cope with shifts in the external environment and problems raised by internal integration efforts. Since the assumptions underlying a culture do not easily change, however, it is important to note that cultural transformation is typically an incremental and evolutionary process (Sathe, 1985; Wilkins and Bristow, 1987). As suggested by the dilemma of cultural manageability (Chapter One), while mergers and acquisitions often require a certain degree of culture change to be successful, true culture change, especially across disparate cultures, is often a time-consuming, financially expensive, and emotionally draining experience (Buono, Bowditch, and Lewis, 1985; Pettigrew, 1986; Trice and Beyer, 1985; Reynolds, 1987; Sales and Mirvis, 1984; Schein, 1985; Van de Ven, 1983). In fact, most successful culture change efforts appear to be based on incremental "redirections" and efforts to "honor" the company's past. As Wilkins and Bristow (1987, p. 225) argue, "changing a company culture is more like pruning trees than remodeling machines or buildings."

Influencing Cultural Change

There are two fundamental ways to effect culture change in an organization: (1) getting organizational incumbents to "buy into" a new configuration of beliefs and values and (2) recruiting and socializing new people into the organization (with an emphasis on those new beliefs and values) while removing past members as necessary. As Figure 2 illustrates, there are five key intervention points and processes that can be utilized to create such change: (1) changing organizational member behaviors; (2) justifying the behavioral changes; (3) communicating cultural messages about the change; (4) hiring and socializing new members who fit in with the desired culture; and (5) removing incumbents who deviate from the desired culture (Sathe, 1985, pp. 386–395). Managers seeking to create change in an organization's culture should intervene at these main points.

Figure 2. A Model of Organizational Culture Change.

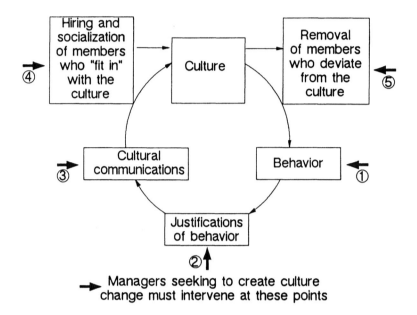

Source: Reprinted from *Culture and Related Corporate Realities* by V. Sathe, p. 385. Copyright by Richard D. Irwin, 1985. Reprinted by permission of Richard D. Irwin.

Behavior Change. Managers attempting to introduce major change in an organization often begin by assessing and then trying to change employee attitudes (Fonvielle, 1984; Sathe, 1985). This approach is consistent with the conventional wisdom that beliefs and values influence behavior. As a significant body of social science research indicates, however, one of the most effective ways of changing beliefs and values is to begin with changes in related behaviors (Aronson, 1976; Bem, 1970; Zimbardo, Ebbesen, and Maslach, 1977). While attitudes do influence behavior, it is important to emphasize that behavior also influences attitudes.

Individual values and attitudes, especially those that are deeply held, are notoriously difficult to change directly, since people's values tend to be part of an interrelated system in which each value is tied to and reinforced by other values. Thus, managers must realize that it is virtually impossible to change a particular value in isolation from an individual's other values. By focusing on relevant behaviors and interactions, managers can begin to shape the outcomes they desire by setting explicit expectations and performance standards, rewarding appropriate behaviors, and providing channels through which people can contribute to goals and objectives. Changes in organizational behaviors in and of themselves, however, do not necessarily translate into culture change. In fact, changes in culture may lag behind behavioral changes for a considerable period of time or in some instances may never occur. Especially when a firm relies solely on extrinsic motivators, organizational members can easily rationalize why they "accepted" the change, leaving present cultural values and orientations intact. But if organizational members can see the inherent value of the change, they are much more likely to accept and identify with what the organization is attempting to accomplish.

Justifying Behavior Changes. While behavior change is an important initial step, for true culture change to take effect, over the longer term the beliefs, values, and attitudes of organizational members must be consistent with and reinforce the new desired behavior (culture change). Indeed, as suggested above, while organizational members may appear to "buy into" proposed changes through their actions, they may be simply rationalizing their behavior because "it was required to keep my job" or "that's what is rewarded." Thus, while they may behave in certain ways desired by the organization, they may still cling to the beliefs and values of their old culture. In this sense, there may be overt behavioral compliance but little, if any, real acceptance of or commitment to the culture change.

If culture change is to take place, therefore, managers should as much as possible support relevant behavioral changes with intrinsic motivators (Sathe, 1985). As part of this process, the culture change must be explained and justified to organizational members. One approach is to convince organizational members to probe their present beliefs and values by showing them that their assumptions conflict with what is happening around them (Schein, 1973). In the Urban-Suburban bank merger, for example, although people were generally satisfied with and had confidence in their respective organizations, most employees were quite aware of the turmoil and problems faced by the industry and the dangers they posed for medium-sized institutions. Largely as a result of this environmental threat, people began to question the feasibility of maintaining the status quo, and these concerns influenced the initial acceptance of the merger. For culture change to take hold, however, managers must also articulate and communicate the new organizational beliefs and values and get people to adopt them.

Using Cultural Communications. Cultural communications take place on both explicit and implicit levels (Sathe, 1985). *Explicit cultural messages* include announcements, memos, speeches, and other direct forms of communication. While managers often rely on these overt forms, *implicit cultural messages*—rituals, ceremonies, stories, metaphors, heroes, logos, decor, dress, and other symbolic actions—also act as significant devices for communicating changes in the organization's culture. Both explicit and implicit forms of communication are important, and both should be used to induce people to adopt the new cultural beliefs and values. The underlying strategy should be to promote a sense of common purpose among organizational members.

A significant problem in bringing about employee acceptance of cultural communications, however, concerns the credibility of both the message and the sender. In mergers and acquisitions, for instance, explicit and implicit communications often conflict with each other as managers say one thing and then do the opposite. In the Urban-Suburban bank merger, employee descriptions of the "Christmas massacre" and characterization of Suburban Bank's CEO's office as "Murderer's Row" reflect the outrage and sense of betrayal brought about by the violation of the "no layoff" promise. The two CEOs pointed to a stronger institution following the merger, with more opportunities and no terminations if people did their jobs and supported the combination (explicit message), but then acted quite differently. Since people interpret such events as symbols of what is important to an organization, these implicit communications significantly affect shared beliefs about the organization and its leadership (Nystrom and Starbuck, 1984). In the bank merger, the "massacre" rapidly became one of the organizational stories concerning the emergent culture and what Merged Bank "really stood for."

Since ongoing, consistent cultural communications are necessary for culture change to occur, it is important that promises, images, and messages be supported by deeds and actions. Reynolds (1987), for instance, describes a computer company that attempted to create an awareness of and commitment to product quality as part of the firm's culture. However, while the idea of high-quality, defect-free products was verbally supported and given a great deal of ballyhoo at company meetings, departments were still shipping defective software packages. Virtually nothing was done to encourage or support employee actions in the quality-improvement area. The result was a highly cynical assessment among employees of the gap between the actual and "official" culture. As one of the company's managers argued, "We do have a zero-defect program: Don't test the product and you'll find zero defects" (Reynolds, 1987, p. 36).

In most instances, actions and symbols have a more potent impact on people than speeches by upper-level managers. The president and CEO of a major health care system that attempted to shift his company's focus from the management of community health resources to the management of regional networks, for example, stresses the importance of transition rituals that allow people to express their feelings and "mourn" the change (Bice, 1986). One of the main values his company expressed—"people matter more than technology"—was reflected in its actions in terms of the way people were supported, trained, and encouraged during these sessions and the change effort. As a way of further getting the "message" across, the firm used a "video newsletter," tapes of employees talking about their experiences and how they are innovating and changing, to relay to other employees what the organization was attempting to accomplish. Overall, the best way to ensure that cultural communications are credible and successful is to back them with consistent actions and behaviors that correspond to the espoused beliefs and values.

Hiring and Socialization. Organizational culture change is also significantly affected by the extent to which newcomers "fit" and are socialized into the new culture. Especially if there are tensions among the present organizational members, it is important to ensure that there are no irreconcilable mismatches between the person being hired and the desired culture (Sathe, 1985). While a "perfect" person-culture fit is highly unlikely and largely undesirable (Falvey, 1987), careful attention should be given to the selection and socialization process. For example, Procter & Gamble (P&G), well known for its "thick" culture, uses an exhaustive application and screening process for new hires (Pascale, 1985). Interviewers are part of an elite, highly trained cadre that not only deeply probe potential applicants—in terms of such qualities as "ability to turn out high volumes of excellent work" and to "identify and understand problems"— but also reveal the reality of working for P&G in terms of its pluses *and* minuses. In this sense, P&G facilitates an applicant's "deselection," on the assumption that the candidate has the best understanding of whether the company meshes with his or her own beliefs, values, and objectives.

In the Urban-Suburban bank merger, new hires during the postmerger period were informed of the realities created by the combination as well as the environmental pressures on the industry. As the 1982 postmerger survey indicates, these people were generally more favorable about organizational conditions than either of the merger partners' employees. It is important to note, of course, that these people did not have any allegiance to the preexisting cultures or administrative systems. In fact, many of them viewed much of the tension and chaos experienced by longer-term members of the two banks as "ridiculous," "petty," and "childish." Thus, by carefully selecting new employees who "fit" the goals and objectives of Merged Bank, its management began to facilitate the culture change.

Removal of Deviants. Finally, employees who continually resist the culture change and what the organization is attempting to accomplish can be removed. While terminations are often involuntary, such as when a person is asked to resign or is fired outright (D. M. Bailey, 1987; Patterson, 1988), in major culture change efforts, some of this turnover will be voluntary, especially among those who feel particular discomfort with the change. Once it became clear that the culture and orientation of Merged Bank would be much closer to those of Suburban Bank than to those of Urban Bank, for example, turnover was significantly higher among former Urban Bank members. In fact, much of the movement toward a psychological merger of the two firms was generated by the gradual exodus of key dissenters.

However, a high degree of turnover, whether voluntary or involuntary, can have negative repercussions. First, it is difficult to assimilate a significant number of new people in a short time (Sathe, 1985). Moreover, a large inflow of new hires can escalate internal political maneuvers as people jockey for position, especially at the managerial levels. Finally, the exodus of significant numbers of employees and the performance downturn that usually follows a merger or acquisition (Pritchett, 1985) can lead to a loss of the very people who are important to the company's future success (Perry, 1984). And even among those who decide to stay with the firm, the withdrawal of key personnel can lead to increased dissatisfaction and lowered morale. As explored in Chapter Nine, culture change through widespread changes in the employee population can be a very expensive strategy.

The Process of Culture Change
in Mergers and Acquisitions

As the discussion of Figure 2 underscores, although culture change is difficult, time consuming, and expensive in terms of the breadth and depth of resources required, it can be accomplished. In a merger or acquisition, however, the actual difficulty of culture change, whether based on a cultural pluralism, blending, or takeover strategy, is compounded by the additional uncertainties, ambiguities, and stress inherent in the combination process (Chapters Four and Five). Moreover, the greater the degree of operational integration desired, the greater the likelihood of cultural tensions as a result of the increase in day-to-day interactions between the different employee groups (Chapter Three). Accordingly, a small but growing number of firms have begun to place a significant emphasis on whether an acquisition candidate meets what it considers to be important cultural criteria. For example, according to Borge Reimer (1985), executive vice-president of Dana Corporation, an engineered-components company based in Toledo, Ohio, the firm will walk away from a potential acquisition candidate if it does not seem to be a good cultural fit with Dana. Instead of attempting a cultural takeover, the corporation attempts to honor the culture and heritage of an acquired firm, gradually getting the firm to buy into the notion of a dual identity—adding a "new" home as part of the Dana "family" while maintaining its own name and legacy. As Reimer (1985, p. 512) argues, "The United States is a melting pot, but in the process of integration, each subculture retains its proud heritage and traditions while at the same time establishing a common identity. . . . Similarly, Dana is also a melting pot, and when a new company joins the Dana Family, it retains its proud heritage and traditions without losing its deep-rooted, time-tested relationships with its people, while at the same time establishing a common identity with its sister divisions within Dana by sharing a common set of beliefs and, consequently, establishing a common identity."

Acculturation and Individual Propensity for Change. In general, resistance to cultural change efforts is related to the degree of change involved; the more radical the change, the greater the likely resistance (Sathe, 1985). Especially when the desired changes involve (1) many important *shared assumptions,* (2) *more central* shared assumptions, and (3) a movement toward *more alien,* less intrinsically appealing shared assumptions in "thick" cultures, difficulties are likely. The result may very well be explicit efforts to preserve one's precombination culture (Berry, 1983; Nahavandi and Malekzadeh, 1988), often at the expense of the other culture and what the organization and its management are attempting to accomplish. In fact, many cases involving postcombination problems and clashes focus on employee resistance to the change and attempts at salvaging remnants of their firm's premerger culture (Buono, Bowditch, and Lewis, 1985; Gaertner, 1986; Manzini and Gridley, 1986; Sales and Mirvis, 1984; Walter, 1985a).

Because of these difficulties, recent work has emphasized the process of *acculturation* in mergers and acquisitions (Nahavandi and Malekzadeh, 1986, 1988; Sales and Mirvis, 1984). Acculturation is typically conceived of as "changes induced in [two cultural] systems as a result of the diffusion of cultural elements in both directions" (Berry, 1980, p. 215). While this definition suggests that acculturation is a reciprocal process, involving a "balanced, two-way flow" between the systems, the reality is that members of one culture often attempt to dominate people in the other (Berry, 1980; Nahavandi and Malekzadeh, 1988). This dynamic is especially the case in mergers and acquisitions, as cultural blending strategies often evolve into cultural takeovers (American Bankers Association and Ernst & Whinney, 1985).

A key factor in both the effectiveness and success of organizational culture change efforts in mergers and acquisitions is the propensity of individuals to accept the change, or to acculturate. The degree to which members of an acquired firm or merger partner want to preserve their identity and culture and the extent to which they are attracted to the acquiring or merging firm appear to influence both the process and the outcome of the culture change effort (Malekzadeh and Nahavandi, 1987; Nahavandi and Malekzadeh, 1986, 1988). These responses can range from outright assimilation and a desire for cultural pluralism to efforts at cultural separation and deculturation (see Figure 3):

1. *Assimilation*—highly attractive acquirer and little desire by the acquired firm to preserve its culture. In essence, this is a unilateral process in which one merger or acquisition partner willingly accepts and adopts the identity and culture of the other.
2. *Cultural pluralism*—highly attractive acquirer with strong desire by acquired firm to preserve its culture. While there may be a high level of integration between the two firms

Figure 3. Acquired Firm's Modes of Acculturation.

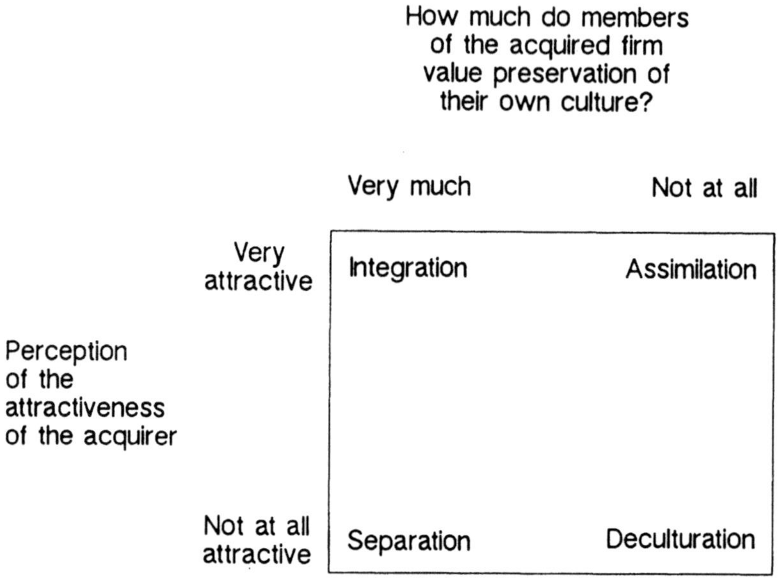

How much do members
of the acquired firm
value preservation of
their own culture?

	Very much	Not at all
Very attractive	Integration	Assimilation
Not at all attractive	Separation	Deculturation

Perception
of the
attractiveness
of the acquirer

Source: Adapted from A. Nahavandi and A. R. Malekzadeh, 1988, p. 83. Reprinted by permission.

in terms of the interaction and adaptation of the companies' members, neither firm experiences a significant loss of cultural identity. As Chapter Six suggests, however, this form of acculturation takes place only when the acquiring firm allows and supports such independence.

3. *Separation*—unattractive acquirer and strong desire by the acquired firm to preserve its culture. Essentially, separation involves attempts to preserve one's culture by maintaining a separate and independent existence from the combined organization's dominant culture.

4. *Deculturation*—unattractive acquirer and little desire by the acquired firm to preserve its culture. In this instance, there is a significant loss of cultural and psychological contact with both the precombination firm and the acquirer or merger partner, with feelings of alienation, loss, and collective and individual confusion (Nahavandi and Malekzadeh, 1988, pp. 82–83).

To illustrate the dynamics involved in such culture change efforts, the remainder of this chapter analyzes the acculturation experience in two combinations: a merger involving cultural separation and the creation of an organizational counterculture and an acquisition involving tendencies toward cultural assimilation. As both these cases illustrate, even in initially favorable situations, if the subtleties and dynamics of the culture change process are not explicitly considered and dealt with, people in the combined institution—consciously and unconsciously—may very well end up working against the combination effort.

Mergers and Organizational Countercultures. Just as societies may have groups whose norms, values, and behaviors sharply contradict dominant societal norms, values, and behaviors (see Cavan, 1961; Roszak, 1969; Yinger, 1960, 1982), organizations may also have subgroups who strongly reject what the organization stands for or what it is attempting to accomplish. As pointed out in Chapter Six, organizations tend to have multiple cultures. While there is typically a dominant culture for a particular firm, divisions, plants, and even departments may have cultures distinct from that of the larger group (Buono and Nichols, 1985; Martin and Siehl, 1983; Wilkins, 1983). In fact, much of the tension concerning the development and transitions that organizations experience is reflected in the language, orientations, and political posturing of these subcultures (Pettigrew, 1986). In terms of culture change efforts, it is important to realize that not all elements of a particular culture will change at the same rate. As a result of a type of "culture lag" (Ogburn, 1922), culture change efforts are often far from perfect. Especially if the status or position of a particular subcultural group is threatened individuals may very well purposefully lag behind the rest of the organization in accepting the culture change (see Mills, 1964).

There are three basic types of subcultures in organizations: enhancing, orthogonal, and counterculture (Martin and Siehl, 1983). *Enhancing* subcultures are enclaves where adherence to the core values of the dominant culture is more fervent than in the rest of the organization. *Orthogonal* subcultures are composed of people who simultaneously accept the core values of the dominant culture and a separate, unconflicting set of values particular to themselves. Thus, the basic content of an orthogonal subculture will be different from, but consistent with, the overall organizational culture. Finally, *countercultures* hold core values that are in direct contrast with and pose a challenge to the dominant culture. Countercultural norms, values, and behaviors sharply contradict the dominant norms, values, and behaviors of the larger organization (see Cavan, 1961; Kephart, 1976; Roszak, 1969; Westhues, 1972; Yinger, 1960, 1982). Dominant organizational cultures and countercultures exist in an uneasy symbiosis, typically taking opposite positions on value issues important to them.

While most organizations have one or more subcultures, these are most often enhancing or orthogonal (Martin and Siehl, 1983). This is usually the case in functionally structured organizations where different orientations may coexist within the dominant culture, such as production managers who value precision and timeliness, R&D managers who place more value on innovation and creativity, and salespeople who are guided more by volume and quotas (Sathe, 1985). True countercultural values and behaviors, however, are inconsistent with what the dominant organization is attempting to accomplish and lead people to either consciously or unconsciously work against the success of the organization.

Countercultures generally combine three forms of protest against the larger group: (1) direct opposition to the firm's dominant values; (2) opposition to the dominant culture's power structures; and (3) opposition to the structural relationships that are supported by the values of the dominant culture (Yinger, 1982, p. 5). They emerge when individuals or groups are living under sets of conditions that they strongly feel cannot provide them with their accustomed or hoped-for satisfactions. In one sense, countercultures can be thought of as calls for help in stressful times, when existing cultural support systems have broken down and people are attempting to regain some sense of control in their lives. Under such conditions of perceived deprivation and frustration of major values, norms and behaviors that oppose the emerging dominant culture may begin to form or strengthen (Cavan, 1961; Yinger, 1960). As indicated in Figure 3, when organizational members desire to preserve their own cultural heritage at the expense of their acquirer's or merger partner's culture, attempts at cultural separation are quite likely. The greater the differences between the cultures and operating philosophies of the precombination firms, the greater the probability and intensity of such countercultural activities, especially in cultural blending or cultural takeover strategies at the operational integration level.

Cultural Loss, Deception, and Cultural Resistance. The merger between Urban and Suburban banks provides a good illustration of merger-related cultural separation and resistance. Even though the merger was to be a collaborative, strategic combination of the two banks, the consolidation precipitated significant declines in employee satisfaction and commitment, an increased sensitivity toward and longing for the "good old days," and a series of behaviors that attempted to work against the transformation. The significant cultural differences between the banks precipitated a "we versus they" orientation between the two groups, negative stereotyping of the other bank's members, and a strengthening and enhancement of the premerger cultures. As a result, responsibility for why things were not going as well as they should, why communication was so poor, or why people were not treated fairly was continually attributed to the other bank.

As discussed earlier, the announced plan was to create a true blending of the two firms. However, it quickly became clear that the orientation and philosophy of Merged Bank would be much closer to that of Suburban Bank than to that of Urban Bank. While the logo and location of the headquarters were hybrids of those of the two original banks, the merged institution retained the name of Suburban Bank, as well as many of its systems and orientations, important symbols of organizational identity. Moreover, as the new chief operating officer (COO) of the merged bank, the former CEO of Suburban Bank was given control over internal decisions and was substantially more visible than his Urban Bank counterpart. As the 1982 postmerger climate data and the responses to merger-related survey questions indicate, both sets of employees were less satisfied after the merger—especially with respect to the subtler, cultural aspects of organizational life (for example, commitment, feelings of job security, job satisfaction, feelings toward upper management). However, the perceived influence of Suburban Bank on the emerging culture of the new institution is reflected by the fact that former Suburban Bank employees felt significantly less alienated and less negative after the merger than did former Urban Bank members.

The initial feelings of loss created by the shift in culture were exacerbated by the "Christmas massacre." The decision to lay off organizational members, despite the public assurances that employees would be secure in their membership in the new organization, was interpreted as a strong symbol of the values of Merged Bank and strengthened resistance to the merger, especially among Urban Bank employees. As one of them reported, "The massacre really destroyed any motivation. People stopped caring about the bank. When you really don't care, you're not going to put any effort into what you're doing."

During this period, Urban Bank's vice-president for human resources, a significant cultural hero in the premerger bank, had a number of value clashes with Merged Bank's COO. While Urban Bank employees looked to the vice-president as someone who "made the bank a great place to work," he was viewed by the new COO as "poisonous to the merger," a "union boss" who was more an "employee representative" than an executive. As it became clear that their management styles were at polar extremes, the COO presented the vice-president with an ultimatum: "change or resign." Choosing the latter, the vice-president went to all Urban Bank employees—from senior vice-presidents to tellers and clerical personnel—to tell them that he was leaving. The day his resignation was announced was dubbed "Black Friday" by Urban Bank employees, who reported that it "gave a clear signal that things were really going to change." While the merged bank's COO viewed this move as a significant step toward merger integration ("a lot of disgruntled employees left after that"), it fueled an increased sense of resentment and loss among those Urban Bank employees who remained with the organization.

Another factor that significantly contributed to the growing dissatisfaction among Urban Bank members was the emerging set of expectations within the bank. The new COO made it clear that he felt that Urban Bank "was a comfortable place to work rather than a competitive institution." His efforts to make the organization "more competitive" and "more in tune with the [financially volatile] times" were interpreted by Urban Bank employees as threats and evidence that he wanted to "use up" people. The outcome of these events was a growing longing for the "good old days," especially among Urban Bank personnel, and increased anger toward the merger.

Boundary-Spanning Grapeviners, the "Out-of-House" Organ, and Countercultural Activity. As the merger and cultural takeover progressed, a number of Urban Bank employees attempted to preserve their cultural heritage and identity, which became increasingly salient in people's minds. In essence, these employees began to develop a counterculture that stood in opposition to the emerging dominant orientation in Merged Bank. An important determinant of the emergence of such groups is effective communication among those with common beliefs, predispositions, and experiences that can form the basis for countercultural values. Potential members need to identify each other, leaders need audiences, and signals to and from the dominant culture are required to give the protestors a sense of identity (Yinger, 1982).

An influential factor in the bank merger was the limited size of the banking community in the metropolitan area—many of those who voluntarily and involuntarily left the bank after the merger went to work for similar institutions in the area. It was not uncommon, for instance, for three or more former Urban Bank members to now be working for the same new organization. Moreover, Urban Bank's vice-president for human resources (the organizational hero referred to earlier) accepted a similar position with a financial services corporation in the area and took a number of his personnel with him. The result was a series of enclaves of former Urban Bank employees throughout the area. These various enclaves not only kept in contact with each other but interacted with the members of Urban Bank who remained at Merged Bank as well. Thus, rather than being isolated, these people served in informal boundary-spanner roles. The resultant intra- and intergroup communication became a chain through which the countervaluative behaviors of these people were linked.

Shortly after the "Christmas massacre," two employees—one who had left the bank and one who remained—created an *Ex-Urban Bank Employee Newsletter*. Financed by contributions from Urban Bank members, it was largely an effort to organize the group, a way of providing information on where people went, what they were doing, how to keep in touch, and so forth. The first issue was published in the spring of 1982, approximately eight months after the merger. Later editions contained information about what was happening at the merged bank along with stories about former Urban Bank members. This communication link provided an important sense of identity for those who left the bank as well as for many of those who remained, since they could serve as a channel of information about what was happening at the institution. Interestingly, while firms use house organs to inform their members about what is happening and to highlight various facets of organizational life, the same was true with the counterculture. Initially published once every six months, the newsletter successfully initiated communication and interaction between both "leavers" and "stayers." Many of these people began to get together informally to talk about what was going on—both in their lives and "back at the bank"—and to reflect on the lost sense of family and togetherness that they had once enjoyed.

As a way of formalizing these get-togethers, a former Urban Bank employee reunion was held in the fall of 1983, attended by more than 100 people—a combination of "leavers" and "stayers." At subsequent reunions held during 1984, 1985, and 1986, approximately 75 people attended. These gatherings served as a way of keeping the old organization alive—through a telling and retelling of organizational stories—as well as a forum for keeping in touch with what was going on in Merged Bank.

Whistleblowing and the Counterculture. While much of the activity of the counterculture was oriented toward keeping Urban

Bank's culture alive and fulfilling the social and psychological needs of its members, the elements of power that were transformed into authority by the merger became prime targets. The outcome was a series of behaviors that attempted to undermine the merger. For example, stories were told to the researchers about Urban Bank employees mistreating Suburban Bank customers, refusing to accept and follow new procedures, and so forth. In viewing these actions, it is important to emphasize that counter-culture ethics contradict the values of the dominant culture. Thus, while one may argue that it is unethical for employees to either covertly or overtly sabotage their employers, in their own interpretations of the situation, they are in the right, and their cause is just (see Yinger, 1982, pp. 114–119).

A significant event that contributed to a sense of power in the counterculture and rapidly became a favorite story at the reunion was a situation that involved alleged coercion, donations to a political action committee (PAC), and whistleblowing. Most cases of whistleblowing—organizational members disclosing illegal, immoral, or questionable practices of their firms—are justified by the frequency and seriousness of the wrongdoing and a sense of personal responsibility to change the situation (Baucus, Near, and Miceli, 1985; Elliston, Keenan, Lockhart, and Van Schaick, 1985). While some incidents of whistleblowing are attributed to retaliation by an individual for perceived personal wrongs, interview data suggest that in the case of the bank merger, the act was based on a desire for *cultural retaliation*.

In the fall of 1984, Merged Bank's COO (formerly the CEO of Suburban Bank) sent a memo to his senior executives to elicit their support for the industry's PACs: "Every single officer of this institution should—must—consider it a part of his or her position to contribute to both [PACs]. Please send your check, not later than next Friday." The memo continued, "Only 19 of the 59 officers in the bank have contributed. This is unacceptable. . . . I hope none of you is so naive as to think that political contributions—even those from PACs, despite all the pious rhetoric—do not play a vital part in the process of such [legislation]. You should, as officers of this bank, all support the PACs." The memo, which was subsequently leaked to the press and reported in the local papers, focused a great deal of negative publicity on the bank. While the COO argued that the memo was "never intended as a threat," local papers reported that employees were "fearful they'll lose their jobs if they don't [contribute]." The incident even fueled a strong editorial in the local press against PACs in general and the bank in particular. The whistleblowing incident led to a probe by the FBI and the Justice Department, and the bank admitted to violating federal law and paid a $17,000 fine.

While the fine was a relatively small one, the outcome was perceived as a major victory for the counterculture. It fueled a significant amount of grapevine activity and served to give the group a sense of empowerment. Although the COO did not, as they hoped, have to resign, they applauded the negative publicity that ensued. Yet perhaps most interesting from a counterculture perspective is the fact that the practice in question was fairly common at both banks prior to the merger. As one of these individuals explained, the Urban Bank CEO "used to make the same type of plea at our staff meetings. [Suburban Bank CEO] did the same thing at one of our meetings. The dollars were real low, so he followed it up with the memo. That's when people felt they had him. It was on paper." Thus, it appears that rather than the main reason underlying the whistle-blowing being the contribution pressure per se, the act was generated by a desire for cultural revenge. Because of the dominance of Suburban Bank's culture and the influence of its CEO on the merged institution, and the desire of members of Urban Bank to remain faithful to their own traditions and values, they attempted to attack and undermine the emerging power structure and cultural orientation of Merged Bank.

Implications. From a managerial perspective, the reactions of these employees to the bank merger underscore the importance of the culture change process illustrated in Figure 2. Although the CEOs initially focused on behavioral change (for example, through the interbank task forces and employee transfer program), these changes were not justified or reinforced by planned cultural messages. In fact, employees received infrequent and

inconsistent messages from their leaders. First, rather than provide employees with ongoing cultural messages about the combination and the orientation of Merged Bank, the CEOs argued
that we "overmet" about the merger and pulled back in their
communication efforts. This decision only served to frustrate
organizational members, who complained that the intergroup
meetings raised many more issues than they resolved and exacerbated tensions between the two groups. Second, a concern
about *deception* was mentioned by many organizational members:
top management's "no layoff" policy, followed by the "Christmas
massacre," resulted in a profound and widespread distrust of
and antagonism toward the new leadership and Merged Bank.
As discussed earlier, there should be consistency in the cultural
messages—both explicit and implicit—that are communicated
to employees. Telling organizational members one thing and
then doing the opposite only serves to undermine management's
credibility and employee support of the change. In essence, the
actions of Merged Bank's top management led to a separation
rather than integration of the two cultures.

In terms of hiring and socializing new members, Merged
Bank's COO did effectively bring in new employees as he replaced those he viewed as cultural deviants. Moreover, many
of the individuals who were the most fervent supporters of the
counterculture eventually left the bank voluntarily. While a
number of former Urban Bank employees still keep in touch
with many "leavers," and the spring 1986 reunion was well
attended, it seems that attempts to sabotage the merger and to
attack its new authority structures reached their peak with the
whistleblowing incident. As illustrated by the sense of loss surrounding "Black Friday," however, removal of deviants can
have unintended, dysfunctional consequences, especially in the
short term. Yet, while management might have alleviated these
difficulties by allowing people to express their feelings and
"mourn" the change, there was no real attempt to help employees work through the sense of loss they experienced.

The counterculture in Merged Bank presented a significant barrier to successful integration of the firms during the first
four years following the merger. Although many of the bank's

employees reported that cultural issues and problems were "behind them" at that point, seeming to indicate a move toward a "psychological merger" between the two institutions, with a new understanding of the psychological contract and renewed organizational stability, anecdotal evidence suggests that this process is not yet complete, as a culture lag still exists. Organizational countercultures reflect more than mere deviation from dominant values and norms, since they constitute detachment from and opposition to the dominant culture. Although such groups might be a minority in a merger or acquisition, since they are culturally removed from the prevailing milieu, various behaviors that would be viewed as deviant by the dominant culture may be perceived as quite tolerable and even lauded by the counterculture. Unless explicit efforts are made to guide the change, especially when there are marked cultural polarities between the two firms, the result may well be significant efforts that work against what the organization is attempting to accomplish.

The Role of Guidance and Trust Building

As the model of combination acculturation (Figure 3) suggests, tendencies of a merger partner or acquisition target toward assimilation should make the culture change effort easier to manage and control. Not all mergers or acquisitions necessarily degenerate into the sort of cultural retaliation and countercultural tensions discussed above. Yet, even if an acquired firm's management and employees are quite willing to accept the change, significant problems can still emerge if the acquiring company or merger partner makes insufficient efforts toward guidance and trust building. The capacity to fully integrate strategic, operational, and cultural orientations requires that each group—acquiring or acquired firm or merger partner—have the requisite intellectual and organizational capabilities to use the skills, knowledge, or resources of the other organization (Jemison, 1986b).

These problems are illustrated by the difficulties faced by the president and vice-presidents of Handy Stores, a fast-food operation involving a large number of franchises that was acquired as part of a conglomerate amalgamation (Shuman and Buono, 1988). In 1984, Retail Corporation, a $5.1 billion conglomerate located in the New England and Middle Atlantic areas, acquired Food Company, a $1.2 billion regional food and drug retailer. Strategically, Retail Corporation wanted to expand its supermarket and drug outlet base and felt that Food Company was a good fit for its growth plans. As part of the acquisition agreement, Handy Stores, a wholly owned subsidiary of Food Company, became part of Retail Corporation's holdings. The situation was similar to TransCo's takeover of Co-op Foods in that Handy Stores was not initially part of Retail Corporation's acquisition strategy. During the years following the acquisition, therefore, Retail Corporation focused its energies and attention on integrating Food Company into its operations. Handy Stores was "put on hold" during this period, and all communication between Retail Corporation and Handy Stores went through Food Company's CEO and COO. The subsidiary, however, was still under the financial control of Retail Corporation and had to respond to various requests from it that were filtered through Food Company's operations.

Postacquisition Tension and Confusion. Shortly after the acquisition, the chairperson and CEO of Food Company, at the request of Retail Corporation, asked Handy Stores' CEO to prepare a strategic audit of the subsidiary that "tells corporate management all about Handy Stores, including future growth plans . . . and not to leave anything out." This rather straightforward request precipitated the first major "aftershock" (Pritchett, 1985) of the acquisition for Handy Stores' top management team. For the first time in his fifteen-year career at Food Company and his three-year tenure as CEO of the subsidiary, Handy Stores' president was confronted with questions concerning his "strategic direction," "growth plans," and "planning agenda." Yet virtually no guidance or support was provided by the company's initial parent or its acquirer.

Although there appeared to be a "fit" between Retail Corporation and Food Company, as with the cases described in Chapter Two, there were significant operating, strategic, and cultural differences between the companies. The preacquisition culture at Food Company, which over time had been totally assimilated into Handy Stores, was an informal, "family business" orientation. This philosophy stood in stark contrast to the "rapid-growth mentality" that was fostered at Retail Corporation (see Table 9). Prior to the acquisition, Handy Stores' "corporate objectives" were to run an efficient operation and to contribute predetermined income levels to its parent's bottom line. The president, who had been promoted out of Food Company's operations area, had even cut back on the number of stores over the previous two years to ensure a "more efficient operation." Since income goals were met during his tenure as president, Handy Stores was allowed to operate on a fully autonomous basis.

**Table 9. Organizational Cultures
of Retail Corporation and Handy Stores.**

	Retail Corporation	*Handy Stores*
Orientation	Strategic planning Corporate growth	Efficient operations Return on investment
Philosophy	Political Conglomerate empire	Familial Part of a privately held family business
Management	High-powered M.B.A.s	"School of hard knocks"
Managerial practices	Management by objectives "Year-round planning"	"Seat of the pants"

The acquisition not only created a shift in strategic orientation from an operations focus to one based on planning and corporate growth but precipitated significant culture shocks as well. Although Retail Corporation's takeover of Food Company was relatively "friendly," Handy Stores' executives interpreted and experienced it as quite threatening. While they felt that the acquisition could open up a number of career possibilities, they had serious concerns about the types of skills and abilities that would be needed to succeed in a much larger corporation. While the president, for example, felt that he had the requisite skills and abilities to continue to effectively and efficiently run Handy Stores as he had in the past, he was uncertain as to whether he was prepared to manage the company under Retail Corporation's rapid-growth strategy. Moreover, his top management team had quite a similar orientation, with little understanding of or appreciation for the political realities of life in a corporate conglomerate. The firm had been, after all, a close-knit "family."

It also became apparent that the first assignment under the new management had a dual purpose. Retail Corporation, which did not have any direct experience with fast-food stores, seemed to want a clearer picture of the subsidiary it had acquired as part of the Food Company takeover. Thus, while the strategic audit and plan would become an important component of Retail Corporation's decision as to whether it would maintain or spin off the operation, at the same time, it was perceived that there was a strong evaluation component in the assignment—that Retail Corporation probably wanted to get a better feel for the management capabilities in its subsidiary. The conglomerate might decide to keep the operation but replace its top people with a different management team. It was clear that the "game was about to change."

During the initial postacquisition period, Handy Stores' CEO sought the assistance of external change agents to facilitate his understanding of the changes taking place through the acquisition and strategic planning as "conceptualized by Retail Corporation." The lack of sufficient guidance in and explanation of these matters—which were not provided by either the acquiring conglomerate or the subsidiary's initial parent—only served to heighten the anxieties, uncertainties, and fears associated with the acquisition. Moreover, many of Retail Corporation's subsequent decisions further contributed to the difficulties experienced by the subsidiary. Retail Corporation initially kept Handy Stores as a division of Food Company instead of shifting it to one of its own divisions. While this may have been a sound strategic decision for Retail Corporation, since the company was undecided as to whether it would maintain or spin off the fast-food-store operation, the organizational arrangement created significant operating problems for Handy Stores. The person at Food Company to whom Handy Stores' CEO reported was naturally quite concerned with his own operation and its integration into Retail Corporation's culture. As a result, Handy Stores' needs and concerns were given less priority than Food Company's, and a strong feeling began to develop at the subsidiary that Handy Stores was little more than an "unwanted stepchild" in the acquisition.

Integration with Retail Corporation. Approximately one year later, Retail Corporation decided to keep Handy Stores as part of its diversification strategy and began its attempts to integrate the company into its operations. At that time, a liaison was appointed at the corporate level to assist the subsidiary with its planning-related projects. While Handy Stores' CEO initially viewed this contact quite favorably, he was also concerned that he could not be fully candid with a Retail Corporation person. The conglomerate still had not laid out its plans for the subsidiary, and he had had no "real" interpersonal contact with the liaison. As he explained to the change agents, "After all, how do I know that I can trust this person? Maybe he is after my job."

During this time, it became apparent that Retail Corporation was interested in the fast-food industry and, in keeping with its growth orientation, wanted to increase both its market area and market share. Moreover, the conglomerate appeared ready to commit the necessary resources to support its strategy. Although initially excited about the possibilities presented by this situation, Handy Stores' CEO quickly became overwhelmed by Retail Corporation's interpretation of "rapid growth": he had submitted a plan to roughly double the operation's stores to 100 within a five-year period; the conglomerate had increased the goal to 250 stores within the same time period.

Escalating Pressures. Thus far during the acquisition, Handy Stores' CEO was under a tremendous amount of pressure as a result of the strategic and cultural changes taking place in the organization. Yet, in an effort to protect his management team, he acted in a type of buffer role. Although corporate performance expectations were changing, for example, the CEO did not make any adjustments in Handy Stores' reward system. It was becoming apparent, however, that while his efforts to "shield the troops" from the culture change made his staff feel more "in control of the situation," they had the dysfunctional effect of intensifying the pressure on the CEO and exacerbating Handy Stores' difficulties in proceeding with its planning efforts. Unfortunately, it also began to be increasingly clear that while "buffering" his management team from the rapid changes that were occurring, the CEO really did not understand the full implications of the changes himself.

During this period, it was almost as if there were two Handy Stores operations: one that interacted (in its communications) with Food Company and its acquirer Retail Corporation and another that operated on a daily basis as it had prior to the acquisition. In effect, the cultural and strategic transference envisioned by Retail Corporation was not taking place. Even though Handy Stores' management was willing to be assimilated into Retail Corporation, given the sudden shift from an operational to a strategic growth focus, they found themselves in an anxiety-provoking, unfamiliar situation. In fact, their situation was quite comparable to what their prior corporate parent was going through. Having always been run as a privately held, family business, Food Company had had a president and CEO who was "old-fashioned" in his ways and managed without any real strategic planning (by "seat of the pants"). Thus, the management team at Food Company found itself dealing with the same uncertainties and tensions faced by Handy Stores' executives. The basic problem, however, was that while Food Company had access to Retail Corporation's expertise, any support from the acquirer was initially filtered through Food Company. This dynamic essentially meant that while they were quite willing to accept the cultural change taking place, Handy Stores' CEO and vice-presidents were receiving guidance from a person at Food Company who was also struggling to deal with the changes and learn the new strategic and cultural orientations of the acquirer. More than a year later, the firm was still struggling—still without any guidance or support from its corporate parent—to assimilate itself into Retail Corporation's "way of doing things." Handy Stores' vice-presidents reported increasing frustration and anxiety; its CEO began quietly to look for a new position.

Implications. There was far less cultural tension and resistance in the Retail Corporation–Handy Stores acquisition than in the Urban-Suburban bank merger. Even though the organizational cultures in each combination were polar extremes of each other, the fact that the plan was for strategic integration (in the form of the growth and expansion program) rather than operational integration reduced the level of threat and tension. At the same time, however, these changes had significant cultural ramifications for Handy Stores' management, who were quite anxious about the combination. Once Retail Corporation decided to keep Handy Stores as part of its operation, its laissez-faire approach sent mixed messages to the newly acquired subsidiary. While the "hands-off" approach might have worked quite well if the conglomerate had decided to maintain financial integration only, the shift to strategic integration required much greater support and guidance than were provided to Handy Stores. While the subsidiary's managers were ready to accept the changes, which they largely viewed as good for their careers, they did not have a good sense of what it would take to "pull off" the program. As a result, there was little real assimilation of the Handy Stores chain, and it continued to operate as it had prior to the acquisition.

Once the decision was made to strategically integrate Handy Stores, Retail Corporation should have provided explicit support and guidance to facilitate the acquired firm's learning process. Especially since Retail Corporation did not have any direct experience in the fast-food industry, the operational expertise of Handy Stores' top managers was important to the conglomerate. Yet the changes that were proposed (addition of 250 stores in five years) required a cultural shift (from an operational to a strategic-planning, growth orientation) on the part of Handy Stores' managers. While this change was communicated through explicit messages (in the form of memos and official communications), the implicit cultural messages these managers received were quite different. For instance, in an effort to keep administrative overhead down, Retail Corporation wanted Handy Stores to use Food Company's legal, real estate, and construction personnel in planning for and adding the new units. At the subsidiary's newly planned growth rate, however, new stores would be added at the rate of forty to fifty per year, almost one a week. Given the time demands already placed on these staff units by Food Company's own growth plans, it became increasingly obvious to Handy Stores' managers that their own needs came well after Food Company's, and they began to increasingly question Retail Corporation's commitment to them and the expansion program. The lack of direction and assistance from the new parent company was also interpreted as a sign that the subsidiary's managers should have already assimilated the orientations of Retail Corporation. They felt that any effort to go to the conglomerate for help would "jeopardize their jobs."

Even though Retail Corporation eventually used a liaison to work with the subsidiary, there appeared to be a fair amount of tension and lack of trust between him and Handy Stores' CEO. As indicated above, the CEO's concerns went so far as to include wondering whether the liaison had his sights on the top position in Handy Stores. If acquiring firms or merger partners hope to successfully influence a culture change—especially when the operational expertise in a subsidiary is important—it is critical to build a climate of trust between the companies through consistent explicit and implicit cultural messages. Even when there is an initial tendency toward cultural assimilation by an acquisition target's members, management in the acquiring firm needs to take the initiative in assisting and guiding the acquired organization's managers and employees through the trying and often turbulent period of adjustment involved in the combination.

Conclusion

Obviously, a merger between two previously autonomous organizations involves an enormous adjustment to change. While such adjustments typically take a long time, mergers and acquisitions take place within a relatively compressed time frame. Yet, during the postmerger period, the development of a new culture that deals with a large share of individual needs and anxieties, facilitates interpersonal relations, accommodates conflicts, and at the same time adapts to new circumstances is an inherently difficult and time-consuming task. Thus, much of the danger in postcombination integration lies in situations where the various elements of organizational life are out of phase with each other. At the extreme, the resultant anxiety and resistance can lead to attempts to preserve the beliefs and values of one or both of the precombination firms through the creation of a counterculture. Yet, even if there is a willingness to accept the change, as illustrated by Retail Corporation's acquisition of Handy Stores, there is still the need for a high level of guidance and trust building between the firms.

This chapter has attempted to outline a process of culture change that can serve as a basic guide to the dynamics and processes involved in mergers and acquisitions, with an emphasis on the problems inherent in such efforts. It is important to realize that culture change is not something that can be totally planned and programmed from beginning to end (Wilkins and Bristow, 1987). In pointing out the difficulty of culture change, for example, Sathe (1985, pp. 404–406) suggests that organizations should critically examine whether the changes they desire can be brought about by creatively utilizing the potential of their prevailing cultures. By moving toward intrinsically appealing beliefs and values that retain as much of the old culture as possible (Bennigson, 1985), instead of more alien beliefs and values, organizations can increase the probability of success in culture change programs. Culture change must be recognized as a time-consuming, evolutionary process that often entails political maneuvering, anxiety-provoking situations, conflicts and tensions, and the need for learning, adjustment, and flexibility.

Eight

Facilitating
Organizational Integration
After the Merger

Considering the myriad merger- and acquisition-related problems and concerns discussed thus far—from individual fears, anxieties, and stress-related reactions to organizational cultural constraints and tensions—it should be clear that postcombination integration is an inherently difficult and time-consuming task. The period following an organizational consolidation is often characterized by "we-they" tensions, power struggles, turnover and absenteeism, and declines in job-related attitudes and performance in the acquired or merged firm that typically require at least one to two years to resolve. Some firms never seem to fully recover from the resulting "psychological pit" and loss of momentum. This type of "postmerger drift"—performance declines, a slow learning process, and general dissatisfaction with the organization—appears to be a basic attribute of virtually all organizational consolidations (Goldberg, 1983; Pritchett, 1985).

While the severity of this "drift" is influenced by the type of combination in question (in terms of the strategic purpose, the degree of friendliness or hostility, and the degree of desired integration discussed in Chapter Three), there is disagreement concerning how much can actually be done to accelerate and facilitate postcombination integration. One position is that *time* is the key factor (Pritchett, 1985; Stybel, 1986): even in friendly mergers, five to seven years must pass before organizational members feel truly assimilated into the new firm; in hostile acquisitions, it can take up to ten years to resolve the lingering bitterness. Until such time has passed, the likelihood is that there will be quite a bit of "we versus they" tensions and mutual distrust between the merger or acquisition partners. As a result, postcombination integration efforts may lead to short-term improvements by providing organizational members with a temporary sense of cohesion, but these efforts are not likely to create true assimilation. There are simply limits to how much the transition process can be hurried along. From this viewpoint, postcombination tensions are essentially symptomatic patterns that are to be expected as part of the cost of merger and acquisition activity.

A competing view is that much of the failure and subsequent divestiture of merger partners and acquisition targets is due to ineffective management of the underlying *process* (Blake and Mouton, 1985; Blumberg and Wiener, 1979; Gordon, 1987; Haspeslagh and Jemison, 1987; Pritchett, 1987b). In effect, many combinations fail because managers "sit back" and wait for time to run its course. Such "sins of omission" are suggested to be the most problematic aspect of merger management (Pappanastos, Hillman, and Cole, 1987). Declining productivity, listlessness among employees, and tension-laden interactions are not necessarily a given, at least not to the extent that the "time-factor" critics suggest. Rather, the process that firms use to integrate their operations is the key. Not only can combination-related failures and difficulties be significantly lowered through an effective use of appropriate transition tools, techniques, and methods, but the integration process can be expedited as well.

To some extent, there is an element of validity in each position. At the same time, however, neither view in its extreme form is accurate, and each may, in fact, contribute to combination-related problems. As suggested in Chapter Five, over the course of a merger or acquisition, organizational members' frames of reference do gradually change. Some people, of course, will refuse to accept the combination and "bail out" of the company. Others, after a sufficient amount of time has passed, will view the combination as fair, just, necessary, and perhaps even worth while. After the feeling that one's psychological contract has been violated has dissipated, mutual understanding between an organization and its members will tend to stabilize once again (Homans, 1974). To simply assume, however, that this sort of transformation will succeed if left to its own devices and that the myriad of issues associated with it will work themselves out in the long run is naive.

One of the realities of mergers and acquisitions is that the main parties often find that they cannot always control the timing or process of combination-related events and interactions. In their research on mergers and acquisitions, for instance, Jemison and Sitkin (1986a) identified three key factors inherent in the combination process that act as constraining factors: (1) involvement of specialists with narrow focuses and independent goals, which can lead to multiple, fragmented views of the agreement; (2) building momentum to close the deal, which can limit consideration of postacquisition integration issues; and (3) an inability to resolve important areas of ambiguity before agreement completion. These factors, compounded by the inherent anxieties and tensions experienced by employees and cultural differences between companies, lead to a difficult, often chaotic period of adjustment once the deal has been signed.

Methods for Postcombination Transition

Most discussions of postcombination integration tend to be rather superficial. Simple prescriptions to "change the culture" of the merger partner or acquisition target often ignore the length of time and inherent difficulties involved in culture change efforts. Advice to "assure your employees" rarely addresses the fragility of the trust that exists in merging or acquired organizations. Recommendations to "build relationships" typically oversimplify the range and depth of such interactions. Reflecting on the difficulties involved in bringing together the key top management personnel of merger or acquisition targets, an administrative partner of Arthur Young & Company (Harvey, 1969, p. 247) argues, ''Few mergers . . . have been successfully consummated without the use of cocktails. Wives should always be included in these get-togethers.'' Surely, there is more to successful merger and acquisition integration than social drinking with the spouse of your combination partner.

This chapter explores a number of methods and considerations that can reduce some of the tension, strain, and discontent associated with the human side of organizational combinations: two-way communication channels, realistic merger previews, combination-related workshops, survey feedback, transition teams, team building and intergroup confrontation, parallel organizational structures, organizational symbols and rituals, employee retention and dismissal, and, in general, attention to the details surrounding the combination. The extent to which an organization will choose to use these mechanisms, however, depends on the nature of the combination. While these transition techniques and concerns provide ways in which the human costs associated with any merger or acquisition can be reduced, they become more significant to merging or acquiring organizations as (1) the level of integration increases from financial to operational and (2) the expertise of managers and employees in an acquired firm or merger partner is important to the overall success of the venture.

Communication Channels

Although it may seem to be a simple verity that communication is an important component of combination success, most managers interpret communication needs in relatively narrow and traditional organizational terms. Mergers and acquisitions, however, place a number of new demands and pressures on the communication process. Because of the high level of uncertainty and insecurity associated with such large-scale organizational changes, combination-related communication needs are qualitatively and quantitatively different from typical business communication requirements. Most firms do not do a very good job of communicating merger- or acquisition-related news to employees. Virtually every case study of a merger or acquisition reports communication shortages at one point or another during the combination process (Bastien, 1987; Buono, Bowditch, and Lewis, 1988; Hayes, 1979; Marks, 1982; Marks and Mirvis, 1985, 1986; Schweiger, Ivancevich, and Power, 1987).

There are two basic types of communication that should be included in the merger and acquisition transition process: (1) communication to keep organizational members informed about the merger, its ramifications, and its implementation and (2) communication to facilitate getting the work done (American Bankers Association and Ernst & Whinney, 1985). During a merger or acquisition, questions usually emerge concerning the nature, extent, and timing of these communications. When should the merger or acquisition announcement be made? How clear and straightforward is the disclosure? Should the announcements indicate a concern for employees? Will top management be retained, and, if so, should that be addressed in any statements? Do communications spell out corporate goals? Do they address basic employee concerns, such as whether there will be layoffs, relocations, job changes, and so forth?

Because of employee anxieties and potential negative repercussions for the firms involved, the initial tendency is to carry out negotiations and combination plans in secret for as long as possible to minimize uncertainty among employees (Graves, 1981). This decision is typically followed by denials about or attempts to suppress any information about the combination. Because of the sensitivity of the issues involved, however, rumors and speculation about an impending consolidation usually leak out and contribute to a heightened sense of anxiety. Any resulting communication gaps are inevitably filled by informal interpersonal communications that the organization has little, if any, control over. Estimates suggest that employees spend approximately two hours per day—roughly one-quarter of their work time—gossiping and worrying about an impending or unfolding merger or acquisition (Cabrera, 1986; Wishard, 1985). Organizational members are more likely to react positively when they are well informed—exposed to unfavorable as well as favorable possibilities—than when they are forced to rely on hearsay and speculation. As a human resource executive involved in mergers and acquisitions argues (American Bankers Association and Ernst & Whinney, 1985, p. 87), "'Bad news' should be disseminated as early as possible. Trauma, uncertainty and dysfunctional behavior will persist if employees are waiting for the other shoe to drop."

Most research suggests that the creation of formal internal communication channels as early as possible in the process may reduce much of the anxiety otherwise fueled by rumors, the office grapevine, or even outside news reports (Bastien, 1987; Buono, Bowditch, and Lewis, 1988; Hayes, 1979; Kanter and Seggerman, 1986; Marks, 1982; Pritchett, 1987b). In order to effectively inform organizational members about the process and planned outcomes of an upcoming merger or acquisition, Taft (1981, p. 32) suggests a *staged approach* to communication. Key managers and executives, for example, should be informed before the announcement is made to middle-level managers, supervisors, and employees. While Securities and Exchange Commission (SEC) guidelines limit what can be told—even to employees—about a merger, as soon as legally possible, organizational members should be informed. The timing of the announcement that a merger or acquisition proposal has been approved should be arranged so that employees hear it first from within the organization. Dull (1986) has suggested that informing employees even only one hour before the combination announcement is made public can lessen the shock and increase trust in future internal communications.

Delta's acquisition of Western Airlines provides a good illustration of a company that followed a carefully planned strategy of communicating accurately and regularly with all organizational members (Kanter, Ingols, and Myers, 1987). Shortly after the acquisition, Delta sent a telex to each Western work unit and soon after that a letter to each employee's home outlining the general plans for postcombination integration. The letter promised additional information on strategies and processes by a certain date, and Delta then fulfilled its promise. The initial letter, for instance, noted that "During the week of February 16, 1987, a bulletin will be distributed containing the following information." As promised, on February 13, a thirty-page report was sent out that included details about such concerns as when job offers would be made, how traveling and moving expenses would be handled, how the transition from one benefit program to the other would be dealt with, and so forth. Throughout the initial combination aftermath period, Delta followed through on its promises. As one of Western's employees commented (Kanter, Ingols, and Myers, 1987, p. 26), "Delta hasn't once had to back up and say 'Hey, that's wrong. We did it wrong.' They're methodical—not fast. But when they give us information it's good, solid." Postacquisition reports about the Delta-Western consolidation suggest that the firm's actions alleviated much employee anxiety and stress and that the combination "got off to a good start."

It is important to emphasize that inaccurate information is worse than no information at all. The congruence of communications with what is actually unfolding has been found to be as important as the quantity and collegiality of communication efforts (Bastien, 1987). In times of stress and insecurity, people's attention to both the detail of the communication ("what does it really say") and its congruence with what they see happening (for example, "they say they're not going to get rid of anybody, and then they start firing people left and right") is substantially intensified. Moreover, the actions by top managers are read by organizational members as a sign of the firm's values and orientations, even though they may not be intended as such. A good example is employee reaction to the "Christmas massacre" in the Urban-Suburban bank merger, which was exacerbated by the "no layoff" statement prior to the consolidation. Organizational members are often quite suspicious of their new owners or merger partners and scan communications for the slightest sign of deception or subterfuge.

While most experts agree that communications should be open, honest, and continuous, there is disagreement as to where communications should come from—existing management or the new parent firm. One position is that communications should come from management of the precombination firm rather than from the merger partner or acquiring firm because of the insecurities associated with the change. The basic rationale is that if organizational members continue to receive information from the existing management structure, they will feel better about the situation (Hayes, 1979). If the communication flow is limited to existing management, however, organizational members are further isolated from their new owners. In Retail Corporation's acquisition of Food Company and Handy Stores, for example, all communication from the conglomerate to Handy Stores was initially filtered through Food Company's management, the fast-food subsidiary's initial parent. While this supported the bonds that existed prior to the acquisition, it also exacerbated the cultural transition of Handy Stores' top managers from an operational to a strategic-growth focus. Since Food Company had been run as a privately held family business, the management team at the company was struggling to deal with the same tensions and uncertainties as Handy Stores' management. Yet, while Food Company had access to Retail Corporation's expertise and guidance, any support to Handy Stores from the acquirer was initially filtered through Food Company. This dynamic essentially meant that Handy Stores' CEO and top managers were receiving guidance from their counterparts at Food Company, who were also grappling with the changes and new strategic and cultural orientations of the acquirer. As a result, there was not only confusion on the part of Handy Stores' managers as to "what is really expected of us" but growing distrust of the new corporate parent as well.

Communication from *both* managements appears to be important. Just ten days after the announcement of Shearson's acquisition of E. F. Hutton, for example, Peter Cohen, Shearson's chairperson and CEO, and his consolidation team visited twenty-two cities to "preach the gospel" of the merger to Hutton's branch managers. Each meeting, described as a "three-hour sales pitch," was followed by a dinner where Hutton employees were encouraged to "let their hair down." Moreover, all retention offers are made directly by Shearson personnel; terminations, however, are handled by the target. While the decisions were made jointly by Shearson and Hutton executives, as Cohen describes, "It's been Hutton people letting Hutton people go—with a lot of guidance from us" (Cowan, 1988, p. F8).

Much of the discussion of communication thus far has stressed one-way communication, largely from management to employees. For mergers and acquisitions to be successful, however, a two-way communication system should be developed that not only informs people but also provides them with the opportunity to raise questions, air fears and concerns, and so forth. Moreover, as successful combination efforts illustrate, effective communication goes far beyond speeches and addresses by the CEO. While such addresses are important, it is necessary to get line managers involved in the communication process as well (Mirvis and Marks, 1987). These needs can be addressed through newsletters, merger hot lines, and group presentations.

Newsletters and Hot Lines. As a way of ensuring that information about an impending or unfolding merger or acquisition is adequately disseminated and questions about it answered, firms are increasingly using in-house newsletters and phone "hot lines" as communication mechanisms. Newsletters can clarify many of the issues surrounding the combination and provide a useful outlet for a "dialogue" about concerns and questions. Similarly, merger and acquisition hot lines provide employees with a channel to anonymously raise questions, express concerns, and offer criticisms and suggestions that they may not feel comfortable doing in person. Usually staffed by people with expertise on the dynamics and processes associated with mergers and acquisitions, these hot lines provide combining organizations with a dual opportunity to both clarify concerns and problems that would otherwise be the subject of rumors and hearsay and inform senior managers about the types of concerns and problems faced by organizational members.

Shortly after Shearson's announcement that it was acquiring E. F. Hutton, for example, the company began publishing a newsletter and running a toll-free hot line for all Hutton brokers (Cowan, 1988). Similarly, during the Delta-Western merger, employees were provided with a toll-free number they could call to hear weekly recordings about the merger and leave their questions. These questions, in turn, often became the subject of subsequent merger updates on the hot line and in the firm's newsletter, *Update,* which was renamed *The Best Get Better* just two weeks after the first merger announcement. Regular features focused on Delta's plans for the merger process as well as comments about the combination by both Delta and Western officials (Kanter, Ingols, and Myers, 1987).

The merger between Connecticut Bank and Trust and Bank of New England also provides a good example of how this approach was used to facilitate the communication process. The newsletter, with the rather lengthy title *Inter-State: News About the Largest Banking Merger of Equals for the Employees of Bank of New England and CBT,* was created shortly after the merger was approved by both boards of directors. Published monthly, *Inter-State* not only informed employees about the combination's progress but attempted to respond to their concerns as well. By including brief open-ended questions that were to be answered anonymously (for example, "What do you want to know about the upcoming merger?"; "What should management pay careful attention to during the merger?"; "What is your biggest concern regarding the merger?"), the firms were able fairly early in the merger process to acquire a general sense of employee reactions. Questions and concerns raised by these comments were discussed in later editions.

Presentations. Another way to alleviate some of the anxiety associated with the uncertainties and ambiguities raised by the merger and acquisition process is to hold a series of group presentations that address employee concerns. While many human resource issues cannot be effectively resolved or even dealt with before a merger or acquisition is actually consummated, a number of issues that employees often interpret as signs of a firm's commitment and intentions can and should be clarified as early as possible. Presentations are also useful as part of a general education effort to get people to understand the transformation process and how it will affect them (Bridges, 1985). Examples range from general orientation sessions about the acquiring or merging organization and discussions about the merger and acquisition process to highly specific presentations on such concerns as compensation, job assignments, and relocation possibilities. As with any type of training effort, these presentations should involve and be supported by key organizational members.

Ilene Gordon (1987, p. 56), vice-president of Packaging Corporation of America, a division of Tenneco, Inc., explains that one of the most effective communication tools in Tenneco's acquisitions is a series of presentations on employee benefits, since they lend "an element of security at an insecure time." Because of the uncertainties and anxieties surrounding an impending combination, it is not sufficient to simply tell people that "your benefits will be equal to or better than what you have now." Specific changes in benefit and compensation plans should be spelled out in a clear and detailed manner (Hayes, 1979), and group presentations provide a direct, economical way of dealing with these concerns. Moreover, by the incorporation of such presentations as part of the combination process, potential problems caused by different interpretations of a merger or acquisition agreement can be confronted and resolved early on. As Joseph Duva (1984, p. 62), director of employee benefits and compensation at SCM Corporation, points out, "Amid demands for pension evaluations, financial reports and employee data, everyone's credibility is questioned. You count yourself lucky if you don't discover some hidden liability that threatens to wreck the deal. You're also lucky if you do not discover, as I did some years ago in reviewing a purchase agreement regarding an overseas acquisition, that not everyone agreed on what the words 'fully funded' mean."

The exact timing and nature of some of these sessions, however, can be problematic because of regulatory constraints that prevent illegal solicitation of merger and acquisition candidates (Dull, 1986). Thus, specific legal advice should be sought before setting up presentations for a merger partner or acquisition target.

Realistic Merger Previews

As noted above, communication about the merger should begin as soon as possible. Accurate information about both favorable and unfavorable developments enables employees to more effectively plan for the future. The communication plan itself, however, should be modified to reflect the nature of any planned changes (Ivancevich, Schweiger, and Power, 1987). If few changes are planned, as might be the case, for instance, in unrelated conglomerate acquisitions such as TransCo's acquisition of Co-op Foods, this intention should be made clear. Similarly, if widespread changes are called for, as in the Urban and Suburban bank merger, the details of such plans should also be communicated to organizational members. In the latter case, initial attempts by the banks' top managers to mask the amount of change that would take place only resulted in a sense of mistrust and betrayal on the part of employees from both companies. At the very least, details about the combination begin to reduce the fear of the unknown; it is even possible that the increased familiarity that results from such communications will lay the foundation for a deeper level of commitment to the new firm (Dull, 1986).

Among the issues and concerns that should be addressed by such early communication efforts are (1) reasons underlying the merger or acquisition decision and what the combination will mean for both the organizations and their members; (2) general facts about and orientation to the merging or acquiring company; (3) changes in company name, structure, and management (chain of command); (4) the elimination of or addition to any functions currently represented in the organization; (5) the possibility of a reduction in force, how decisions will be made, and whether there will be outplacement assistance; (6) detailed changes in compensation and benefit packages and management perquisites (expense accounts, company cars); (7) job-related changes, including new roles and assignments; (8) transfers to new job assignments or geographical areas; (9) possible changes in career paths; (10) changes in working relationships (colleagues, reporting relationships, departmental interactions); (11) how business will be conducted during the transition period; and (12) general changes in company policies (Barrett, 1973; Imberman, 1985; Ivancevich, Schweiger, and Power, 1987).

Accurate and honest responses to questions about these issues should provide organizational members with a realistic assessment of what the merger or acquisition will mean for them personally and for the new organization. The concept of such realistic merger previews emerges from earlier research and theory on realistic job previews (Schweiger and DeNisi, 1987; Schweiger and Ivancevich, 1985). Realistic job previews are based on the premise that accurate, realistic communication about job duties and responsibilities is an important component of socializing newcomers to an organization (Wanous, 1980). People entering an organization need to know what to expect on their jobs so that they can properly prepare themselves to effectively cope with job-related pressures and demands. Moreover, employees who receive an accurate appraisal of what their jobs will be like are less likely to be disappointed when unrealistic expectations go unfulfilled. Research on realistic job previews indicates that, in general, people who are provided with factual depictions of what their jobs will be like tend to be more satisfied and committed to their firms, with less stress and likelihood of turnover, than employees who do not receive such information (Premack and Wanous, 1985).

While more research on realistic merger previews is needed, a seminal study in this area (Schweiger and DeNisi, 1987) shows promising results. Two closely matched but geographically separate manufacturing plants of one company that was being merged with another were provided with different information about the combination. One plant was provided with a detailed, realistic (positive and negative) appraisal of what the merger would mean; the other plant received more traditional, limited communications. The researchers found that the levels of satisfaction, commitment, trust, and self-reported performance efforts at the plant receiving the realistic merger preview remained stable after the merger, while there was a marked decline in these measures in the second plant. These results suggest that realistic communications about an impending merger or acquisition may minimize some of the negative repercussions on the firms' human resources. To some extent, a comparison of the attitude findings in the Urban-Suburban bank merger with the findings in the TransCo-Co-op Foods acquisition further supports these findings. Additional research is needed to determine whether such realistic assessments are essentially only temporary remedies, cushioning organizational members from the initial shock of the merger but wearing off over time. Continued open communication throughout the combination process, however, seems to hold promise as a way to reduce some of the shocks and negative repercussions of a merger or acquisition.

Workshops and Counseling

Even if realistic and accurate information about an impending merger or acquisition is communicated to employees, over the course of the combination, employees will still tend to experience conflicting emotions, ranging from shock, anger, disbelief, and helplessness to hope, excitement, and even high expectations about what the future may hold (Bowditch and Buono, 1987; Marks and Mirvis, 1985; Schweiger, Ivancevich, and Power, 1987). As noted in Chapters Three and Four, individual reactions can vary widely depending on the type of combination, how it unfolds, and the experiences of different employees. However, as discussed in Chapter Five, following a merger there is typically a mourning or grief period similar to that experienced when a family member dies (Fried, 1963; Sinetar, 1981). Because of the traumas, anxieties, and tensions associated with such change, organizational members usually need some help in dealing with the resultant stress in their lives.

In the merger between Urban and Suburban banks, for example, people became quite nostalgic about their former bank affiliations during the initial aftermath period. Employees from both merger partners expressed an active dislike of their merger partner counterparts, the other bank's managers, and its policies and cultural orientations. As discussed in Chapter Five, the idealization of a ''lost'' company is a typical grief reaction and part of the process of ''working through'' the loss. Yet, while this may be a normal response, as part of this process, employees often display a general depressive tone and somatic symptoms, experience a sense of helplessness, and express both direct and displaced anger. The significance of such feelings was not even acknowledged by Merged Bank's management, and the resulting tensions affected virtually all interfirm interactions.

From a managerial perspective, it is important to assist employees in dealing with such feelings because residual anger can persist on the part of employees for years following a merger or acquisition (Levinson, 1970). Thus, an important component of the postcombination process is how the company "manages" the grieving process. When Delta Airlines acquired Western, for example, many of the latter's employees reported that the reality of the merger and the loss of identity with their company did not take hold until they saw the company logo being removed from the airplanes (Kanter, Ingols, and Myers, 1987). Despite the apparent goodwill that was developed by the extensive and open communication during the early merger stages, this sense of personal loss, exacerbated by the general upheaval created by almost 2,000 cross-country relocations, began to create a high level of stress and anxiety throughout Western. As a way of dealing with these feelings, the company used its Health Services Program (HSP), a joint union-management employee assistance venture, to help employees deal with the stress and anxiety caused by the acquisition through individual counseling, "rap" sessions, and workshops.

Workshops. The main purpose of combination-related workshops is to provide organizational members with ways to understand what is happening and regain some sense of control over their work lives and careers. While most of these workshops focus on how to cope with the stress and anxiety created by mergers and acquisitions, other programs for organizational members include seminars on organizational culture and culture change, how to manage under conditions of uncertainty, career development, and so forth. Participation in these seminars should be voluntary (Schweiger and Ivancevich, 1985); however, direct support from the parent firm is needed if they are to be effective over the long term. In the UNISYS (Burroughs-Sperry) consolidation, "merger syndrome" workshops were used to prepare people for the types of emotional stress and anxieties that are typically confronted during a merger or acquisition (Mirvis and Marks, 1987). In Retail Corporation's acquisition of Handy Stores, outside consultants were hired to conduct a series of workshops and individual counseling and training sessions to assist Handy Stores' managers to (1) understand organizational culture and culture change and how they explicitly applied to the acquisition; (2) comprehend the nature of Retail Corporation's orientations and expectations; and (3) assist individual managers in meeting changing expectations and coping with the concomitant stress and anxiety.

A major difference between the Burroughs-Sperry workshops and the Retail Corporation–Handy Stores effort was support from the top of the organization. In the UNISYS venture, the workshops were instituted by the corporation's top management team; anecdotal reports suggest that they have been quite effective during the initial aftermath period (Mirvis and Marks, 1987). In the Retail Corporation–Handy Stores acquisition, in contrast, the seminars were initiated by Handy Stores' CEO as a "cry for help." Since the firm did not receive any support or guidance from its new parent (Retail Corporation), the workshops and counseling efforts were part of the CEO's attempt to cope with the magnitude and rate of change taking place (Shuman and Buono, 1988). The result was limited to a stabilization of Handy Stores' managers' performance and attitudes over the *short term*. Without any direct guidance or support from Retail Corporation, however, the situation began to unravel.

Counseling. While group workshops are an economical way of meeting the needs of a number of people and creating a support system among co-workers, these efforts may not always be sufficient to develop an individual's ability to cope with merger-related stress and anxiety. Accordingly, individual counseling efforts may be required to help people "get a grip" on what is happening in the organization and their lives. Counseling can be quite useful both to differentiate between the real and imagined effects of a merger and to help employees clarify their own needs and expectations in regard to their role in the organization and their careers.

Combination-related counseling efforts can be broken down into three categories (Schweiger and Ivancevich, 1985, pp. 58–60): personal adjustment counseling (focusing on a person's emotional responses to the combination); educational counseling (providing employees with information on the combination and its underlying processes); and career counseling (attempting to clarify issues dealing with choices and opportunities). It is important to note that these three types are not necessarily independent of each other, and in most instances there is considerable overlap in practice. Success depends on the skills of the individual counselors involved, their ability to effectively listen, understand, and communicate, their knowledge of the two organizations, and their ability to develop rapport with their clients.

Survey Feedback

Diagnostic surveys, used extensively in organizational change programs, are an important source of information with which to build and implement appropriate interventions to facilitate integration between merging companies. A typical reaction in many merging or acquiring firms, however, is a reluctance to initially undertake any activities that go beyond basic adjustments in financial controls, strategic orientations, or human resource policies such as benefit packages and compensation systems. With managers not wanting to overburden an already complicated situation, the general sentiment seems to be "let's let the dust settle down a little before taking any action" (Pritchett, 1985, p. 108).

While this position appears to be reasonably sound, the resulting inaction often compounds rather than resolves employee tensions and concerns. While an acquiring firm might view such decisions as "in the best interests of all involved," employees may well have a very different interpretation of the situation. When SteelCo acquired Petro, for example, the parent company's management was initially wary about tampering with the target's scientists and engineers. While the conglomerate made extensive changes in Petro's accounting and human resource areas, the acquisition plan was to allow the technical experts to operate as they had prior to the acquisition. This decision was communicated to the specialists through routine channels. Given the extensive changes in other departments, however, the scientists and engineers readily questioned the validity of the "no change" promise and began to "bail out" of the company, according to one company official, "in droves." SteelCo's CEO was bewildered by the exit of these valued employees, and the conglomerate was faced with the onerous task of "turning the tide around."

Through organizational surveys, an acquiring or merging firm can develop a foundation to understand the reactions of organizational members to the combination. Such opinion data are quite useful as the base line on which postcombination integration plans can be built. If SteelCo had employed such a survey early on in the acquisition, the company could have been alerted to the uneasiness and concerns of the technical experts. It is important to assess this information as quickly as possible, as a way of understanding the range and scope of interventions required to successfully combine the firms and achieve strategic goals.

One approach to survey feedback, illustrated in Figure 4, involves five interrelated stages that form the basis of a participative process of data gathering and organizational action (Bowditch and Buono, 1982):

1. *Entry phase* of the program, which involves initial discussion and decisions about the scope and parameters of the survey, the timetable, the type of information desired, who will have access to the data and in what form, how feedback will be handled, and a preliminary assessment of problem areas. This phase is often referred to as "contracting."
2. *Planning and development phase,* in which meetings with key human resource personnel and cross-sectional small-group sessions with randomly selected employees are used to identify important combination-related concerns and issues. This input forms the basis of the questionnaire.
3. *Implementation and administration phase,* during which the questionnaire is pilot tested and then administered to all organization members (preferable) or, in very large firms, a sample of employees.

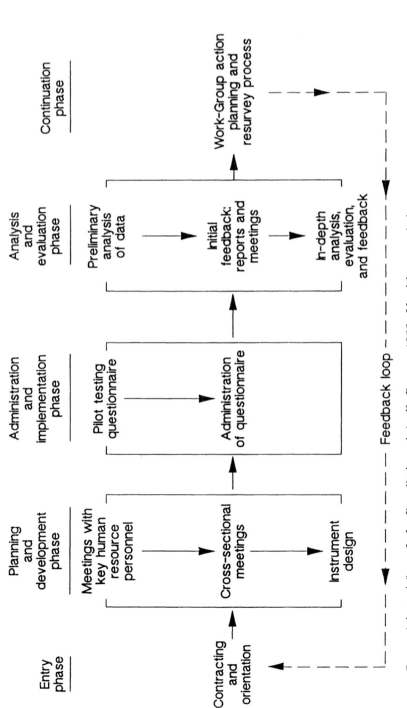

Figure 4. An Integrated Survey Feedback Model.

Entry phase

Contracting and orientation

Planning and development phase

Meetings with key human resource personnel → Cross-sectional meetings → Instrument design

Administration and implementation phase

Pilot testing questionnaire → Administration of questionnaire

Analysis and evaluation phase

Preliminary analysis of data → Initial feedback: reports and meetings → In-depth analysis, evaluation, and feedback

Continuation phase

Work-Group action planning and resurvey process

Feedback loop

Source: Adapted from J. L. Bowditch and A. F. Buono, 1982. Used by permission.

4. *Analysis and feedback phase,* in which a preliminary analysis
    of the data is undertaken and fed back as early as possible
    through reports and meetings, followed by more in-depth
    analyses and feedback to work-group planning committees.
5. *Reassessment and change,* when the information generated
    through the survey process is used to deal with combination-
    related concerns and problems. The process should be re-
    peated every two years.

As these stages suggest, the social processes underlying the
design, administration, and application of a combination-related
survey and its results are just as important as the technical content in terms of questionnaire design and analysis.

Typical areas of concern in merger- and acquisition-
related surveys are attitudes toward such facets of organizational
life as organizational commitment; job satisfaction (in terms of
both content and context); interpersonal relations, including interactions between co-workers, departments, and the companies;
job security; management policies and style; one's immediate
supervisor; advancement and career concerns; compensation
and benefits; and underlying processes and outcomes of the combination itself. As suggested in Chapter Five, another important dimension to consider in combination-related surveys is the
expectations of the employees. Understanding employee expectations about what will happen in a merger or acquisition is quite
important, especially in the context of creating and assessing
realistic merger previews and communications about the combination. The expectations of Petro's scientists and engineers
that SteelCo would drastically change their operation appeared
to be unfounded. Yet, since SteelCo's management was unaware
of this apprehension, they were oblivious to the need to further
clarify and reinforce their intention for the technical staff. Unfortunately, this situation seems to be fairly commonplace.
Despite growing realization about the importance of employee
expectations (Barclay, 1982; Davis and Luthans, 1980; Porras
and others, 1982), even if organizations use surveys, they do
not generally gather data on employee expectations about upcoming events (Pond, Armenakis, and Green, 1984).

As with any organizational survey effort, combination-related surveys entail a certain amount of risk. While the mere implementation of a survey is often interpreted by organizational members as a sign that management is concerned about their thoughts and opinions, it is important for managers to work with employees in dealing with the results of the survey. Once an organization solicits employee opinions about a merger or acquisition, people generally expect that something will be done with the data. Organizations that are not prepared to take action on the results are perhaps wiser not to undertake the survey in the first place. "What, another attitude survey?" is usually the reply when employees feel that nothing has really changed since the last data-gathering exercise. By involving organizational members in the planning, development, and implementation of the survey and its results, however, managers can provide the foundation for successful postcombination integration.

Transition Teams

Obviously, not all organizational members can or should be involved in bringing about combination-related changes. While participation and involvement are key strategies for getting people to accept organizational changes, it is simply not practical to have everyone included in the process. At the same time, however, it is important to involve as many people as feasible where legitimate, appropriate, and supported by top management. Much of the initial success of the UNISYS merger, for example, is credited to the involvement of hundreds of Burroughs and Sperry employees in an interlocking series of task forces focused on different aspects of the merger. Yet one of the "lessons learned" from the consolidation was that even more people should have been involved even earlier in the process (Mirvis and Marks, 1987).

Especially if some interfirm transition teams focus on results from organizational surveys, these groups can undertake many of the integrative functions necessary for merger success. Moreover, they can serve as conduits of accurate information and be identified as sources that employees can turn to. By meeting periodically for a specified period of time—for at least six to eight months, but often longer, depending on the task involved—the resulting interaction also provides an opportunity for managers to get to know each other and gives employees from both firms a way to interact and exchange ideas with management. This association can begin to resolve much of the "we versus they" mentality that inhibits the integration process (DeMeuse, 1986, 1987; Gordon, 1987).

Such transition teams, however, will not automatically begin to resolve combination-related problems. In the merger between Urban and Suburban banks, for example, the two CEOs set up a series of transition teams during the initial combination process period with the explicit function of dealing with specific operational concerns, such as which computer system, forms, and operating procedures Merged Bank would use. As described in Chapter Two, however, discussions at transition team meetings were largely characterized by defensiveness on the part of each group as to why "their way" was better. Because of the extreme cultural differences between the two banks and related ethnocentric attitudes, little of any real substance emerged from these transition team efforts. In fact, they actually served to reinforce people's awareness of the disparate cultural orientations.

Part of the difficulty in getting transition teams to work effectively together is caused by such cultural strains and clashes. Yet, if properly acknowledged and dealt with, these tensions can be minimized. Marks and Mirvis (1986), for example, report on two hospital management teams that worked closely together during a merger of the two organizations. The groups met regularly, and instead of simply focusing on operational issues and concerns, members attempted to explicitly clarify each firm's values, philosophy, and approaches to health care as well as their own impressions of the other's operation. As these perceptions were uncovered and confronted, the teams found widespread stereotyping by both management teams—in a situation quite similar to what happened in the Urban-Suburban bank merger and the CompServe-NetCo joint venture, each team valued its own culture while deriding the culture of the other. These insights, however, were then used as a guide on how to handle the merger. Points where the two cultures were compatible were the first areas the teams attempted to integrate. In areas with clashes and potential resistance, however, movement was more cautious and slow, each management team attempting to respect the differences and the orientation of the other.

The potential for working through cultural and psychological concerns when focusing on operational and technical combination-related needs is further illustrated by the success of one of the later transition teams in the Urban-Suburban bank merger. During the postcombination aftermath period, a human resource–based communications committee (HRC) composed of a cross section of eleven employees and supervisors, elected by their peers, was formed. Although Merged Bank's COO (formerly CEO of Suburban Bank) initially resisted the idea, because of the growing discontent among and problems between members of the two banks, he eventually gave the team his support. The committee met with the new vice-president for human resources every other month to raise problems, discuss solutions, and pass on information to upper-level management and employees. In preparation for the meetings, each team member polled his or her ''constituency'' about their concerns and any current or anticipated problems. This information shaped the agenda of the next meeting. To prevent the polling and meetings from becoming simply unfocused gripe sessions, however, one of the team's ground rules was that all complaints had to be accompanied by suggestions on how the situation could be improved. As a result of the involvement of team members and their constituencies in both identifying and proposing solutions to existing and potential problem areas, people from both banks slowly began to identify more with the merged institution and develop a more realistic set of expectations about the difficulties involved in resolving many merger-related problems. Interview data suggest that the HRC had a positive effect on the movement toward psychological combination. Rather than being left until organizational difficulties reach the proportion they did in Merged Bank, such interfirm transition management structures should be incorporated into the combination process as early as possible.

Intergroup Mirroring and Team Building

   As indicated by the initial interbank tensions in the transition teams in the Urban-Suburban bank merger, simply providing such groups with clearly defined objectives will not necessarily ensure that the tasks will be accomplished. Stresses and strains between employees of consolidating firms, individual fears and anxieties, and disparate cultural identities and ethnocentric attitudes often undermine the potential of joint task forces. The experiences of the hospital merger team and the HRC discussed above suggest, however, that if the interactions between members of combining firms focus initially on identifying major human problems and concerns raised by the combination, it seems that organizational, operational, and procedural concerns can then be more easily resolved. A recognition of cultural differences through intergroup mirroring interventions, followed by team-building efforts, is applicable here.

   Intergroup mirroring attempts to bring to the surface the root causes of conflict between two groups and to create conditions under which mutual problem solving can occur. Each group develops and shares an image of itself and the other in an attempt to reveal stereotypes and assumptions that naturally exist about "them" and "us." The groups then focus on their uniqueness, differences, and similarities as they work through their perceptions of each other's image, motivations, and competencies. This process is accomplished in three basic phases (Plovnick, Fry, and Burke, 1982, p. 90):

1. *Imagery:* Each group develops an image of itself and the other group. When the groups acknowledge and discuss stereotypes and untested assumptions about each other, many of the myths surrounding merging or acquiring organizations can be eliminated.
2. *Confrontation:* Each group admits to its uniqueness and differences from the other. The basic goal is to delineate the differences that are accepted as valid and those that are causing conflict. Without sufficient clarification and definition of the conflict, meaningful resolution is unlikely.

3. *Bonding:* Groups experiencing irresolvable conflicts with each other can begin to collaborate and address problems as they become more alike in their understanding of (1) perceived and real injustices experienced by each other; (2) motivations of each group to succeed; (3) competencies and resources each has to offer; and (4) a need to work together or to depend on one another.

Through drawing out the *goals* of the new organization, the *roles* that organizational members will play, the *process and procedures* through which the firms will interact, and *interpersonal relationships and interactions,* stronger team identities can begin to be established (Beckhard, 1971). Since the emerging culture of the new institution evolves slowly over time as a product of shared experience, the greater the number of these shared experiences that can be produced early on in the process, the faster a set of symbols and shared meanings will develop with which organizational members can begin to identify.

There are differences of opinion, however, as to whether such outright confrontations are the most effective way to build team identities, especially in such stressful situations as organizational combinations. On the one hand, the type of intergroup process of observation, assessment, and feedback discussed above has been shown to be quite beneficial in mergers and acquisitions (Blake and Mouton, 1981, 1985). On the other hand, a more task-oriented approach may keep personal remarks and assessments at a minimum and create an agenda that focuses on informational rather than perceptual exchanges. This approach attempts to minimize the risk of uncovering and mobilizing fears and frustrations between the two groups (Beckhard, 1971; Walter, 1984).

The task-centered approach appears to generate more of a "conference" than a confrontational atmosphere in intergroup mirroring efforts (Walter, 1985b). However, while this environment may create the ability to exchange data in a more comfortable setting, it also limits the true exchanges and understandings that can emerge from intergroup confrontation sessions. Thus, many of the problems between the two firms will remain unresolved. It seems that the potentially most effective team-building efforts between merging firms or an acquirer and its target can be accomplished through an eclectic combination of interactions focused on planning, work relations (individual and cultural), task procedures, and other legitimate task issues. The main goal is to create mutual comprehension and understanding between the two groups.

As part of the goal-setting process, it is also useful to institute a time frame and related responsibilities. In Shearson's acquisition of E. F. Hutton, for example, a series of "conversion meetings" were held regularly during which progress on all responsibilities and assignments was reviewed—each of the 225 managers involved in the transition had to publicly explain why his or her group failed to accomplish the assigned task within the assigned time (Cowan, 1988). Such meetings, while stressful in themselves, can be an effective way of exerting external pressure to complete the assigned tasks.

Parallel Organizational Structures

During a merger or acquisition, managers and executives are faced with a number of important and immediate tasks and decisions. As described earlier, organizational combinations often have a frenetic quality, characterized by escalating momentum, cascading minor changes, rising tensions and conflicts, and stressful uncertainties. As a result, combination managers can be so swamped by what appear to be urgent priorities and demands that they often do not have the time to focus on how well the transition itself is going, how communications are being handled, and so forth. Thus, no one takes full responsibility for what is happening, what needs to be done, or what should be re-evaluated or modified (Carcione, 1984; Mayers, 1986a, 1986b). While transition teams alleviate some of this chaos, the efforts of one group often fail to be integrated with the efforts of another.

As a way of formalizing the integration of different transition teams working on combination-related issues, *parallel organizational structures* can be highly beneficial in mergers and acquisitions. Parallel organizations have enjoyed wide success in the 1980s as part of systemwide incentive plans and quality-of-work-life approaches (Moore, 1986). Their main purpose is to fill in the gaps created by traditional bureaucratic structures by focusing on employee concerns, data gathering, diagnosis and problem solving, organizational interventions, strategy planning, and implementation. In a sense, parallel organizations represent the ultimate effort to incorporate organization development as part of a long-term effort to improve a company's problem-solving and renewal processes.

A parallel organizational structure creates a series of rotating task forces directed by a steering committee. Similar to a matrix organization, these structures undercut traditional authority relations, since those involved hold two simultaneous positions and roles. This situation can be quite beneficial in a merger or acquisition, since people often find that they cannot simply rely on their functional authority or status to resolve various problems. Unlike matrix organizations, however, parallel structures are not anchored in projects per se as much as they are in the ongoing reexamination and reevaluation of organizational routines, exploring new options and developing new techniques, tools, and approaches for dealing with changing organizational conditions (Kanter, 1983; Moore, 1986).

The role of a parallel organizational structure in a merger or acquisition can perhaps best be described in terms of a combination-oriented steering committee, responsible for tracking the combination, uncovering and resolving conflicts and dilemmas, and attempting to ensure its acceptance by both groups of employees. In the UNISYS consolidation, for example, a merger coordination council was used to oversee the general dynamics and processes associated with the combination (Mirvis and Marks, 1987). The human resource–based communication committee (HRC) in the Urban-Suburban bank merger was a similar type of task force, oriented toward the successful integration of the two banks.

While such parallel structures appear to hold promise as transition facilitators, there is a danger in making such committees top-heavy. In the joint venture between CompServe and NetCo, for example, an advisory committee composed of two members from each board of directors, the two presidents, and two of their senior vice-presidents was designated to oversee the interfirm endeavor. Through formal and informal meetings, the committee was to ensure that all combination-related concerns, from strategic and operational issues to interactions between members of the firms, were dealt with in a mutually satisfactory manner. Formal meetings were to be held monthly, and committee members agreed to be available to deal with specific problems as they arose. Unfortunately, the advisory committee was almost completely ineffective in dealing with problems raised by the joint venture and questions about a possible merger between the companies. Despite many of the obstacles and difficulties that emerged during the initial combination aftermath period, the committee never officially met after its initial "kickoff" meeting. Although a number of meetings were scheduled, each was canceled because of "scheduling problems" or other commitments of the group's members. It was also apparent that these people were too far removed from the realities of the combination as experienced by members of the two firms.

If such steering committees are to be successful, they must have an explicit emphasis on data gathering, problem finding, and problem solving. Moreover, it is important that the task force's members are integrated both laterally (involving different functions and departments at the same level) and vertically (involving different levels). While it is critical to have the support and guidance of top management, if the membership of such structures is restricted to those at the top echelons, much of the potential and effectiveness of these groups will be minimized. Membership of the HRC in the Urban-Suburban bank merger appears to be more in line with both the intent and objectives of parallel organizational efforts.

Organizational Symbols and Rituals

Since a merger or acquisition typically involves a significant amount of individual and collective loss, the ways in which organizational symbols are managed—through transition rituals, stories, and artifacts—play a key role in assisting people to deal with the change. As Chapters Six and Seven discuss, much of the tension and conflict in a merger or acquisition is associated with managing the threat to the companies' cultures and managing conflicts involved in cross-cultural interaction. As part of this process, it is important for managers to understand how the symbolic and expressive aspects of their actions, decisions, or policies reinforce or undermine the cultural identities in the firms.

Especially given the amount of change involved in most mergers and acquisitions, new patterns of behavior and cultural identities must often be created. Even in unrelated acquisitions where a low level of operational integration is planned, people must acclimate themselves to being part of a new organization. Similarly, cultural pluralism strategies still entail some degree of reorientation and acculturation. The social interactions required to create and establish such new identities and orientations are reflected in the concept of "rites of creation." These relatively elaborate, dramatic, and planned sets of activities combine various forms of cultural expression in an effort to establish new patterns of behavior and embed them in existing organizational interactions and arrangements (Beyer and Trice, 1987). At the same time, however, such creation also means that organizational members have to let go of the old entity and, what is usually more difficult, the old identity that went with it (Bridges, 1986). Reports of successful culture change efforts in mergers and acquisitions focus on the role played by such disengagement efforts as "grieving meetings," where people are encouraged to openly discuss their feelings and emotions, and superficial-appearing but symbolically important "hoopla activities" such as ceremonies and rituals that honor, reward, and emphasize valued behaviors (Sales and Mirvis, 1984; Tichy and Ulrich, 1984a, 1984b).

The ways in which organizational symbols are constructed and managed create compelling images of the new organization. Properly handled, such symbols can readily influence the cognitive maps that people use to understand their organizations (Ashforth, 1985). In a process similar to the socialization process used for newcomers to an organization (Pascale, 1985), organizational members can be indoctrinated into a merger or acquisition through a series of mutually reinforcing processes, such as stories and myths that reinforce a particular management philosophy, ceremonies and rituals that signify passage from one state to another, and actions that bring organizational values to life (Deal and Kennedy, 1982; Peters, 1978). In the Burroughs-Sperry merger, for example, people were involved in a "Name the Company" contest. Members from both firms wore baseball caps with company names on them to signify the change. When the new name for the company was chosen, organizational members were given caps with the UNISYS name. These caps became important symbols of the goals and objectives of the merger. Whenever a manager would start building up one company at the expense of the other, he was told to put on his baseball cap. The slogan "Have your corporate hat on" became a symbol of the intent to reinforce a partnership between the two companies and to form bonds of allegiance between Burroughs and Sperry employees to the merged company (DeMeuse, 1987; Mirvis and Marks, 1987).

Symbolic gestures can also be used to reinforce direct communications to organizational members. In a combination involving two entertainment companies, for example, the acquiring firm (Movies, Inc.) made a conscious effort to understand the cultural orientations of the acquired firm (Acme, Inc.) and to transmit its own cultural values to it (Siehl, Ledford, Silverman, and Fay, 1987). Following the public announcement of the acquisition, a formal meeting at Acme headquarters was held to present the rationale for the merger. The meeting was designed as a major ceremony, to which employees and their spouses were invited. Immediately after the presentations and question-and-answer period, a banquet was held during which a team of Movies, Inc., executives circulated around the room to discuss the acquisition and respond to concerns such as continued job security, career opportunities, and potential combination-related changes. Instead of a sit-down dinner, the gathering was held as a stand-up affair to facilitate mixing and to increase the number of people that Movies, Inc.'s president could personally meet. While the parent company used formal channels to inform Acme employees about the value of "family" and the importance of communication at Movies, Inc., its espoused values were more memorably demonstrated by the banquet, the invitations to spouses, and the communication efforts at the affair than by simply being verbalized.

As the Movies-Acme acquisition illustrates, management actions during the combination signify a great deal about the values and orientations of the new firm. People interpret such events as signs of what is important to the organization, and, as a result, such events can significantly affect the shared beliefs about an organization and its management (Nystrom and Starbuck, 1984). These "signals," however, are not always interpreted positively. In the merger between Urban and Suburban banks, for example, the "Christmas massacre" readily became a symbol of the emerging cultural orientation of Merged Bank. While the CEOs may have intended the "no layoff" promise as an initial way of gaining momentum and support for the merger, the resulting sense of betrayal when layoffs were announced contributed to the significant rise in employee disaffection. Moreover, given what were perceived to be the new values of Merged Bank (for example, "people are our least important resource"), many organizational members, especially from Urban Bank, readily rationalized the countercultural retaliation and efforts to undermine the merger discussed in Chapter Seven.

Ironically, the use of symbols and rituals seems less of an innovative technique than a return to an earlier form of management—the role of the charismatic leader (Heller, 1985). The distinction between the "transformational leader" and the "transactional manager," for example, underscores the importance of strong corporate leaders who can develop a shared sense of values and mission among organizational members (Burke, 1986; Tichy and Ulrich, 1984b). Transformational leaders are increasingly being called upon to create something new out of something old. They must be able to create a vision of the desired future state of the firm, articulate that vision to organizational members, and work with those members to ensure their acceptance of and identification with that vision. Transactional managers, in contrast, make only minor modifications in the organization's mission, structure, and human resource system. Given the scope and magnitude of change involved in mergers and acquisitions, it seems that the more executives are able to effectively manage and control the symbolic and expressive aspects of the combination, the greater the probability of post-combination integration success.

Retaining and Dismissing Employees

Explicit efforts at employee retention following a merger or acquisition, whether at the managerial or the operational level, are not necessarily a good or bad strategy. In organizational rescues or "bailouts," for instance, existing management is generally held responsible for the poor performance and asked to leave. In collaborative unrelated acquisitions, by contrast, the expertise of the other firm's managers and employees is usually quite valuable. Thus, retention strategies depend on the type of merger or acquisition involved, its strategic intent, and what the dominant firm hopes to accomplish (Hayes, 1979). The way in which combination-related reductions in force are managed, however, sends clear signals about the new organization's values to employees.

It is inevitable that in any merger or acquisition there will be some overlap of function, duties, or responsibilities. The obvious outcome is some level of job terminations and resulting bitterness among employees who are asked to leave as well as those who remain. Research suggests, however, that it is not staff reductions and layoffs in and of themselves that generates dissatisfaction and bitterness, but rather the way in which such terminations are handled (Schweiger, Ivancevich, and Power, 1987). Unfortunately, most people involved in mergers and acquisitions feel that termination decisions are handled in an arbitrary and ineffective manner. In the merger between Urban and Suburban banks, for example, the "Christmas massacre" and what were reported as cavalier ways of dismissing employees fueled significant resentment toward and dissatisfaction with Merged Bank and its management and precipitated a rise in

voluntary turnover. In a similar situation, within one year after
a horizontal acquisition by North Carolina National Bank, only
one of the combination partner's department heads was still
employed by the institution. The resentment created by these
large-scale layoffs generated such ill will toward the firm that
with the next acquisition, approximately half of the top 300
officers left voluntarily within eighteen months of the combination (Heylar, 1986).

Even firms that have developed good reputations for han-
dling merger and acquisition integration often run into difficulties
in dealing with employment terminations. In Shearson's acquisition of E. F. Hutton, for example, Shearson conversion managers assigned their counterparts at Hutton to one of three lists:
the "A list" (those who would get jobs), the "B list" (those
who would be offered a bonus to stay through the transition),
and the "C list" (those whose employment would be terminated).
Yet, since these lists were "based on hastily arranged interviews," the process was criticized by many of those who were
involuntarily dismissed. Many of those on the "C list" reported
that they were given one day to vacate their offices. For newly
hired employees, severance compensation amounted to just two
weeks' pay. Moreover, much of the bitterness seems to have
emerged from the sheer timing of the layoffs—ironically, as in
the case of the "massacre" in Merged Bank, during the Christmas holiday season. Shearson's chair was quoted as saying that
the way the press dealt with the layoff announcements was similar to how it dealt with "Vietnam war body counts" (Cowan,
1988, p. F8).

Termination decisions, however, do not necessarily have
to be disruptive for the combined firm. During TransCo's acquisition of Co-op Foods, for example, a number of middle
managers were let go for performance reasons. Although no
promises concerning managerial job security were made by
TransCo, these terminations initially fueled apprehension and
anxiety on the part of many employees. However, it was also
clear to most people that the terminations were based on performance factors rather than arbitrary standards or cultural differences, and they were largely accepted. Pritchett (1985, p. 65)

argues that not only does terminating the employment of poor performers send a message to other employees about job-related expectations, but it is usually accepted by the better performers who are "weary of having to carry the load that should have been borne by others." In such instances, it is still important for the organization to aid those being let go with outplacement assistance, counseling, and related job search and support services.

While his emphasis is on senior management personnel, Jay's (1968) advice about retention strategies seems applicable to organizational members in general. In a merger or acquisition, you should do one of two things: (1) welcome the managers and employees of the firm warmly, encouraging them, supporting them, and showing them that they are to be an important part of the "new" company, or (2) terminate their employment as quickly as possible. While such termination decisions should still be handled in a supportive, humanistic manner, if you send indecisive signals to people you risk losing key managers and employees.

The SteelCo acquisition of Petro illustrates problems that can emerge when an acquiring firm fails to send clear messages to valued employees. Since the acquisition was part of SteelCo's diversification strategy, the positions of the technical experts, engineers, and scientists at Petro were not threatened. In fact, SteelCo had acquired the firm largely to secure the expertise of these people. During the postcombination aftermath period, however, as operational consolidation of basic functional areas—human resources, accounting, and finance—began to take place, many of the technical staff interpreted the terminations and changes in other sections of their company as a "sign of things to come." The result was a high level of voluntary turnover among the very people that influenced SteelCo's decision to buy the company in the first place. By not communicating the importance of these individuals to the firm, underscoring its commitment to them and to their R&D efforts, SteelCo found itself in control of the petrochemical company but without many of the petrochemical experts that made the organization a desirable acquisition target.

When it is decided that a reduction in force is needed, all terminations and outplacement services should be handled with dignity and respect (Ivancevich, Schweiger, and Power, 1987; Schweiger, Ivancevich, and Power, 1987). It is important to remember that the way in which people are let go has a powerful effect on those who stay. The popular belief, of course, is that poor performers, those who are fearful that their deficiencies will be uncovered and that they will lose power and status, are the ones most likely to "bail out" following a merger or acquisition. Research, however, has shown the exact opposite—the better employees, whose skills and expertise are valuable to the company, are the ones most likely to leave. These people tend to be quite marketable and enjoy the most career options (Marks and Mirvis, 1985). As a result, they are the ones who are immediately approached by "headhunters" and search firms. While technical specialists and key managers are often disinclined to consider leaving their firm for another job, the stress and uncertainty surrounding a merger or acquisition often open them up to other possibilities. Many people simply opt for a securer position with another company, as a way of both guaranteeing their immediate situation and avoiding much of the stress and anxiety associated with living through the combination. Ironically, not only do such decisions weaken the combined firm, they typically strengthen the firm's competitors (Magnet, 1984a).

Some of the organizational stress and tension associated with job loss can be minimized by following well-developed plans. It is important to realize, however, that regardless of how well such efforts are managed or how supportive the organization is to those it lets go, the impact on people who are dismissed can be quite severe. Especially in collaborative ventures, initial reductions in force should be as voluntary as possible. Through attractive severance packages, early retirement plans, and employee attrition, much of the sting of job loss can be reduced. When involuntary termination is required, all decisions should be as objective as possible and supported by outplacement assistance, counseling, and related job search and support services. Yet, in the mergers and acquisitions we studied, no outplacement services or support were available. While management in the merger between Urban and Suburban banks did offer some counseling, the support for those leaving was minimal.

When termination decisions are made, especially for over-lapping positions, it is important to use participation and decisions that are as nonpartisan as possible in selecting the most qualified person for the job (Borucki, Tichy, and Trullinger, 1987). Many people involved in mergers and acquisitions, for example, feel that job performance evaluations, fairness, and honesty *should be,* but typically are not, used in making such decisions. While this reaction might be dismissed as part of human nature, in that we tend to blame others or the "system" for many of our own shortcomings, consider the following comment from a manager in a recently acquired firm (Schweiger, Ivancevich, and Power, 1987, p. 130): "What a bunch of con artists! They told us that the performance record is the key to retention. Well, why did 25 of my coworkers get terminated because of redundancy? The other firm kept their own 25 people in what they refer to as redundant jobs." As a result, many people who initially survive job cuts often begin to question whether it makes sense to remain with the company, especially considering the way it handled the termination process.

Attention to Detail

It is clear that managing the consolidation of two firms into one involves a multitude of responsibilities, concerns, and tasks. One of the realities of organizational combinations is that it is virtually impossible to predict every concern that needs to be dealt with or exactly how organizational members will react to the various interventions and processes that will occur. Effective management of the merger and acquisition process, however, emerges from the ability to evaluate the relative successes and failures of each step of the transition (Bridges, 1985). What types of changes and procedures smoothed the transition? Which ones served only to intensify problems? What should have been done differently? How might this vary in different situations? Unfortunately, research indicates that few managers and organizations learn from their combination-related mistakes (Haspeslagh and Jemison, 1987; Yunker, 1983).

Attention to the details involved in a merger or acquisition requires a concern for both obvious and less apparent matters. Indeed, many of the "little things" in an organizational combination signal the intention and concern of the acquiring firm. PCA/Tenneco, for example, has a policy about housecleaning during a merger or acquisition—not "cleaning house" of the other firm's managers and employees but rather literally cleaning the building. As one of the company's vice-presidents argues (Gordon, 1987, p. 56), "A fresh coat of paint, new carpeting, maybe even a walled-in office for the boss show new employees they're not going to be forgotten stepchildren. . . . When employees and management see equipment replaced and offices remodeled, it instills a great deal of confidence in their new corporate relationship."

Shearson's acquisition of E. F. Hutton further illustrates the level of detail and difficulty involved in consolidating two firms (Cowan, 1988). Approximately 225 managers were entrusted with overseeing the combination, guided by a 1,200-step acquisition manual. As Peter Cohen, Shearson's chair and CEO, comments, "There's no one grand stroke that does it. It's a lot of little steps." The firm, which has thus far acquired twenty-one other companies, focuses on matters from such evident concerns as picking the right partner and deciding which employees will be let go to such minute issues as ordering stationery and how phones should be answered. The steps range from the obvious to the unexpected—for instance, the manual stipulates that the corporation's international branches have to "review office leases"; the over-the-counter trading function is instructed to "publish new market-maker list"; and unit trust people are directed, among their many other responsibilities, to "look for toaster for Tuesday morning staff meeting" (Cowan, 1988, p. 8). Virtually no part of the acquisition is taken for granted, and the company continuously modifies its acquisition plans and guidebook. Not only does this serve to facilitate present combination efforts, but it becomes a useful framework for thinking through future merger and acquisition activities.

Conclusion

There is no single approach or technique that will guarantee the successful consolidation of two organizations. As the introduction to this chapter suggests, to some extent much of the disruption and dislocation created by organizational combinations requires a sufficient amount of time to stabilize and develop into new routines. At the same time, however, merging or acquiring organizations that approach an impending combination with a well-planned, well-prepared strategy are more likely to minimize much of the tension and trauma inherent in the process. Simply adopting a "hands-off" policy will not necessarily ensure that discontent, bitterness, and conflict between merger partners or an acquirer and its target will be avoided.

The difficulties involved in consolidating two firms into one are exemplified by the fact that even firms that have developed good reputations for undertaking mergers and acquisitions have problems. To some extent, there is a predicament of what might be termed "managerial diseconomies" associated with such consolidation efforts. To the extent that firms get larger, they become that much more difficult to oversee, integrate, and manage. Extensive management hierarchies often create communication problems between managers at corporate headquarters and those at divisional or subsidiary locations. These general difficulties are exacerbated by the ambiguities and uncertainties, stresses and strains, and culture conflicts and change-related obstacles associated with organizational combination efforts.

As indicated by the various interventions discussed in this chapter, there is a need to develop an eclectic perspective when thinking about postcombination integration. The focus and intent of these techniques and interventions, of course, are collaborative. Hostile raids and financial takeovers typically involve a quite different set of dynamics and desired goals. If such consolidations are to be truly effective, especially when strategic and operational integration is desired, the human processes underlying mergers and acquisitions must be supported by as many means as possible.

Nine

Understanding the Hidden Costs
of Combining Organizations

One of the main themes of this book is that mergers and acquisitions create significant upheaval in the lives of organizational members. The disruption caused by combination-related stress and anxiety, culture shocks and tensions, and job loss, relocation, or realignment, among other difficulties and concerns, obviously entails a number of human costs. What is often overlooked, however, is that mergers and acquisitions not only disrupt the lives of individuals but inevitably destabilize the organizations involved as well. The result is often general declines in post-combination employee performance (Buono, Bowditch, and Nurick, 1987; Sinetar, 1981) and what has been referred to as "postmerger slump," characterized by losses in productivity, revenues, opportunities, and human resources (Pritchett, 1985, p. 102). Yet most observers of the merger and acquisition process overlook the financial impact of such combination-related attitudes and behaviors.

Merger and acquisition plans are typically accompanied by optimistic feasibility studies and pro forma financial statements that project a rosy future for the new company, without any estimates of the cost effects of a disaffected work force, a dissatisfied customer base, or the need to replace departed employees. As noted in Chapter Five, however, mergers and

acquisitions can significantly and abruptly alter existing organizational arrangements, with consequent alteration of the unwritten expectations that develop over time betweeen organizations and their members, as well as written rules and procedures.
The psychological contract, in effect, must be renegotiated, and
during the process, especially where there are a large number
of ambiguities to be clarified, productivity may suffer and
customers may look elsewhere, resulting in significantly lower
financial performance for the organization (see Cascio, 1987;
Mirvis and Lawler, 1977). The stress, trauma, and anxiety
caused by mergers and acquisitions also lead to a number of
unproductive employee behaviors that reduce the overall effectiveness of the combined firm. Organizational members often
spend disproportionate amounts of time worrying and gossiping about the merger, battling co-workers over relatively petty
issues, thinking about their own futures and careers, and, in
general, procrastinating in their work efforts.

It is quite difficult to place an exact monetary value on
corporate losses in overall organizational effectiveness and productivity due to the merger-related stress and problems experienced by individual employees (Matteson and Ivancevich,
1982). Yet, as related research has documented, the financial
costs of such merger-related realities as tardiness, absenteeism,
turnover, reduced output, and other destructive behaviors can
be quite high (Cascio, 1987; Mobley, 1982). Moreover, there
are also a number of subtle or hidden costs with respect to the
declining morale, loyalty, commitment, and trust of those who
remain in the postcombination firm. These particular consequences often have immense costs for the firm in terms of future
productivity, the eventual turnover of key organizational members, and a loss of opportunities that were not seized because
of the general malaise created by the combination (Buono,
Bowditch, and Nurick, 1987; Ivancevich, Schweiger, and Power,
1987; Walsh, 1988). It often takes years, for example, for corporate statistics to accurately reflect how problems during the
combination aftermath period enabled competitors to gain an
edge in a particular market or markets. Yet top managers involved in a merger or acquisition rarely put a price tag on the

decrease in productivity and effectiveness that can continue for years following organizational consolidation efforts (Pritchett, 1985; Stybel, 1986).

Employee Attitudes, Work-Related Behaviors, and Postcombination Performance

Empirical studies have found that, other things being equal, there is a relationship between employee attitudes and a number of work-related behaviors, such as turnover, absenteeism and tardiness, strikes and grievances, and quality of job performance (Mobley, 1982; Mobley, Griffith, Hand, and Meglino, 1979; Porter and Steers, 1973; Smith, 1977). As research has also indicated, while nonproductive work-related behaviors have significant costs for organizations, savings can be realized by the introduction of changes focused on improving employee satisfaction, commitment, and motivation (Lawler, Seashore, and Mirvis, 1983; Likert and Bowers, 1973). However, determining ways to (1) actually measure the financial impact of such attitudes and behaviors and (2) link this impact with the overall performance of the firm has been a particularly vexing problem for organizational researchers. Indeed, despite some thirty-five years of research on the general subject of determining the cost of human resources, there is still no generally accepted procedure for employee valuation or for assessing its relationship to organizational performance (Cascio, 1987; Flamholtz, 1972; Mirvis and Lawler, 1983).

It is clear, however, that employee attitudes are related to such key organizational concerns as absenteeism, turnover, and productivity. The conflicting views concern *the extent to which* these attitudes affect the bottom line of an organization, not whether they affect performance outcomes. Since the problems associated with relating attitudes and behaviors to financial costs and organizational performance are largely methodological in nature, they are beyond the scope of this book (see Cascio, 1987, for a good summary). For our purposes, it seems sufficient to emphasize that as organizations attempt to transform their operations through mergers, acquisitions, or related restructuring efforts, the complex relationship between employee attitudes and the overall performance of the firm is a significant factor in the overall success of the venture.

The Urban-Suburban bank merger, for example, precipitated a severe decline in employee satisfaction and commitment to the combined institution. While one might dismiss these declining feelings as part of the human costs of creating a leaner, more competitive institution, there was also a sharp decline in favorable opinions about the quality of customer service during the year following the merger. As research has underscored, especially in service-oriented businesses such as banking, poor employee attitudes can negatively affect customer service and satisfaction (Mobley, 1982; Schneider, 1980). Thus, if bank employees report a deterioration in service quality, we can also expect that customers will sense a similar decline.

The White House Office of Consumer Affairs has recently released some startling statistics that emphasize the importance of the employee attitude–customer satisfaction link: 96 percent of dissatisfied customers do not complain about poor quality to the organization or its management. Instead, they simply choose to take their business elsewhere and spread their dissatisfaction among friends and acquaintances (Kelley, 1987). Similarly, according to a study by *American Banker,* other than changing residence, most surveyed customers reported that the major reason they changed financial institutions was what they considered to be poor service and errors in the way in which their accounts were handled ("Changing Banks," 1987, p. 31). A significant determinant of poor service is employee perception of poor management. Since organizational members generally treat customers the way they are treated by management, if employees feel that top management does not care about them, that they are unvalued and unimportant to the firm, they will tend to treat customers in the same way. Thus, if managers want to improve service quality, it is important for them to treat their employees as they want their employees to treat customers (Kelley, 1987). Considering the tensions and traumas experienced by organizational members during a merger or acquisition, unless specific actions are taken to help employees deal with the change, combining firms risk losing an important portion of their customer base.

Postcombination Productivity and Profitability

Evaluating merger and acquisition performance is quite a complex task, since a number of intervening and moderating variables can influence productivity and profitability outcomes (see Michel and Shaked, 1985). Organizational and financial performance during a merger or acquisition, however, is likely to suffer during the initial combination aftermath period, particularly in mergers involving significant operational integration. DeMeuse (1987, p. 1) has used the analogy of "corporate surgery" to describe the process during what might be termed the postcombination recuperative period: "Just as a patient needs to recover from major surgery, an organization needs time to regain its strength. It takes time for people to understand their new roles, their new positions, to understand the new linkages, and get productive again." During this time, much of the anticipated synergy expected to result from operational effectiveness and economies of scale is often undermined by cultural differences between the firms and the psychological reactions and repercussions experienced by individual organizational members. Figure 5, based on a compilation of merger and acquisition performance data, illustrates the typical pattern of organizational productivity and profitability during the years immediately following an organizational combination. As this graph suggests, however, while there is a general drop in organizational performance following a merger or acquisition, there is a significant difference between well-managed and unattended combinations (see Chapter Eight).

In the Urban-Suburban bank merger, the initial aftermath period was characterized by significant "we-they" feelings, related tensions, and feelings of personal loss. Each employee group viewed its counterpart from the *other* bank as an "invading enemy" rather than a co-equal partner. Members of both organizations distrusted their counterparts from the other bank, and a great deal of time and energy was spent dealing with the

Figure 5. Postcombination Recovery Period.

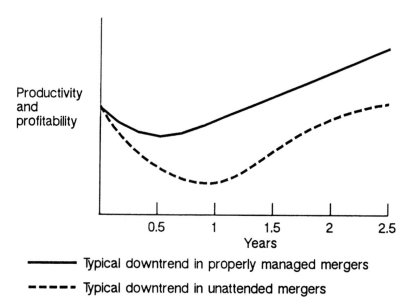

—————— Typical downtrend in properly managed mergers

- - - - - Typical downtrend in unattended mergers

Source: Reprinted from *After the Merger: Managing the Shockwaves* by P. Pritchett, p. 103. Copyright by Dow Jones–Irwin, 1985. Reprinted by permission of Dow Jones–Irwin.

ambiguities and strains brought on by the merger. The "no layoff" promise and the "Christmas massacre" described in earlier chapters greatly exacerbated the situation. As the 1982 postmerger survey indicates, there were marked declines in employee satisfaction with the subtle aspects of organizational life—a sense of pride and organizational commitment, feelings of job security, attitudes toward upper-level management, job satisfaction, and customer service. There was also a substantial drop in the overall performance of the institution during this period.

Using traditional financial performance criteria, Table 10 compares a variety of performance measures of the two premerger banks and Merged Bank with a performance index of all banks in the state from 1979 to 1985. Using net income as a percentage of total assets as a simple measure of profit, Figure 6 compares the profit performance of Merged Bank with

Table 10. Comparative Analysis of Financial Data: Merged Bank Versus All Banks.

	1979			1980			1981		1982		1983		1984		1985	
	Suburban Bank	Urban Bank	All Banks	Suburban Bank	Urban Bank	All Banks	Merged Bank	All Banks	Merged Bank	All Banks	Merged Bank	All Banks	Merged Bank	All Banks	Merged Bank	All Banks
Surplus as % of assets	5.99%	7.87%	7.98%	6.18%	7.67%	7.81%	6.75%	7.80%	6.13%	7.49%	5.61%	7.73%	16.07%	7.57%	15.52%	7.65%
Surplus as % of deposits	6.60%	8.72%	8.94%	6.77%	8.49%	8.99%	7.63%	8.86%	7.21%	8.45%	6.16%	8.63%	17.62%	8.53%	16.89%	8.63%
Stock yield	7.27%	9.12%	7.81%	8.24%	10.72%	8.66%	13.44%	8.99%	10.95%	9.83%	20.33%	7.78%	22.49%	8.22%	11.70%	5.89%
Bond yield	10.73%	13.18%	8.60%	8.67%	17.23%	9.69%	11.04%	11.10%	9.77%	10.74%	8.17%	10.92%	3.77%	11.09%	4.60%	8.39%
Loan yield	8.16%	7.94%	8.50%	9.09%	8.60%	9.11%	9.95%	9.78%	10.20%	10.42%	9.63%	10.80%	8.73%	11.30%	4.12%	8.56%
Net income	2,432	-2,322	95,587	901	548	40,041	-5,550	654	-5,939	-13,563	-1,596	98,885	4,462	115,588	3,221	230,324
As % of total assets	0.45%	0.36%	0.47%	0.17%	0.06%	0.20%	-0.48%	0.00%	-0.52%	-0.06%	-0.13%	0.41%	0.35%	0.44%	0.35%	0.81%
As % of operating earnings	5.27%	-4.41%	5.74%	75.08%	63.41%	0.22%	-219.89%	0.03%	-257.43%	-0.59%	-1.40%	4.03%	0.46%	4.01%	3.46%	9.88%
Growth rate Deposits	-2.11%	-4.09%	2.93%	-0.49%	0.71%	2.25%	-4.14%	3.60%	0.07%	7.79%	11.65%	11.01%	2.42%	8.86%	0.95%	7.79%
Surplus	8.15%	-5.95%	6.36%	2.02%	-1.92%	2.95%	-5.19%	2.03%	-4.27%	9.14%	-0.87%	8.37%	193.21%	8.37%	-3.20%	9.15%
Real estate foreclosures and possessions as % of total assets	0.00%	0.19%	0.39%	0.29%	0.27%	0.35%	0.32%	0.33%	0.07%	1.14%	0.03%	0.79%	0.00%	0.79%	0.00%	na
Spread—gross interest margin less interest cost	2.20%	7.20%	5.94%	1.46%	1.78%	7.01%	8.55%	7.98%	0.53%	1.89%	1.54%	2.68%	0.85%	3.18%	2.68%	2.87%

Figure 6. Net Income as a Percentage of Total Assets.

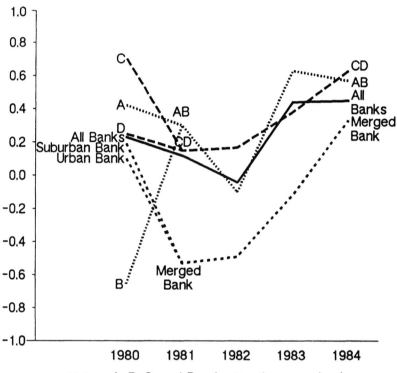

Note: A, B, C, and D refer to other area banks;
        AB and CD refer to the merged banks

that of two comparable savings banks in the state that merged during the same period and with the all-bank index from 1980 to 1984. There are, of course, numerous problems involved in both reporting and interpreting such data. Indeed, despite myriad efforts devoted to empirical evaluations of postcombination performance, there is considerable disagreement concerning appropriate methodologies, performance data, and outcomes for analysis (see Ford and Schellenberg, 1982; Lubatkin, 1983; Michel and Shaked, 1985; Mullins, 1981; Young, 1981). The general consensus, however, seems to be that while the techniques used to assess merger and acquisition performance are imperfect and fraught with inherent difficulties, they are useful nonetheless, since they provide insights into the relationship between the combination process and firm performance. For banks, net income (net interest income after provisions for losses minus erosion and income taxes) and spread (gross interest margin minus interest cost) are typical measures of performance. Thus, such financial data, especially if compared with similar data from comparable organizations in the same geographical area, can provide a general overview of how the institution fared during the merger.

As Figure 6 indicates, the merging banks experienced declines in performance during the initial combination aftermath period. While net income trends for these banks generally followed the all-bank net income index, it seems that industry-wide trends were exacerbated during the aftermath phase. Moreover, the net income of only one of the banks improved during the immediate postmerger period (1981–82). While most related-business mergers show performance declines for a six- to eight-month period following the physical-legal combination (Pritchett, 1985), however, it took Merged Bank almost four years to become profitable.

While employee attitudes and their impact on productivity and customer service are important, performance is also affected by key business decisions made by merging or acquiring companies. For example, Lanvin–Charles of the Ritz, a maker of cosmetics and fragrances, was in good business and financial shape until it merged with Squibb Corporation, a drug manufacturer and food processor (Louis, 1982, pp. 88–89). After completing the combination, Squibb brought in a textile executive as head of the Lanvin subsidiary. After dismissing Lanvin executives, the new top manager brought in a team of outsiders inexperienced in the cosmetics business. One of the management team's initial decisions—offering the Jean Naté line of toiletries to retailers at discount with the intent of sharply boosting sales volume—nearly destroyed the successful product. Lanvin's new management group apparently did not realize that in cosmetics a discount is perceived as a sign that the product has failed. Many buyers turned away from Jean Naté, and it took years to recapture premerger sales volume.

While such questionable judgment may be more typical

of unrelated-business mergers and acquisitions, management decisions in horizontal combinations can also create postconsolidation performance problems. In assessing the Urban-Suburban bank merger, it is important to isolate the effects of interest rate changes on the bank's performance. Accordingly, the spread (see Table 10) becomes a useful measure of how a bank manages its funds in financially volatile times. During periods of rising interest rates, the spread will tend to decrease, because the average cost of liabilities increases faster than the average return on assets. By comparing the performance of an individual bank with the performance of other banks in the region, however, we can begin to isolate the effects of interest rate change and management decisions on the financial performance of the institution. Although Merged Bank's spread improved relative to the performance of the premerger firms and the all-bank index during the physical-legal combination stage, from 1982 to 1984 performance was roughly at one-fourth to one-half the all-bank index. In contrast, by 1985, when Merged Bank was beginning to experience psychological combination, the institution's performance rate was better than 90 percent of the all-bank index. While there was a favorable interest rate change during this period, Merged Bank's spread improved significantly, as compared to a slight decline in the all-bank index.

As suggested earlier, although it is difficult to decide which profitability index provides the fairest representation of what is going on in a service organization such as a bank (as opposed to a manufacturing or sales organization), the variety of performance measures presented in Table 10 shows that Merged Bank took years to become profitable. Moreover, even after it became profitable, it lagged behind the all-bank index on most measures. Part of the initial performance decline, however, was a result of management's decision to take advantage of the common wisdom that a merger or acquisition will result in such decline. Merged Bank's leaders, for example, chose to use the merger to write off a number of problem loans, thus artificially depressing the institution's profit during the year after the combination. This decision is comparable to the recent practice of many U.S. banks of gradually writing off uncollectible Third

World loans during profitable quarters to minimize the impact of questionable management judgments over a number of years (Cohen, 1986). In subsequent years, it should have become easier for Merged Bank to make a profit, especially since a greater percentage of "good" loans was carried on the books. Yet Table 10 and Figure 6 indicate that Merged Bank went through a longer period of unprofitability than did other merging banks in the area and that it lost more money than did banks in general.

In sharp contrast to the bank situation, where operational integration of the two merger partners took place, is the experience of Co-op Foods. Even though there were three changes in ownership in an eighteen-month period, the fact that the supermarket chain remained basically autonomous under the two parent companies and management buyout might account for the relatively strong and consistent financial performance (see Table 11). Additionally, while employee satisfaction was relatively stable during both the Aero and TransCo ownership periods, it improved slightly across most dimensions during the management buyout era.

It is difficult, of course, to assess the extent to which the financial performance of Merged Bank and Co-op Foods may be attributed to general industry conditions, management decisions, or the impact of the combination per se. Moreover, the two cases involve highly disparate industries, making comparative assessments problematic at best. As suggested earlier in this chapter, most evaluations of postmerger and acquisition performance underscore the analytical difficulties involved. There are, however, a number of similarities between the *general patterns* of data for postcombination employee attitudes and the financial performance of the firms. Thus, while we are not suggesting a causal relationship, there does appear to be a link between organizational climate as measured by the combination surveys and employee attitudes and behaviors that could influence the productivity and ultimate profitability of the merged and acquired firms.

In the Urban-Suburban bank merger, hidden costs related to the combination ranged from subtle slowdowns in customer

Table 11. Co-op Foods Ratio Analysis.

	1986	1985
Index or ratio		
Current ratio[a]	1.20	1.32
Quick ratio[b]	.36	.34
Working capital	$17,114,000	$22,570,000
Activity		
Average collection	5.48	13.964
Accounts receivable turnover	65.66	25.78
Inventory turnover	10.41	4.22
Inventory turnover in days	4.14	1.76
Profitability		
Return on assets	.028	.008
Return on equity	.223	.112
Profit margins	.0068	.0046
Earnings per share	.88	.23
Leverage		
Debt to assets	.87	.93

$$^{a}\text{Current ratio} = \frac{\text{Current assets}}{\text{Current liabilities}}$$

$$^{b}\text{Quick ratio} = \frac{\text{Current assets} - \text{inventories}}{\text{Current liabilities}}$$

Note: Current ratio and quick ratio reflect a firm's liquidity, that is, its ability to meet its short-term obligations. Many financial experts argue that the ultimate test of business success lies in a firm's ability to meet its obligations when they fall due.

service and a high level of intergroup conflict to the formation of the counterculture and whistleblowing incident discussed in Chapter Seven. The Co-op Foods situation, in contrast, did not involve similar types of problems or employee backlash. Although it is difficult to generalize from two examples, these cases underscore the paradox of strategic significance discussed in Chapter One. A tenable conclusion, therefore, is that when operational integration is required, it should be done deliberately but slowly. One of the major problems the bank encountered was that as the situation was changing, it was unclear what the final outcome would be for employees, particularly for managers. The personal and cultural ambiguities remained for a long time after the merger was completed and clearly affected the performance of bank employees. Co-op Foods, on the other hand, suffered relatively few ambiguities as a result of the successive buyouts. Even the department most affected by the unrelated-business acquisitions, the accounting department, remained on an even keel during this period, even though it was required to make numerous financial reporting changes because of the changes in ownership.

Assessing the Costs of Mergers and Acquisitions

As earlier chapters have noted, mergers and acquisitions often involve a number of human costs, ranging from a disruption of social ties and working relationships to lowered perceptions of job satisfaction, security, and organization commitment to job displacement, anxiety, stress, and psychosomatic disorders. There are also a number of related costs for the combined organization that are typically overlooked in such assessments. The myriad, often hidden costs associated with merger and acquisition activity include such factors as (1) absenteeism, turnover, and related hiring and training expenses; (2) time and associated expenses involved in combination-related activities and meetings; (3) time lost in interfirm employee arguments, trying to decide "which boss really counts," and related infighting and office politicking; (4) conscious and unconscious efforts to restrict personal performance because of fears of layoffs, changes in perceptions of promotion opportunities, lowered feelings of commitment, a sense of cultural betrayal, and a decline of trust in the organization's leadership; and (5) customer frustration with new policies and procedures.

Obviously, postcombination productivity and profitability are influenced by a variety of other factors, including the strategic purpose of the merger or acquisition, the level of integration desired and the degree of friendliness or hostility involved, the combination process itself, industry conditions, and management strategic and operational decisions. As suggested by Figure 7, however, employee attitudes and behaviors and cultural conflicts

Figure 7. Moderating and Intervening Factors That Influence Postcombination Productivity and Profitability.

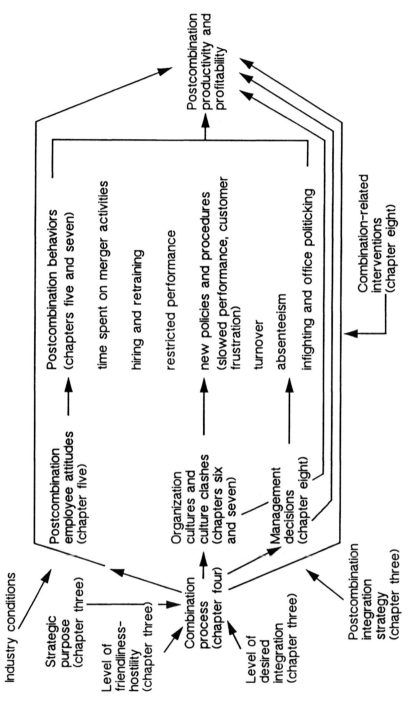

between the companies constitute important determinants of company performance as well. As discussed in Chapter Eight, the negative repercussions of these human concerns can be reduced through carefully planned interventions. Yet, although the costs of organizationally dysfunctional employee perceptions and actions are quite real for combining firms, they are usually buried within strategic, financial, and operational assessments and thus are frequently overlooked or ignored during precombination feasibility studies and planning of the combination process.

As an example of some of the consequences of dysfunctional combination-related behaviors, this section concludes with a brief discussion of the hidden costs of employee turnover. As earlier chapters mentioned, there is often a high degree of voluntary and involuntary managerial and employee turnover following a merger or acquisition. In horizontal combinations, of course, a reduction in force is often the planned result of eliminating identical job assignments and overlapping responsibility. As part of the process of culture change, however, top managers will sometimes dismiss proficient employees whose jobs are still necessary, and then rehire others who "fit" the desired culture of the combined institution. Frequently, managers want their own people in positions of responsibility and perceive employees who have gone through the transition as having questionable loyalty to the "new team." Just as often, significant departures result from employee "bailouts" because of unfavorable expectations of what is likely to occur. SteelCo's experience with the exodus of Petro engineers and scientists is an example of this situation. Whatever the reasons, organizational combinations often result in fewer people remaining with the organization than are needed to sustain it, forcing management to hire new employees.

As an illustration of the costs involved, consider a typical situation following a merger between two organizations that each has 300 employees. Let us assume that the merged entity loses 200 employees at various levels but subsequently hires 200 new members and over time ends up with roughly the same number of employees the firms started with—600 people. As a result, the combined firm is faced with separation costs for the old employees and replacement and training costs for the new employees. Given a conservative estimate of cost factors involved (Cascio, 1987), *separation costs* include such considerations as (1) administrative costs associated with termination, including exit interviews and related organizational functions, such as pension assessments, discontinuation of life, disability, and medical insurance, and so forth; (2) separation and severance pay; and (3) unemployment tax.

Although the expenses associated with terminating employment can be substantial, probably the most expensive aspect of human resources turnover is *replacement costs,* including (1) communicating and advertising job availability; (2) fulfilling pre-employment administrative functions, such as screening prospective candidates, entrance interviews, and testing costs; (3) travel and moving expenses; and (4) dissemination of information on such varied concerns as medical benefits, pension planning, life insurance, educational benefits, and company policies in general. Finally, since replacement employees are not likely to be fully trained, indoctrinated, or socialized as to the nature of the job or the new organization, there will ordinarily be *training costs* for each replacement worker. These include informational literature about the organization, instruction in formal training programs, specific on-the-job training efforts, and costs related to lost productivity during the learning process.

As the above discussion suggests, a high level of turnover can be quite expensive for combining organizations. At the same time, it is important to note that organizations without any turnover are likely to be rather unproductive for some time. Firms often need "new blood" and new ideas in order to continually improve organizational effectiveness and efficiency. The broad shifts in human resources that ordinarily accompany mergers and acquisitions, however, are usually *very* costly and, just as usually, overlooked in calculating combination-related costs and benefits.

Conclusion

It is clear that any consolidation involving the integration of two separate organizations or parts of organizations into one functioning unit entails a number of costs that can manifest themselves in decreased productivity and profitability during the postcombination aftermath period. At the same time, however, it does not make sense to conclude that a merger or acquisition should not occur because of potential declines in postcombination performance. The stand-alone organizations might not be able to survive the competition, and over the long term, some form of interfirm consolidation may very well be a sound strategy. As emphasized in this chapter, however, it is important to be aware of the myriad costs involved in the merger and acquisition process. Although the costs of mergers and acquisitions cannot be eliminated entirely, there are ways to reduce the dysfunctional impact of employee dissatisfaction and the resulting effect on performance that can contribute to declines in the combined firm's productivity and profitability.

Ten

Facing the
Human Resource Consequences
of Mergers and Acquisitions

Given the processes and dynamics underlying the different mergers and acquisitions discussed in this book, even friendly, collaborative combinations can precipitate significant individual and collective conflicts and adjustments in a relatively short period of time. Even the mere potential of merger-related changes in procedures, locations, and policies, threats of job redundancies and layoffs, conflicts and shocks arising from culture clashes, and the stresses and strains experienced by individuals generate a high degree of tension at all organizational levels. In fact, as many observers of the merger and acquisition process argue, it may very well be that regardless of how thoughtfully and sensitively human resource issues are handled, some degree of turmoil and dislocation is inevitable.

This book has urged the point that the human resource dimension of mergers and acquisitions should be accorded the same emphasis and attention given financial, legal, operational, and strategic concerns. Just as experts in accounting and finance are needed to deal with financial planning and tax considerations, and legal matters require attention by corporate lawyers, human resource and organization development professionals are needed to actively work with managers and employees in dealing with the changes and uncertainties that will inevitably emerge from the combination. A status quo approach to human resource decisions and issues neglects many of the developmental needs and requirements of the combined firm (Pappanastos, Hillman, and Cole, 1987). The talents and expertise necessary for the success of the venture must be identified through careful analysis and assessment and then nurtured and supported by top management. As SteelCo's problems with the Petro acquisition illustrate, a status quo approach to valued organizational members may very well result in the loss of such employees.

It is important to approach the myriad human resource issues and concerns that are raised by organizational combinations with an open mind and an appreciation for the complexity of the issues involved. Unfortunately, there is no simple set of answers or panaceas that will automatically create effective, efficient, and smoothly integrated mergers and acquisitions. Instead, combination planning should be viewed as an iterative process. As suggested in Chapter Eight, perhaps the best way to proceed is to approach such transformations with an eclectic perspective, realizing that there is no single model for change nor one intervention that will encompass all concerns and issues.

Although many of the human problems associated with mergers and acquisitions—fears and uncertainties, stresses and tensions—cannot be eliminated or totally prevented from disrupting individual lives and organizational performance, managers can exert influence on both the integration process and consolidation outcomes. It is important to remember, however, that a number of dilemmas and paradoxes concerning the rate of change, information sharing, the manageability of organizational culture, strategic significance, postcombination strategies, and the illusion of managerial control pervade the combination process. As a way of summarizing these problems, much of the tension underlying the human side of mergers and acquisitions may be attributed to five key concerns and dilemmas—each with a strong ethical component:

1. *Competing claims,* arising from the reality that mergers and acquisitions involve multiple parties, each with its own interests and needs.

2. *Secrecy versus deception* in combination-related communication—that is, the managed release of information in an open, honest, and timely manner as opposed to the controlled release of information to distort the truth and manipulate people.
3. The distinction between *coercion and participation*—forcing people into certain situations as opposed to providing them with a true opportunity to take part in discussions and decisions.
4. How the processes of *grief, loss, and termination* are handled.
5. The *level of respect* accorded to organizational members and other key constituents as individuals.

Competing Claims

Although it has long been recognized that mergers and acquisitions involve multiple parties with their own competing and at times conflicting interests, historically this conflict has been framed in terms of the investment of the acquiring and acquired firms' stockholders (Gillis and Casey, 1985). The traditional business gospel is that a company is essentially a piece of private property owned by those who hold its stock. Accordingly, firms have sacrosanct and inviolable obligations to these people. Employees are viewed as servants of the firm, functioning as technical instruments in production, marketing, finance, and so forth (Buono and Nichols, 1985; Freeman and Reed, 1983). Under this model, the idea of "legitimate" competing claims is viewed largely in terms of the interests of the two stockholder groups. Consequently, corporate officials are "duty bound" to define and pursue the best interests of these groups (Richman, 1984). Even our contemporary understanding of stockholders as investors rather than owners retains these distinctions.

A more recent perspective argues that many groups in society—employees, customers, suppliers, local communities, interest groups, and regulators, among others—are materially involved with the corporation through different types of transactions. Referred to as the *stakeholder model,* this perspective views corporations as having responsibilities to these claimant groups that often go beyond the immediate interests of stockholders. Employees are regarded as people with a wide range of legitimate needs in which the corporation must take an interest. Stockholders continue to occupy a place of prominence, but their interests and desires are no longer absolutely decisive in determining corporate conduct (Buono and Nichols, 1985; Freeman, 1984; Mitroff, 1983). With respect to merger and acquisition decisions, the stakeholder model suggests that a utilitarian orientation (that is, the greatest good for the greatest number of stakeholders) should help to resolve the difficulties posed by such competing claims (Richman, 1984).

In many instances, however, the "greatest good" in a merger or acquisition is difficult to determine (Hosmer, 1987). Stockholders as a group have one set of concerns. Senior executives of both firms and key outside advisers, such as investment bankers and consultants, typically have others. Moreover, managers and employees, especially in the target company, focus on quite different issues, as do indirect constituents, such as suppliers and local communities (Haspeslagh and Jemison, 1987). Simply put, what might be beneficial for a firm's stockholders might not be in the best interests of its senior management team. And what might be in the best interest of the organization and its senior-level managers might not be in the best interest of employees or local communities, and so forth.

Culture Conflict as a Competing Claim. While the tensions between these different interests and concerns obviously exacerbate combination-related difficulties, the subtle nature of many competing claims further clouds the consolidation process. The Urban-Suburban bank merger and the CompServe-NetCo joint venture were complicated by extreme cultural differences between the organizations. The different realities of organizational life in the firms had existed for a long time, they shaped and were shaped by quite divergent values and beliefs, and they were accepted as "the way things should be." The bank consolidation was supposed to be a "merger of equals." Similarly, the computer services joint venture was planned as an "equal partnership," with a collaborative merger in mind. Yet each employee group felt that its culture and orientation were superior to those of the other. In their minds, each group felt that it had a legitimate claim that the culture of the combined firm should be closer to its own culture than to the culture of its merger or joint venture partner. Despite these competing "perceived rights," upper-level management overlooked these differences in both combination planning and integration. The cultural differences were sufficiently strong, however, that they undermined attempts to resolve potential operating difficulties and facilitate interaction between employees and contributed to drastic declines in employee satisfaction and commitment in the bank merger and serious reservations about the joint venture.

In these instances, the issue is not whether the different employee groups were "right" or "wrong" in their attempt to support their culture at the expense of the other. Rather, the key point is the way in which management attempted the cultural integration in dealing with the "collision" of different philosophies, values, and styles. Indeed, rather than recognizing the legitimacy of different cultural orientations and values, the CEOs showed little concern for the views of their employees. As the CEO of Suburban Bank, who became chief operating officer of Merged Bank, repeated on a number of occasions, "I don't give a damn what they think. If they don't like it, [expletive deleted] them." CompServe's CEO held similar attitudes, arguing, "if any employees can't cope with the change, it's their problem." While the reality of such organizational combinations underscores the legitimacy and importance of employee perceptions and perspectives, key CEOs of the merger and joint venture partners dismissed these beliefs and attitudes as insignificant compared to the "greater good" they felt would result from the combinations.

In the TransCo-Aero–Co-op Foods acquisition, in contrast, instead of attempting to blend the different cultures, the conglomerate followed a "cultural pluralism" orientation (see Chapter Six). Both TransCo and Aero allowed for maximum flexibility in letting Co-op Foods operate autonomously, permitting cultural diversity to exist within a shared strategy for growth. Thus, the "claim" to the supermarket chain's cultural heritage was not challenged by the acquisition. Indeed, the fact that TransCo did not attempt to change Co-op's culture was continually mentioned by the supermarket's employees as a significant determinant of their relatively stable levels of satisfaction and commitment following the acquisition. This approach, however, seems to be more typical of unrelated-business combinations where operational integration is not required.

With a fully integrated horizontal merger such as the bank consolidation, of course, there is a much higher probability of culturally oriented competing claims than would tend to be found in an unrelated conglomerate acquisition. As exemplified by the paradox of strategic significance (Chapter One), in related combinations, upper-level managers in acquiring organizations tend to think that they have a much greater understanding of the workings of the acquired firm than they actually do. To complicate matters, they are usually oblivious to the reality that they are often viewed as uninformed and ignorant by members of their acquisition target (Blake and Mouton, 1985). As a result, the opportunity for true collaboration between the firms is greatly reduced. For instance, even though Co-op Foods enjoyed a supportive relationship with TransCo, being permitted to maintain its cultural heritage and identity after the acquisition, the lesson seemed lost on its management. Following the leveraged management buyout of the company, Co-op Foods found itself in the reverse role of *acquirer* as the company bought five supermarket stores from Spot Company. Yet, instead of allowing the new stores to be gradually assimilated into Co-op's structure and culture, the firm followed a "rape and pillage" strategy in its dealing with the Spot stores and their management teams. Especially in related acquisitions, the parent firm is likely to intervene and assume control over the target to ensure that the intended outcomes of the combination are achieved. Ironically, the nature of such control undermines the iterative, evolutionary nature of the integration process (Jemison, 1986b) and exacerbates competing claims between employee groups.

As emphasized in Chapters Six and Seven, culture change is one of the most difficult transitions for people to accept.

Indeed, one of the underlying dilemmas that managers face in a merger or acquisition concerns management of different organizational cultures and the tensions between them. Given the assumption that all mergers and acquisitions—even those based on a cultural pluralism strategy—will involve some degree of culture change, however, cultural diagnosis on two levels is necessary (American Bankers Association and Ernst & Whinney, 1985; Siehl, Ledford, Silverman, and Fay, 1987). First, it is important for the parent company to have a good understanding of its own culture. The next step is an audit and diagnosis of the target firm's culture. The process should begin during the early stages of merger or acquisition negotiation and continue in more depth as the negotiations continue. If the acquiring firm has audited and diagnosed its own culture prior to merger or acquisition efforts, it will have a better understanding of those aspects of organizational life and processes that are important to it, what characteristics it wants more of, and how possible acquisition targets or merger partners might either conflict with or reinforce desired cultural characteristics. By supporting this assessment with explicit diagnosis of the merger or acquisition target, management can prevent or at least prepare for severe cultural mismatches. Unfortunately, since the period following a merger or acquisition is often chaotic and frenzied, the tendency is to avoid such cultural self-examinations.

Conflicts of Interest. Potential conflicts of interest can also emerge from competing claims in merger and acquisition situations. In the Urban-Suburban bank merger, for example, questions were raised concerning the extent to which the self-perceived career needs of the CEOs disproportionately influenced the merger decision. Urban Bank's CEO, nearing retirement, wanted to exert more influence on industrywide issues and felt that being part of a larger institution would afford him the opportunity to be more visible at the national level. Suburban Bank's CEO, by contrast, wanted to be in control of a larger, more influential bank. The merger, which created a dual top management structure, provided both officers with their desired opportunities.

Following the consolidation, Urban Bank's CEO assumed the role of CEO of Merged Bank but was rarely around the institution, instead devoting his time and energies to national industry association activities. Suburban Bank's CEO became chief operating officer and assumed control of all internal decisions. While these were the preferred sets of activities for both officers, extending back to their presidencies of the premerger banks, employees felt that each CEO was more interested in fulfilling his own agenda than in doing what was good for the bank as a whole. Many employees, for example, reported that their former president had "sold them out," which further contributed to the decrease in commitment and satisfaction after the merger.

In sharp contrast, during the buyout at Co-op Foods, the top management team emphasized—both publicly and privately—the important role played by the supermarket's employees. Ironically, questions concerning potential conflicts of interest are often raised about leveraged management buyouts (Paine, 1987; Wright and Coyne, 1985). Yet, while Co-op's management had an obvious interest in obtaining control over the company through the buyout from TransCo, employees did not perceive a "hidden agenda" on top management's part as they did in the bank merger. Co-op's executives attempted to make themselves available to their employees, supporting their efforts and responding to their questions. The overall effectiveness of their efforts is reflected in the relatively stable attitudes of employees across the changes and the high productivity and profitability of the venture. Despite a period of relatively high inflation, interest rates, and unemployment, the company was able to consistently increase sales and earnings. The bank, by contrast, took longer than other banks merging during the same period to become profitable. As discussed in Chapter Nine, while such financial comparisons cannot be attributed solely to differences in employee attitudes and behaviors, such attitudes and behaviors can have a significant effect on performance outcomes, especially in service-oriented organizations. Moreover, when these two combinations are compared, it seems clear that organizational members at Merged Bank felt much more strongly about hidden agendas on the part of the CEOs (conflict of interest between personal career needs and those of the banks) than was the case in the management buyout of Co-op Foods.

Secrecy Versus Deception

When managers are faced with a merger or acquisition, basic questions emerge in their minds concerning the nature and timing of communication to employees. As discussed in Chapter Eight, while the tendency is to carry out all negotiations and discussions in secret to minimize uncertainty among organizational members, it seems that the creation of formal internal communication mechanisms as early as possible may greatly limit the anxiety otherwise fueled by rumors, the grapevine, or even outside news reports. Managers, however, face a number of legal and operational dilemmas that affect decisions about information sharing.

First, Securities and Exchange Commission guidelines limit what can be told—even to employees—about merger or acquisition plans. Second, since the actual details of a merger have to be worked out over a period of several months or even years after the combination, management rarely has accurate answers to many employee questions. Finally, even despite efforts to openly and honestly inform organizational members about what is likely to happen, the high level of stress and anxiety involved means that employees often maintain feelings of suspicion and never feel fully informed.

Unfortunately, managers often attempt to use such constraints and realities to deceive and manipulate employees. The standard approach to merger communication is to inform employees that little will actually change in the day-to-day operation of the company, even when it is known that major changes will probably occur. But telling employees that little or nothing will change and then implementating a series of combination-related changes only undermines the credibility of upper management. This is illustrated by the ''no layoff'' promise and subsequent ''Christmas massacre'' in the Urban-Suburban bank merger. Yet, even in the wake of the turmoil, dissatisfaction, and widespread distrust of the new leadership and bank created by the "massacre," Merged Bank's COO argued that he would use the same tactic again, in order to "gain time and momentum" for the merger. This reasoning seems to be more the rule than the exception, as exemplified by the recent firing of the top management team of another bank *one day* after an acquisition, even though some of them had been given personal assurances that their jobs were secure (D. M. Bailey, 1987). As a result of such actions, savvy employees rarely believe anything they are told by their managers about combination-related changes.

In the TransCo-Aero–Co-op Foods acquisition and subsequent management buyout, by contrast, a concerted effort was made to ensure that all communications were as accurate and honest as possible. With the support of TransCo, a series of well-timed memos and bulletins were sent out to keep people "officially" apprised. Additionally, managers actively used the office grapevine to "keep people informed every step of the way." While management did not have "all the answers" and employees still wondered exactly how and when things were going to change and how they would be affected, most people reported that the acquisition and the management buyout were "handled with care" and that they appreciated the "accurate grapevine."

Open communication channels are an important factor in minimizing people's fears and creating a positive image of the acquiring or merging firm. Since mergers and acquisitions typically produce a high degree of stress and confusion for organizational members, people have a basic need for a great deal of information about the combination. Even when not intentionally attempting to deceive employees, top managers, in an effort to avoid alerting competitors or worrying employees, often put up a "shield of confidentiality" to protect their interests (Gerard, 1986). Despite efforts to maintain confidentiality, however, word leaks out anyway, and rumor mills and the grapevine work overtime, leading to more anxiety and, in many instances, counterproductive behaviors. Often based on fears rather than reality, these rumors can significantly exacerbate employee anxiety, tensions, and stress.

The importance of developing and maintaining a high level of communication with respect to the transformation and its underlying processes cannot be overly stressed. Information needs during a merger or acquisition are qualitatively and quantitatively different from those during normal, everyday interactions. In the Urban-Suburban bank merger, although both CEOs reported that "we overmet" before and during the physical merger period, it was clear that they felt that there were many misunderstandings and instances of poor communication after the merger had taken place. Similarly, organizational members reported that communication concerning the merger was too infrequent and that it raised more issues than it resolved. Such information should be as accurate and honest as possible; while it may continue to increase uncertainties and tensions to some degree, in those areas where decisions have not yet been made, acquiring companies are best advised to tell organizational members just that—the combination does indeed raise questions about restructuring, personnel, compensation, and other work-related issues, and these concerns will be addressed over the next year or two as the merger or acquisition unfolds (Stybel, 1986).

Coercion Versus Participation

While most premerger statements and discussions about postmerger integration emphasize the importance of participation in bringing about organizational change, studies have indicated that the process is usually tightly controlled by top management (Barmash, 1971; Buono, Bowditch, and Lewis, 1988; Gillis and Casey, 1985; Sales and Mirvis, 1984). It is argued, for example, that merger-related restructuring is typically *done to* rather than *done by* employees (Kanter and Seggerman, 1986). Because of the chaotic events and bursts of activity that generally accompany mergers and acquisitions, the potential for enlightened management of people and the change process is often lost in the shuffle.

In the mergers and acquisitions discussed in this book, there was a sharp contrast between participative and coercive orientations during the combinations. As related earlier, shortly after the Urban-Suburban bank merger, Merged Bank's COO was infuriated when he returned from a trip to find a number of former Urban Bank officers leaving ''on time.'' Given the changing competitive circumstances in the thrift industry, he decided that if Merged Bank was to survive, it would be necessary to impose Suburban Bank's task-oriented culture on the new institution. His subsequent efforts to ''weed out'' key Urban Bank officers and managers and to make the organization ''more competitive'' and ''more in tune with the times'' were interpreted by many organizational members as threats and evidence that he wanted to ''use up'' people. Urban Bank members emphasized that they were being forced to either accept ''his rules'' or leave the institution. While employees of both merger partners expressed dissatisfaction following the merger, the significance of the COO's efforts is shown by the fact that, in virtually all instances, Urban Bank employees' responses in the postmerger climate surveys were significantly less favorable than those of Suburban Bank members. The ramifications of such dissatisfaction are reflected in the countercultural activities and whistleblowing incident discussed in Chapter Seven. The underlying reason for the whistleblowing appears to have been a desire for cultural revenge for the coercive way in which the postmerger integration process was managed.

A low level of employee participation was also found in the CompServe-NetCo joint venture, SteelCo's acquisition of Petro, and the Retail Corporation–Food Company–Handy Stores consolidation. Throughout the changes in ownership of Co-op Foods, in contrast, a specific attempt was made to involve employees in the transformation process. During both the TransCo acquisition and the leveraged buyout, for example, Co-op maintained an advisory council of employees that had been in place since 1976. While employees argued that the success of the council was ''dependent on the people on it,'' they acknowledged it as an important vehicle for communication and input during the changes. Virtually all the supermarket's officers emphasized its importance during the transition both as a sounding board and as a way of providing mutual assistance and guidance between employees and management.

TransCo (in its acquisition of Aero/Co-op) and Co-op (in its leveraged management buyout) chose a highly participative change strategy compared to the more coercive tactics employed in the bank merger. Co-op Foods, of course, did not have to be operationally integrated into a similar firm. When the company undertook its horizontal acquisition of the Spot stores, in contrast, the supermarket chain pursued a "rape and pillage" approach. Although TransCo had allowed it to maintain many of its own systems and policies after the acquisition, the entire Spot tradition and system were abruptly ended after Co-op took over the firm.

The attitudinal, operational, and financial outcomes in these mergers and acquisitions, as well as other research (Akin and Hopelain, 1986; Nurick, 1982, 1985; Sashkin, 1984), demonstrate that participative methods are related to more favorable organizational climates and productivity than result from coercive approaches. The eventual use of an employee involvement strategy in the Urban-Suburban Bank merger, for example, was a significant force in the gradual move toward a psychological combination of the merger partners. Yet, ironically, the paradox of strategic significance suggests that the mergers and acquisitions most likely to benefit from such information sharing and employee involvement tend to be characterized by coercion by the dominant firm.

Management of Grief, Loss, and Termination

As described in Chapter Five, during a merger or acquisition, employees generally experience conflicting emotions ranging from shock, disbelief, anger, and helplessness to hope, excitement, and high expectations about the future. Depending on how the acquisition unfolds and the experiences of employees, of course, individual reactions can vary widely. Following an organizational consolidation, however, there is often a mourning or grief period during what is referred to as an "ending phase" (Bridges, 1986). Common metaphors used by acquisition members to describe their feelings include death and dying, bereavement, loss of a limb, painful and unwanted divorce, destruction of a home, and even the end of the world. This process is exemplified by the Urban-Suburban bank merger, where employees often become quite nostalgic about their prior organizational affiliations during the initial aftermath period.

The idealization of a lost entity is a typical grief reaction and part of a person's attempt to "work through" the loss. This process is especially seen in contested mergers and acquisitions where employees' behavior can resemble reactions to death and dying—denial, anger, bargaining, and eventual acceptance (Harshbarger, 1987; Marks and Mirvis, 1986). As part of the move toward such gradual acceptance, however, people may display a general depressive tone or somatic symptoms, experience a sense of helplessness, and express both direct and displaced anger (Fried, 1963). Such feelings and residual anger can persist on the part of employees for years following a merger or acquisition. Unless they are acknowledged and dealt with, the outcomes are typically manifested in such dysfunctional behaviors as voluntary turnover, decreased productivity, lowered commitment, increased office politicking, and, as exemplified by the countercultural efforts in the Urban-Suburban bank merger, efforts to undermine the combination.

As emphasized in Chapter Eight, the way in which employee terminations and staff reductions are handled also sends clear signals about management's values to the employees. As discussed earlier, it does not appear to be staff reductions and layoffs per se that create dissatisfaction and bitterness, but rather the way in which these terminations are handled. Where possible, job redundancies should be managed through attrition, early retirement, and attractive severance packages. When involuntary termination is necessary, decisions should be as objective as possible and supported by outplacement assistance, counseling, and related job search and support services. While the obvious intent is to minimize the trauma for the individuals being terminated, the way in which the process is handled has a significant influence on those organizational members remaining with the firm. It may very well sway their own decisions about whether to become productive, contributing members of the combined firm or to look for other positions.

Respect for Employees as Individuals

Historically, the relationship between employer and employee has been governed by the employment-at-will doctrine: the employment contract is terminable at will by either party at any time and for any reason. Although this perspective has been challenged by questions of public policy based on the greater "social good," it has led to the rather simplistic view that employees have only those rights that they negotiate with their employers (Elliston, Keenan, Lockhart, and Van Schaick, 1985). Employees and employers, however, are not mere abstractions, and, as individuals, organizational members have a moral right to be treated with respect and dignity (DeGeorge, 1986; Gillis and Casey, 1985). Still, in large-scale organizational change efforts, employees are often viewed as mere replaceable parts in the overall production or service process. As a result, the respect and dignity they might normally be given are neglected for the "greater good" that is projected to result from the transformation.

In the Urban-Suburban bank merger, for example, top management continually asserted a utilitarian view that, while there might be "some pain for certain individuals," the overall success of the institution was dependent on the success of the consolidation. The lack of respect for employees as individuals is exemplified in such tactics as deceiving them about job security after the merger, ignoring their "perceived rights" and cultural orientations during the integration period, and using coercive strategies to force change. While these decisions may have been made with such admirable ends in mind as creating a stronger bank to serve the local community or securer jobs for the employees who remained, it is in a firm's long-term self-interest to be open and progressive with a concern for justice in its dealings with organizational members (Buono and Nichols, 1985).

As noted in Chapter One, mergers have less than a 50-50 chance of being successful, and much of the failure is increasingly attributed to mismanagement of the firms' human resources. By ignoring the rights of organizational members or questions of fairness in dealing with them, managers precipitate unrest, dissatisfaction, alienation, and decreases in commitment and work efforts. Even in the CompServe-NetCo joint venture, the input and concerns of many professional-level employees were dismissed as unimportant early on in the process; when the venture did not fulfill the initial expectations, merger talks were put on "indefinite hold." In contrast, the case of the TransCo-Aero–Co-op Foods acquisition and buyout demonstrates that if these issues are attended to, the outcome can be more stable employee attitudes and work efforts and potentially greater productivity and profitability.

A Final Word

It is clear that mergers, acquisitions, and related downsizing and divestiture activities are continuing to have a major impact on the lives and orientations of our work force. From relatively friendly collaborative ventures to hostile corporate takeovers and raids, organizational consolidations and combinations have been front-page headlines for so long that we almost take them for granted. That is, of course, until they happen to us. The relatively stable world we once knew and lived in literally vanishes before us as we are confronted with the potential of job loss, geographical relocation, status changes, new expectations and demands, different cultural beliefs, values, and norms, and new identities.

The general focus of this book is on such psychological and cultural concerns and dynamics and ways in which these issues can be dealt with openly and positively. The intent is to increase our awareness and insight into how the human side of such combinations can be successfully managed. As discussed in Chapter Three, postcombination integration strategies vary from such "love and marriage" tactics in truly collaborative mergers to much more hostile "rape and pillage" strategies in raids and financial takeovers. Yet, as a cursory scan of virtually any newspaper or popular business magazine readily reveals, the simple fact is that the latter are much more common than the former.

At times, we have used the TransCo-Aero–Co-op Foods acquisition as an indication of what can be done to ameliorate some of the human problems inherent in mergers and acquisitions. The decisions and actions taken by TransCo in this acquisition, however, were far from exemplary. Obviously, the unrelated nature of the acquisition and basic questions as to whether Co-op Foods fitted into its overall strategic plans influenced many of its decisions. Yet, in comparison with the other mergers and acquisitions we studied, this combination process was managed relatively well. This situation appears to say more about the manner in which mergers and acquisitions are handled in general than about TransCo's combination-related acumen.

Part of the hidden agenda underlying corporate takeovers has been characterized as a type of modern-day rape of the Sabine women by the Romans (Thurow, 1988). The tactics involved in raids and takeovers—managerial firings, restructurings, divestiture of units, and related pillaging efforts—are usually justified under the rationale of improving organizational effectiveness and efficiency. The reality, however, is that such actions rarely lead to these expressed outcomes. Instead, what they actually do is serve to reinforce the power of the new leadership, prove that the new boss is indeed "in charge," and make money for the raiders. As Thurow (1988, p. 30) argues, "If one comes back two or three years later, after all those jobs will have been filled, there will have been no reduction in white-collar overheads and those new managers will not be outperforming the old managers." Furthermore, as discussed in Chapter Nine, replacement and training costs will be high.

Given the increasing level of hostility involved in many takeovers and related restructurings, downsizings, and divestitures, recent advice for corporate managers is to "pack your own parachute" (Hirsch, 1987). Hirsch calls for managers to become "free agents" in the sense that, like professional baseball players, they should look out for themselves, find out how much they are worth, and regularly consider offers from other firms. Managers, in effect, should "loosen the psychological ties" that bind them to any one particular organization. Loyalty no longer pays off; self-interest does.

This message and its ramifications are frightening when placed in the broader context of increased global competition, consumer demands for higher-quality products and services, and calls for longer-term views of corporate profit and growth. Our business system increasingly seems to rely on such short-term financial solutions to long-term behavioral problems (Kilmann, Covin, and Associates, 1988). Consolidations, restructurings, downsizings, and divestitures do little to generate adaptive, innovative, and market-driven orientations. Instead, they undermine loyalty and turn once-committed employees into ''free agents.'' A myopic focus on the financial efficiencies that can be derived from organizational consolidation serves only to disrupt the human fabric of an organization, a firm's true resource in a postindustrial world. Such efforts are far from the trust, subtlety, and intimacy envisioned in the world of Theory Z organizations (Ouchi, 1981) or the sort of ''corporate renaissance'' necessary to ''reawaken our spirit of enterprise'' (Kanter, 1983). Instead, it may be, as a *Business Week* cover story (''The End . . . ,'' 1986) posited, ''the end of corporate loyalty.''

The simple fact, which is not so simple to deal with in practice, is that mergers and acquisitions precipitate significant life changes for organizational members. While we have drawn some brief examples from hostile ventures where one would expect disruption, dislocation, and upheaval in people's lives, the dominant orientation of the cases presented here is toward collaborative ventures, albeit with different strategic purposes and planned levels of integration. Yet, as the material in this book has emphasized, even friendly, collaborative ventures that should seemingly result in stronger, more competitive institutions involve costs and sacrifices for both the organizations and their members. If mergers and acquisitions are to be successful over the long term, the basic nature of such change as a human process—with its inherent problems, interactions, and ramifications—must be acknowledged, understood, and integrated into the planning process. The human side of mergers and acquisitions has been neglected for too long.

Appendix

Companies Studied
and Research Methods Used

This book is based on eight years of research involving longitudinal and cross-sectional field study, interviews, organizational surveys, archival research, and bibliographical search of the merger and acquisition literature. Throughout our efforts, the focus has been on the human side of such organizational combinations in terms of (1) the personal issues involved in mergers at both the psychological and cultural levels; (2) the organizational issues that these personal concerns raise; and (3) implications for managing the merger and acquisition process. While we have used anecdotal accounts and research reports on other mergers and acquisitions as a way of extending our discussion and analysis, our research base consists of the results of three primary and two secondary data-collection efforts:

Primary
1. *Urban-Suburban bank merger:* a collaborative merger between two medium-sized savings banks in the Northeast that resulted in an institution with more than $1 billion in assets
2. *TransCo-Co-op Foods acquisition:* an unrelated-business acquisition involving a $4.6 billion conglomerate
3. *CompServe-NetCo joint venture:* a joint venture agreement with a merger stipulation between two small, entrepreneurial computer services firms

Secondary

4. *Retail Corporation–Handy Stores acquisition:* a product-extension acquisition involving a $5.1 billion retail conglomerate
5. *SteelCo-Petro acquisition:* a product-extension acquisition that created one of the largest engineering and construction firms in the nation

Primary Data Sites

A multimethod field approach employed in longitudinal and cross-sectional designs was used to gather data on the precombination organizations, the transformation process, and the postcombination experience. Information on the organizations, their culture profiles, and the combination process was obtained through in-depth interviews with organizational members, observations, and archival data. Lengthy interviews with the chief executive officers (CEOs), upper- and middle-level managers, supervisors, and employees in each company focused on such items as (1) personal descriptions of the organization; (2) organizational history; (3) types of people working at the firm; (4) what type of place the company is to work at; (5) management style before and after the combination; (6) policy and procedural changes; (7) the combination process itself; (8) outcomes of the combination; (9) individual reactions to the combination; and (10) general facets of organizational life. Following grounded theory (Glaser and Strauss, 1967) and phenomenological approaches to organizational research (Sanders, 1982), the researchers examined transcripts of the interviews for concepts and themes that could characterize the different organizations. These "emergent hypotheses" were then tested in discussions with members of the research team and the companies to develop shared perceptions of each organization's culture and the combination process. Additional information on the companies was obtained through observations and archival data gathered throughout the study period. The researchers studied the physical settings of the organizations (for example, office location and decor, consistency of decor across departments and levels), meetings and interactions between organizational members, and each institution's own statements about itself (annual reports, copies of the house organ, internal memos, and so forth).

Organizational climate surveys were undertaken with the populations and stratified random samples of the different organizations. The surveys focused on employee perceptions about various facets of organizational life, including the combination and related processes, job satisfaction, organizational commitment, interpersonal relations, management and supervisory behavior and relations, compensation, job security, advancement, working conditions, and interfirm relations.

Urban-Suburban Bank Merger. Our research effort began with climate surveys administered to the populations of the two banks during late 1979 and early 1980. The survey used in Urban Bank (N = 325) was part of an internally developed quality-of-work-life and organization development program (see Bowditch and Buono, 1982), while a nationally developed survey form was used with Suburban Bank (N = 188). These initial data-gathering processes to obtain information on the premerger organizational climates differed in that Urban Bank relied on a more participatory approach with small groups of employees providing input into the formulation of a Likert-type survey, while Suburban Bank provided a standard, commercially available questionnaire for its employees to complete. In spite of the different approaches, however, both surveys focused on the basic items mentioned above, and there were a number of identical or very similar questions, so that clear climate profiles of the two premerger institutions were obtained (Buono, Bowditch, and Lewis, 1985). Because of a serendipitous research opportunity, these data were collected *prior to* any merger-related discussions.

Data on the organizational climate of Merged Bank were collected through a survey questionnaire administered in 1982 and 1984. The instrument, developed to include the items covered by the 1979 and 1980 surveys, was administered to a stratified random sample of postmerger bank employees: in 1982, 100 employees (45 former Urban Bank employees, 45 former Suburban Bank employees, and 10 new employees); in 1984, 140 employees (50 former Urban Bank employees, 50 former Suburban Bank employees, and 40 new employees). In 1983, a questionnaire was mailed to 90 employees who had left the bank following the merger (response rate 65 percent). While the "leaver" survey included both employees who left voluntarily and employees who left involuntarily, no significant differences were observed. Phone interviews were subsequently conducted with 28 of these people to provide qualitative information about their perceptions of the merger experience. Finally, from 1980 to 1986, information was gathered through in-depth interviews with the CEOs, upper- and middle-level managers, supervisors, and employees of both banks; observations; and assessments of archival data.

Co-op Foods Acquisition and CompServe-NetCo Joint Venture. Both these data-collection efforts used a process similar to that used for the Urban-Suburban bank merger: organizational culture profiles were based on in-depth interviews, observations, and archival reports, while climate profiles were based on organizational surveys. The two climate surveys, however, were cross-sectional instead of longitudinal. While the structure of the questionnaires was similar to that of the one used in the bank merger, the researchers used the Bowditch and Buono (1982) model for survey development, in which questions were also created from issues raised in cross-sectional, diagonal groups where employees discussed salient issues and concerns. In the Co-op Foods study, 300 questionnaires were distributed in 1987 to the headquarters and accounting-comptroller groups of the firm; 278 usable questionnaires were returned (response rate 93 percent). These groups were targeted since they were the ones most affected by the acquisition. Most questions directed employees to compare their attitudes during three periods in the supermarket chain's history: (1) when the company was owned by Aero Corporation; (2) the time of the acquisition by TransCo; and (3) the present, management buyout era.

In 1987, surveys were also administered to all CompServe and NetCo employees ($N = 22$) shortly after their joint venture agreement. Organizational members were instructed to compare and contrast their attitudes about their companies prior to the joint venture and during its initial aftermath. Thus, in these two sites, retrospective rather than actual precombination attitude data were used to create climate profiles of the precombination firms. Similarly, retrospective accounts were used to create composites of the cultures of the different organizations. Although a basic criticism of such data is that they become less accurate with the passage of time between a given situation and the subsequent survey, evidence indicates that if the information is collected within a couple of years of the studied event, there does not appear to be an accuracy or bias problem (Gutek, 1978). Moreover, within the context of the present research, studies suggest that any threat to an organization's existing culture can readily make it clearer and more significant to organizational members (Sales and Mirvis, 1984). As a result of contrasts between the ''old'' and ''new'' cultures following the mergers and acquisitions in the present study, for instance, members of the combined institutions freely discussed sharp recollections about salient aspects of the culture of their former company and of the combined firm, and their relative satisfaction at different times (climate).

As much as possible, uniformity of data-collection efforts was attempted across the primary study sites. Our analysis was guided by what Lawler (1985) has referred to as *participative research,* in which key organizational members assisted in interpreting the data. Overall, these three organizations were quite open and more than generous with us in allowing interviews, surveys, observations, and access to archival data. At times, however, constraints were placed on us that limited our ability to continue to probe certain areas. In the Urban-Suburban bank merger, for example, during the 1984 postmerger follow-up survey, we were allowed to focus only on quality-of-work-life issues. Merged Bank's chief operating officer felt that the specific merger-related questions asked during the 1982 survey (see Chapter Two, Table 3) would only ''reopen old wounds'' and stir up ''unpleasant memories.'' Similarly, while we had planned a final survey intervention in 1986, we were informed that the ''timing'' was not right for another survey.

Secondary Data Sites

In our assessments of the Retail Corporation–Handy Stores and SteelCo-Petro acquisitions, interviews were our main source of information. While we attempted to use a research design similar to the one described above, we were denied such extensive access to a broad cross section of organizational members. The basic nature and focus of the questions, however, were similar to those used at our primary data sites.

The Retail Corporation–Handy Stores project was initiated two months after the acquisition at the request of Handy Stores' president. Over a three-year period, a series of in-depth interviews were undertaken with the subsidiary business unit's CEO and his senior staff. Data were also gathered through group training seminars and individual planning and development discussions with this group. These interventions, which were designed to assist the subsidiary in coping with the acquisition and the process of organizational change, included (1) organizational culture and culture change assessments of Retail Corporation and Handy Stores; (2) strategic planning seminars and assessments of the acquiring firm's orientation to planning; and (3) creation of an annual operating plan in line with Retail Corporation's expectations.

The SteelCo-Petro acquisition project was strictly limited to interviews with SteelCo and Petro managers from November 1986 to April 1987. These discussions centered on the high level of voluntary turnover among Petro's valued engineers and scientists during the combination aftermath period. Throughout both projects, attempts were made to collect as much information as possible about the acquisition process and its effects on the companies involved. The research on our secondary sites is limited, however, to certain sides of the story. By agreement with our organizational contacts, interviews and interventions were undertaken only with specified management personnel. While written reports and archival data were used to obtain further information, no personal contacts with members of some of the firms (for instance, Retail Corporation, Food Company,

Spot stores) or departments (for example, Petro's human resource department) were undertaken. These limitations obviously increase the subjectivity of the data and the possibility of distortion in descriptions of the acquisition process. Yet, at the same time, this subjectivity provides a powerful indication of the ways in which key managers viewed the parent companies and the acquisitions and the reasons underlying their decisions on how to handle the transition (see Sales and Mirvis, 1984).

References

Ackerman, L. S. "Transition Management: An In-Depth Look at Managing Complex Change." *Organizational Dynamics,* Summer 1982, pp. 46–66.

Adams, J. S. "Inequity in Social Exchange." In L. Berkowitz (ed.), *Advances in Experimental and Social Psychology.* New York: Academic Press, 1965.

Akin, G., and Hopelain, D. "Finding the Culture of Productivity." *Organizational Dynamics,* 1986, *14,* 19–32.

Alarik, B., and Edstrom, A. "Post-Merger Integration as a Process of Conflict Resolution." In W. H. Goldberg (ed.), *Mergers: Motives, Modes and Methods.* Aldershot, England: Gower, 1983.

Allaire, Y., and Firsirotu, M. E. "Theories of Organizational Culture." *Organizational Studies,* 1984, *5* (3), 193–226.

American Bankers Association and Ernst & Whinney. *Implementing Mergers and Acquisitions in the Financial Services Industry: From Handshake to Hands On.* Washington, D.C.: American Bankers Association, 1985.

Ansoff, I., Bradenburg, R. G., Portner, F. E., and Radosevich, H. R. *Acquisition Behavior of U.S. Manufacturing Firms, 1946–1965.* Nashville, Tenn.: Vanderbilt University Press, 1971.

Argyris, C. *Understanding Organizational Behavior.* Homewood, Ill.: Dorsey Press, 1960.

Aronson, E. *The Social Animal.* San Francisco: W. H. Freeman, 1976.

Ashforth, B. E. "Climate Formation: Issues and Extensions." *Academy of Management Review,* 1985, *10* (4), 837–847.

Bailey, D. M. "Home Owners Fires 4 Top Officers at Union Warren." *Boston Globe,* Oct. 7, 1987, p. 71.

Bailey, J. "A Bad Marriage? Chicago Law Firm Tries to Overcome Merger Troubles." *Wall Street Journal,* Sept. 24, 1987, p. 29.

Barclay, L. "Social Learning Theory: A Framework for Discrimination Research." *Academy of Management Review,* 1982, *7,* 587–594.

Barmash, I. *Welcome to Our Conglomerate—You're Fired.* New York: Dell, 1971.

Barnes, L. B. "Managing the Paradox of Organizational Trust." *Harvard Business Review,* 1981, *59* (2), 107–116.

Barnouw, V. *An Introduction to Anthropology.* Homewood, Ill.: Dorsey Press, 1975.

Barnouw, V. *Culture and Personality.* Homewood, Ill.: Dorsey Press, 1979,

Barrett, P. F. *The Human Implications of Mergers and Takeovers.* London: Institute of Personnel Management, 1973.

Bastien, D. T. "Common Patterns of Behavior and Communication in Corporate Mergers and Acquisitions." *Human Resource Management,* 1987, *26* (1), 17–33.

Baucus, M. S., Near, J. P., and Miceli, M. P. "Organizational Culture and Whistleblowing." Paper presented at the 45th annual meeting of the Academy of Management, San Diego, Calif., Aug. 1985.

Beam, A. "For Gillette, Life Not the Same After Arrival of Perelman." *Boston Globe,* June 19, 1987a, pp. 69–74.

Beam, A. "Polaroid Discourages Raiders." *Boston Globe,* Sept. 18, 1987b, p. 25.

Beam, A. "More Cuts Expected at Savings Bank." *Boston Globe,* Oct. 9, 1987c, p. 23.

Beam, A. "Gillette a Takeover Target for the Fourth Time in 2 Years." *Boston Globe,* Feb. 12, 1988, pp. 1, 69.

Beckhard, R. "Optimizing Team Building Efforts." *Journal of Contemporary Business,* 1971, *1* (3), 23–32.

Behr, P., and Vise, D. A. "More Firms Are Shedding a Few Extra Pounds: Their Employees." *Washington Post National Weekly,* 1986a, *3* (51), 21.

Behr, P., and Vise, D. A. "Not with My Company You Don't: Managers Are Mobilizing to Stave Off Takeovers." *Washington Post National Weekly,* 1986b, *4* (3), 17.

Bem, D. J. *Beliefs, Attitudes and Human Affairs.* Monterey, Calif.: Brooks/Cole, 1970.

Bennigson, L. A. "Managing Corporate Cultures." *Management Review,* Feb. 1985, pp. 31–32.

Berg, N. *General Management: An Analytical Approach.* Homewood, Ill.: Irwin, 1984.

Berman, R. J., and Wade, M. R. "The Planned Approach to Acquisitions." In S. J. Lee and R. D. Colman (eds.), *Handbook of Mergers, Acquisitions and Buyouts.* Englewood Cliffs, N.J.: Prentice-Hall, 1981.

Berry, J. W. "Social and Cultural Change." In H. C. Triandis and R. W. Brislin (eds.), *Handbook of Cross-Cultural Psychology.* Vol. 5. Boston: Allyn & Bacon, 1980.

Berry, J. W. "Acculturation: A Comparative Analysis of Alternative Forms." In R. J. Samuda and S. L. Woods (eds.). *Perspectives in Immigrant and Minority Education.* Lanham, Md.: University Press of America, 1983.

Bettis, R. A., and Hall, W. K. "Diversification Strategy, Accounting Determined Risk, and Accounting Determined Return." *Academy of Management Journal,* 1982, *25* (1), 254–264.

Betts, S. "New NEH Corporation Marks Entry into 'For Profit.'" *Courier-Gazette* (Rockland, Me.), Nov. 12, 1987, p. 1.

Beyer, J. M., and Trice, H. M. "How an Organization's Rites Reveal Its Culture." *Organizational Dynamics,* 1987, *15* (4), 4–25.

Bhagat, R. S., and McQuaid, S. J. "Role of Subjective Culture in Organizations: A Review and Directions for Future Research." *Journal of Applied Psychology,* 1982, *67* (5), 653–685.

Bice, M. O. "The Organizational Transformation of Lutheran Health Systems." Paper presented at the Managing Organization-wide Transformations Conference, University of Pittsburgh, Oct. 1986.

Blake, R. R., and Mouton, J. S. "The Merger Laboratory." *Gridupdate,* Fall 1981, pp. 3–6.

Blake, R. R., and Mouton, J. S. "How to Achieve Integration on the Human Side of the Merger." *Organizational Dynamics,* 1985, *13* (3), 41–56.

Blumberg, A., and Wiener, W. K. "One from Two: Facilitating an Organizational Merger." In L. D. Goodstein, B. Lubin, and A. E. Lubin (eds.), *Organizational Change Sourcebook II: Cases in Conflict Management.* La Jolla, Calif.: University Associates, 1979.

Boland, R. J. "Merger Planning: How Much Weight Do Personnel Factors Carry?" *Personnel,* Mar.-Apr. 1970, pp. 8–13.

Borucki, C., Tichy, N., and Trullinger, J. "Managing a Mega-Merger: Strategic and Tactical Issues Involved in Integrating RCA Corporation in the General Electric Company." Paper presented at the 47th Annual Meeting of the Academy of Management, New Orleans, La., Aug. 1987.

Bowditch, J. L., and Buono, A. F. *Quality of Work Life Assessment: A Survey Based Approach.* Boston: Auburn House, 1982.

Bowditch, J. L., and Buono, A. F. "Great Expectations: When Hopes for a Better Life Following a Merger Turn Sour." Paper presented at the 47th annual meeting of the Academy of Management, New Orleans, La., Aug. 1987.

Boyle, S. E. "Pre-Merger Growth and Profit Characteristics of Large Conglomerate Mergers in the U.S., 1948–68." *St. Johns Law Review,* 1970, *44,* 152–170.

Bradford, W. D. "Savings and Loan Association Mergers: Analysis of Recent Experience." *Review of Business and Economic Research,* Fall 1977, pp. 1–18.

Breaugh, J. A. "The Measurement of Job Ambiguity." Paper presented at the 43rd annual meeting of the Academy of Management, Dallas, Tex., Aug. 1983.

Brenner, M., and Shapira, Z. "Environmental Uncertainty as Determining Merger Activity." In W. H. Goldberg (ed.),

Mergers: Motives, Modes and Methods. Aldershot, England: Gower, 1983.

Bridges, W. "How To Manage Organizational Transition." *Training,* Sept. 1985, pp. 28–32.

Bridges, W. "Managing Organizational Transitions." *Organizational Dynamics,* Summer 1986, pp. 24–33.

Brief, A. P., and Atieh, J. M. "Studying Job Stress: Are We Making Mountains Out of Mole Hills?" In J. A. Pearce and R. B. Robinson, Jr. (eds.), *Academy of Management Best Paper Proceedings, 1986.* Academy of Management, 1986.

Brozen, Y. *Mergers in Perspective.* Washington, D.C.: American Enterprise for Public Policy Research, 1982.

Buono, A. F., and Bowditch, J. L. "Organizational Countercultures: The Dark Side of Post-Merger Integration." Paper presented at the 46th annual meeting of the Academy of Management, Chicago, Aug. 1986.

Buono, A. F., Bowditch, J. L., and Lewis, J. W. "When Cultures Collide: The Anatomy of a Merger." *Human Relations,* 1985, *38* (5), 477–500.

Buono, A. F., Bowditch, J. L., and Lewis, J. W. "The Cultural Dynamics of Transformation: The Case of a Bank Merger." In R. H. Kilmann, T. J. Covin, and Associates, *Corporate Transformation: Revitalizing Organizations for a Competitive World.* San Francisco: Jossey-Bass, 1988.

Buono, A. F., Bowditch, J. L., and Nurick, A. J. "The Hidden Costs of Organizational Mergers." In A. Larocque and others (eds.), *Psychologie du travail et nouveaux milieux de travail* [Work psychology and new work environments]. Quebec: University of Quebec Press, 1987.

Buono, A. F., and Nichols, L. T. *Corporate Policy, Values and Social Responsibility.* New York: Praeger, 1985.

Burke, W. W. "Organizational Culture and Climate Are Not the Same." Paper presented at the 45th annual meeting of the Academy of Management, San Diego, Calif., Aug. 1985.

Burke, W. W. "Leadership as Empowering Others." In S. Srivastva and Associates, *Executive Power: How Executives Influence People and Organizations.* San Francisco: Jossey-Bass, 1986.

Cabrera, J. C. "The Human Resource Side of Mergers and Acquisitions: Potential Costs and Benefits." *Asset Based Financial Journal,* 1986, *7,* 27–30.

Cameron, K. S., and Whetten, D. A. "Perceptions of Organizational Effectiveness over Organizational Life Cycles." *Administrative Science Quarterly,* 1981, *26,* 525–544.

Caplan, R. D., and Jones, K. W. "Effects of Work Load, Role Ambiguity and Type A Personality on Anxiety, Depression and Heart Rate." *Journal of Applied Psychology,* 1975, *60,* 713–719.

Carcione, S. G. "The Merger Managers: Caught in the Crossfire." *Bank Marketing,* Apr. 1984, pp. 18–25.

Cascio, W. F. *Costing Human Resources: The Financial Impact of Behavior in Organizations.* (2nd ed.) Boston: Kent, 1987.

Cates, D. C. "Banks Are Paying Too Much to Merge." *Fortune,* Dec. 23, 1985, pp. 151–152.

Cavan, R. "The Concepts of Tolerance and Contraculture as Applied to Delinquency." *Sociological Quarterly,* 1961, *2,* 243–258.

Chandler, A. D. *Strategy and Structure.* Cambridge, Mass.: MIT Press, 1962.

"Changing Banks." *Wall Street Journal,* Oct. 16, 1987, p. 31.

Chatterjee, S. "Types of Synergy and Economic Value: The Impact of Acquisitions on Merging and Rival Firms." *Strategic Management Journal,* 1986, *7,* 119–139.

Child, J. "Culture, Contingency, and Capitalism in the Cross National Study of Organizations." In L. L. Cummings and B. M. Staw (eds.), *Research in Organizational Behavior.* Vol. 3. Greenwich, Conn.: JAI Press, 1981.

Cohen, B. J. *In Whose Interest? International Banking and American Foreign Policy.* New Haven, Conn.: Yale University Press, 1986.

Cohen, L. P. "Failed Marriages: Raytheon Is Among the Companies Regretting High-Tech Mergers." *Wall Street Journal,* Sept. 10, 1984, pp. 1, 18.

Cole, R. J. "When Two Old Friends Make a Friendly Merger." *New York Times,* Nov. 21, 1982, pp. 6F–7F.

Conn, R. L. "The Failing Firm/Industry Doctrines in Conglomerate Mergers." *Journal of Industrial Economics*, 1976, *24* (3), 181–187.

Connolly, T. "Information Processing and Decision Making." In B. M. Staw and G. Salancik (eds.), *New Directions in Organizational Behavior*. Chicago: St. Clair Press, 1977.

Cook, T. D., Crosby, F., and Hennigan, K. M. "The Construct Validity of Relative Deprivation." In J. Suls and R. Miller (eds.), *Social Comparison Processes*. New York: Wiley, 1977.

Council for Community Development. *Investigation of the Impact of Acquisition on the Acquired Firm*. Washington, D.C.: Economic Development Association, 1981.

Cowan, A. L. "Swallowing Hutton in 1,200 Bites." *New York Times*, Jan. 10, 1988, pp. F1, F8.

Cox, C. A. "Marshalling the Combined Resources." In S. J. Lee and R. D. Colman (eds.), *Handbook of Mergers, Acquisitions and Buyouts*. Englewood Cliffs, N.J.: Prentice-Hall, 1981.

Crosby, F. *Relative Deprivation and Working Women*. New York: Oxford University Press, 1982.

Crosby, F. "Relative Deprivation in Organizational Settings." In B. M. Staw (ed.), *Research in Organizational Behavior*. Vol. 6. Greenwich, Conn.: JAI Press, 1984.

Dalton, D. R., and others. "Organization Structure and Performance: A Critical Review." *Academy of Management Review*, 1980, *5* (1), 49–64.

Darlin, D., and Guiles, M. G. "Whose Takeover? Some GM People Feel Auto Firm, Not EDS Was the One Acquired." *Wall Street Journal*, Dec. 19, 1984, pp. 1, 20.

Davis, J. A. "A Formal Interpretation of the Theory of Relative Deprivation." *Sociometry*, 1959, *22*, 280–296.

Davis, T. V., and Luthans, F. "A Social Learning Approach to Organizational Behavior." *Academy of Management Review*, 1980, *5*, 281–290.

Deal, T. E., and Kennedy, A. A. *Corporate Cultures: The Rites and Rituals of Corporate Life*. Reading, Mass.: Addison-Wesley, 1982.

Deal, T. E., and Kennedy, A. A. "Culture: A New Look Through Old Lenses." *Journal of Applied Behavioral Science,* 1983, *19* (4), 498–505.

DeGeorge, R. T. *Business Ethics.* (2nd ed.) New York: Macmillan, 1986.

DeMeuse, K. P. "Merger Mania: Anatomy of a Corporate Takeover." Paper presented at the 94th annual meeting of the American Psychological Association, Washington, D.C., Aug. 1986.

DeMeuse, K. P. "Corporate Surgery: The Human Trauma of Mergers and Acquisitions." Paper presented at the 95th annual meeting of the American Psychological Association, New York, Aug. 1987.

"Do Mergers Really Work?" *Business Week,* June 3, 1985, pp. 88–100.

Dohrenwend, B. S., and Dohrenwend, B. (eds.). *Stressful Life Events: Their Nature and Effects.* New York: Wiley, 1974.

Dull, J. H. "Helping Employees Cope with Merger Trauma." *Training,* Jan. 1986, pp. 71–73.

Duva, J. W. "Benefit Manager's Role Is Vital in Acquisitions." *Business Insurance,* Nov. 12, 1984, pp. 62–63.

Elliston, F., Keenan, J., Lockhart, P., and Van Schaick, J. *Whistleblowing: Managing Professional Dissent in the Workplace.* New York: Praeger, 1985.

"The End of Corporate Loyalty?" *Business Week,* Aug. 4, 1986, pp. 42–49.

Evan, W. M., and Klemm, R. C. "Interorganizational Strategies and Structures of Hospitals: A Comparative Study of a Consortium, a Joint Venture, a Merger and a Corporate Management System." In W. H. Goldberg (ed.), *Mergers: Motives, Modes and Methods.* Aldershot, England: Gower, 1983.

Falvey, J. "Best Corporate Culture Is a Melting Pot." *Wall Street Journal,* Apr. 6, 1987, p. 28.

Federal Trade Commission, Bureau of Economics. *F. T. C. Statistical Report on Mergers and Acquisitions.* Washington, D.C.: U.S. Government Printing Office, 1975.

Firth, M. A. *Share Prices and Mergers.* Westmead, England: Saxon House, 1976.

Flamholtz, E. G. "Toward a Theory of Human Resource Value in Formal Organizations." *Accounting Review,* 1972, *47,* 666–678.

Fonvielle, A. "Behavior Versus Attitude: Which Comes First in Organization Change?" *Management Review,* Aug. 1984, p. 14.

Ford, J. D., and Schellenberg, D. H. "Conceptual Issues of Linkage in the Assessment of Organizational Performance." *Academy of Management Review, "* 1982, *7* (1), 49–58.

Franzen, D. "Problems in International Integrations: When Culture, Industry, and Spirit Are Different." Paper presented at the 47th annual meeting of the Academy of Management, New Orleans, La., Aug. 1987.

Fray, L. L., Down, J. W., and Gaylin, D. "Acquisitions and Divestitures." In W. D. Guth (ed.), *Handbook of Business Strategy.* Boston: Warren, Gorham & Lamont, 1985.

Freeman, R. E. *Strategic Management: A Stakeholder Approach.* Boston: Pitman, 1984.

Freeman, R. E., and Reed, D. L. "Stockholders and Stakeholders: A New Perspective on Corporate Governance." *California Management Review,* 1983, *25,* 88–106.

French, W. L., and Bell, C. H. *Organizational Development: Behavioral Science Interventions for Organizational Improvement.* (3rd ed.) Englewood Cliffs, N.J.: Prentice-Hall, 1984.

Fried, M. "Grieving for a Lost Home." In L. J. Duhl (ed.), *The Urban Condition.* New York: Basic Books, 1963.

Gaddis, P. O. "Taken Over, Turned Out." *Harvard Business Review,* 1987, *65* (4), 8–10, 14–16, 18, 22.

Gaertner, K. N. "Colliding Cultures: The Implications of a Merger for Managers' Careers." Paper presented at the 46th annual meeting of the Academy of Management, Chicago, Aug. 1986.

Geber, B. "The Forgotten Factor in Merger Mania." *Training,* 1987, *24* (2), 28–37.

Gerard, K. N. "After the Merger Comes the Hard Part." *Across the Board,* 1986, *23* (7/8), 50–54.

Gereau, D. D. "What Is the Role of HRD in a Merger?" *Training and Development Journal,* Apr. 1986, pp. 20–22.

Gillis, J. G., and Casey, K. L. "Ethical Considerations in Take-overs." *Financial Analysts Journal,* 1985, *41* (2), 10–12, 18.

Glaser, B. G., and Strauss, A. L. *Discovery of Grounded Theory: Strategies for Qualitative Research.* Chicago: Aldine, 1967.

Goldberg, W. H. (ed.). *Mergers: Motives, Modes and Methods.* Aldershot, England: Gower, 1983.

Gordon, I. S. "Smoothing Out Transitions for New Ventures." *Management Review,* Sept. 1987, pp. 54–56.

Graves, D. "Individual Reactions to a Merger of Two Small Firms of Brokers in the Reinsurance Industry." *Journal of Management Studies,* 1981, *18* (1), 89–113.

Gupta, A. K., and Govindarajan, V. "Business Unit Strategy, Manufacturing Characteristics and Business Unit Effectiveness at Strategy Implementation." *Academy of Management Journal,* 1984, *27* (1), 25–41.

Gurr, T. R. *Why Men Rebel.* Princeton, N.J.: Princeton University Press, 1970.

Gutek, B. A. "On the Accuracy of Retrospective Attitudinal Data." *Public Opinion Quarterly,* 1978, *42,* 390–401.

Hackman, J. R. "The Transition That Hasn't Happened." In J. R. Kimberly and R. E. Quinn (eds.), *Managing Organizational Transitions.* Homewood, Ill.: Irwin, 1984.

Hall, E. T. *The Silent Language.* New York: Doubleday, 1959.

Hall, G. E. "Reflections on Running a Diversified Company." *Harvard Business Review,* 1987, *65* (1), 84–92.

Halpern, P. "Corporate Acquisitions: A Theory of Special Cases? A Review of Event Study Cases Applied to Acquisitions." *Journal of Finance,* 1983, *2,* 297–318.

Harris, P. R., and Moran, R. T. *Managing Cultural Differences.* Houston: Gulf, 1979.

Harshbarger, D. "Takeover: A Tale of Loss, Change, and Growth." *Academy of Management Executive,* 1987, *1* (4), 339–343.

Harvey, J. L. "Planning for Postmerger Integration." In J. L. Harvey and A. Newgarden (eds.), *Management Guides to Mergers and Acquisitions.* New York: Wiley-Interscience, 1969.

Haspeslagh, P. C., and Jemison, D. B. "Acquisitions—Myths and Reality." *Sloan Mangement Review,* Winter 1987, pp. 53–58.

Hayes, R. H. "The Human Side of Acquisition." *Management Review*, 1979, *8* (11), 41–46.

Hayes, R. H. "What Happens to My People After I Sell? The Human Side of Acquisition." In S. J. Lee and R. D. Colman (eds.), *Handbook of Mergers, Acquisitions and Buyouts.* Englewood Cliffs, N.J.: Prentice-Hall, 1981.

Heller, T. "Changing Authority Patterns: A Cultural Perspective." *Academy of Management Review,* 1985, *10* (3), 488–495.

Hennessy, E. L., Jr. "Our Takeover Economy: The Raiders Make It Harder to Compete." *New York Times,* Mar. 13, 1988, p. F3.

Heylar, J. "Regional Trend: In the Merger Mania of Interstate Banking, Style and Ego Are Key." *Wall Street Journal,* Dec. 18, 1986, pp. 1, 10.

Hickson, D. J., and others. "A Strategic Contingencies Theory of Organizational Power." *Administrative Science Quarterly,* 1971, *16,* 216–227.

Hirsch, P. *Pack Your Own Parachute: How to Survive Mergers, Acquisitions, and Other Corporate Disasters.* Reading, Mass.: Addison-Wesley, 1987.

Hirsch, P., and Andrews, J. A. Y. "Ambushes, Shootouts, and Knights of the Roundtable: The Language of Corporate Takeovers." In L. Pondy, P. Frost, G. Morgan, and T. Dandridge (eds.), *Monographs in Organizational Behavior and Industrial Relations.* Vol. 1: *Organizational Symbolism.* Greenwich, Conn.: JAI Press, 1983.

Homans, G. C. *Social Behavior: Its Elementary Forms.* (2nd ed.) New York: Harcourt Brace Jovanovich, 1974.

Hopkins, T. H. *Mergers, Acquisitions, and Divestitures: A Guide to Their Impact for Investors and Directors.* Homewood, Ill.: Dow Jones–Irwin, 1983.

Hosmer, L. T. "Ethical Analysis and Human Resource Management." *Human Resource Management,* 1987, *26* (3), 313–330.

"How to Survive Your Company's Merger." *Business Week,* Sept. 17, 1979, pp. 146–148.

Howard, R. L. "Mergers in the Savings and Loan Industry."

Unpublished doctoral dissertation, Ohio State University, Columbus, 1978.

Howell, R. A. "Planning to Integrate Your Acquisition." *Harvard Business Review,* 1970, *48* (6), 66–76.

Hubbart, W. S. "Inside a Company Merger." *Administrative Management,* Sept. 1982, pp. 22–23, 52–54.

Humpal, J. S. "Organizational Marriage Counseling: A First Step." *Journal of Applied Behavioral Science,* 1971, *7* (1), 103–109.

Imberman, A. J. "The Human Element of Mergers." *Management Review,* June 1985, pp. 35–37.

Ingrassia, L. "Employees at Acquired Firms Find White Knights Often Unfriendly." *Wall Street Journal,* July 7, 1982, p. 23.

Ivancevich, J. M., Schweiger, D. M., and Power, F. R. "Strategies for Managing Human Resources During Mergers and Acquisitions." *Human Resources Planning,* 1987, *10* (1), 19–35.

Janis, I., Mahl, G. F., Kagan, J., and Holt, R. R. *Personality.* New York: Harcourt Brace Jovanovich, 1969.

Jay, A. *Management and Machiavelli: An Inquiry into the Politics of Corporate Life.* New York: Holt, Rinehart & Winston, 1968.

Jelinek, M., Smircich, L., and Hirsch, P. "Introduction: A Code of Many Colors." *Administrative Science Quarterly,* 1983, *28* (3), 331–338.

Jemison, D. B. "Process Constraints on Strategic Capability Transfer During Acquisition Integration." Research Paper no. 914, Graduate School of Business, Stanford University, 1986a.

Jemison, D. B. "Strategic Capability Transfer in Acquisition Integration." Research paper no. 913, Graduate School of Business, Stanford University, 1986b.

Jemison, D. B., and Sitkin, S. B. "Acquisitions: The Process Can Be the Problem." *Harvard Business Review,* 1986a, *64* (2), 107–116.

Jemison, D. B., and Sitkin, S. B. "Corporate Acquisitions: A Process Perspective." *Academy of Management Review,* 1986b, *11* (1), 145–163.

Jensen, M., and Ruback, R. "The Mark for Corporate Control: The Scientific Evidence." *Journal of Financial Economics,* 1983, *11* (1), 5–50.

Jenster, P. V. "Integration Problems and Consultants: A Theoretical Perspective." Paper presented at the 47th annual meeting of the Academy of Management, New Orleans, La., Aug. 1987.

Kahn, R., and others. *Organizational Stress: Studies in Role Conflict and Ambiguity.* New York: Wiley, 1964.

Kanter, R. M. *The Change Masters: Innovation for Productivity in the American Corporation.* New York: Simon and Schuster, 1983.

Kanter, R. M., Ingols, C., and Myers, P. "The Delta-Western Merger: 'The Best Get Better.'" *Management Review,* Sept. 1987, pp. 24–26.

Kanter, R. M., and Seggerman, T. K. "Managing Mergers, Acquisitions, and Divestitures." *Management Review,* Oct. 1986, pp. 16–17.

Kay, E. "The Impact of Mergers, Acquisitions and Downsizing." Speech presented at the New England Society of Applied Psychologists, Chestnut Hill, Mass., Sept. 1987.

Keenan, M. "Valuation Problems in Service-Sector Mergers." In M. Keenan and L. J. White (eds.), *Mergers and Acquisitions: Current Problems in Perspective.* Lexington, Mass.: Lexington Books, 1982.

Kelley, R. E. "Poorly Served Employees Serve Customers Just as Poorly." *Wall Street Journal,* Oct. 12, 1987, p. 20.

Kelly, J. *How Managers Manage.* Englewood Cliffs, N.J.: Prentice-Hall, 1980.

Kephart, D. *Extraordinary Groups.* New York: Free Press, 1976.

Kilmann, R. H., and Covin, T. J. "Conclusions: New Directions in Corporate Transformation." In R. H. Kilmann, T. J. Covin, and Associates, *Corporate Transformation: Revitalizing Organizations for a Competitive World.* San Francisco: Jossey-Bass, 1988.

Kilmann, R., Covin, T. J., and Associates. *Corporate Transformation: Revitalizing Organizations for a Competitive World.* San Francisco: Jossey-Bass, 1988.

Kimberly, J. R., and Quinn, R. E. "The Challenge of Transition Management." In J. R. Kimberly and R. E. Quinn (eds.), *Managing Organizational Transitions.* Homewood, Ill.: Irwin, 1984.

Kitching, J. "Why Do Mergers Miscarry?" *Harvard Business Review,* 1967, *46* (6), 84–101.

Kowal, D. "Mergers Often Alienate Employees." *Worcester Telegraph,* Oct. 26, 1986, pp. 23B–24B.

Kozmetsky, G. *Transformational Management.* Cambridge, Mass.: Ballinger, 1985.

Krekel, N. R. A., Van der Woerd, T. G., and Wouterse, J. J. *Mergers: A European Approach to Technique.* London: Business Books, 1969.

Kroeber, A. L., and Kluckhohn, C. "Culture: A Critical Review of Concepts and Definitions." *Papers of the Peabody Museum of American Archeology and Ethnology,* 1952, *47* (1), 36–47.

Kubler-Ross, E. *On Death and Dying.* New York: Macmillan, 1969.

Labaton, S. "For the States, a Starring Role in the Takeover Game." *New York Times,* May 3, 1987, p. F8.

LaGesse, D. "Boost Is Seen for S&L Buys in New Deals." *American Banker,* 1984, *149,* 1, 18.

Lawler, E. E. "Theory and Practice in OD." Paper presented at the 45th annual meeting of the Academy of Management, San Diego, Calif., Aug. 1985.

Lawler, E. E., and Porter, L. W. "Antecedent Attitudes of Effective Managerial Performance." *Organizational Behavior and Human Performance,* 1967, *2,* 122–142.

Lawler, E. E., Seashore, S. E., and Mirvis, P. H. "Measuring Change: Progress, Problems, and Prospects." In S. E. Seashore and others (eds.), *Assessing Organizational Change.* New York: Wiley-Interscience, 1983.

Lazarus, R. S., and Folkman, S. *Stress, Appraisal, and Coping.* New York: Springer, 1985.

Lee, S. J., and Colman, R. D. (eds.). *Handbook of Mergers, Acquisitions and Buyouts.* Englewood Cliffs, N.J.: Prentice-Hall, 1981.

Lefkoe, M. "Why So Many Mergers Fail." *Fortune,* July 20, 1987, pp.113–114.

Lenzner, R. "Corporate Empire Builders Have $16b in Play." *Boston Globe,* Feb. 2, 1988, p. 39.

Lev, V., and Sundar, S. "Methodological Issues in the Use of Financial Ratios." *Journal of Accounting and Economics,* 1979, *1* (3), 187–210.

Levin, D. P. "Fearing Takeover of Gulf Oil, Employees Are Showing Myriad Symptoms of Stress." *Wall Street Journal,* Feb. 28, 1984, p. 35.

Levinson, H. *Men, Management and Mental Health.* Cambridge, Mass.: Harvard University Press, 1962.

Levinson, H. "A Psychologist Diagnoses Merger Failures." *Harvard Business Review,* 1970, *48* (2), 139–147.

Levy, A. "Second-Order Planned Change: Definition and Conceptualization." *Organizational Dynamics,* Summer 1986, pp. 5–20.

Lewin, K. "Group Decision and Social Change." In T. M. Newcomb and E. L. Hartley (eds.), *Readings in Social Psychology.* New York: Holt, Rinehart & Winston, 1947.

Lewin, K. *Field Theory in Social Science.* New York: Harper & Row, 1951.

Likert, R., and Bowers, D. G. "Improving the Accuracy of P/L Reports by Estimating the Change in Dollar Value of the Human Organization." *Michigan Business Review,* Mar. 1973, pp. 15–24.

Linton, R. *The Study of Man.* East Norwalk, Conn.: Appleton-Century-Crofts, 1936.

Linton, R. *The Cultural Background of Personality.* East Norwalk, Conn.: Appleton-Century-Crofts, 1945.

Litterer, J. *Introduction to Management.* New York: Wiley, 1978.

Louis, A. M. "The Bottom Line on 10 Big Mergers." *Fortune,* May 3, 1982, pp. 84–89.

Lubatkin, M. "Mergers and the Performance of the Acquiring Firm." *Academy of Management Review,* 1983, *8* (2), 218–225.

Lubatkin, M., and O'Neil, H. M. "Merger Strategies and Capital Market Risk." *Academy of Management Journal,* 1987, *30* (4), 665–684.

Lubatkin, M., and Shrieves, R. E. "Towards Reconciliation of Market Performance Measures to Strategic Management Research." *Academy of Management Review,* 1986, *11* (3), 497–512.

Lundberg, C. C. "Strategies for Organizational Transitioning." In J. R. Kimberly and R. E. Quinn (eds.), *Managing Organizational Transitions.* Homewood, Ill.: Irwin, 1984.

McCaskey, M. B. "The Hidden Messages Managers Send." *Harvard Business Review,* 1979a, *57* (6), 135–148.

McCaskey, M. B. "The Management of Ambiguity." *Organizational Dynamics,* Spring 1979b, pp. 30–48.

Mace, M. L., and Montgomery, G. G., Jr. *Management Problems of Corporate Acquisitions.* Boston: Division of Research, Graduate School of Business Administration, Harvard University, 1962.

McLeod, D. "Mergers Create Human Resource Problems." *Business Insurance,* Apr. 21, 1986, p. 30.

Magnet, M. "Acquiring Without Smothering." *Fortune,* Nov. 12, 1984a, pp. 21–26.

Magnet, M. "Help! My Company Has Just Been Taken Over." *Fortune,* July 9, 1984b, pp. 44–51.

Magnet, M. "What Merger Mania Did for Syracuse." *Fortune,* Feb. 3, 1986, pp. 94–98.

Malekzadeh, A., and Nahavandi, A. "The Fit Between Strategy and Culture in Mergers." In F. Hoy (ed.), *Academy of Management Best Paper Proceedings 1987.* Academy of Management, 1987.

Management Analysis Center. *Making Mergers Work in the Financial Services Industry.* Boston: Management Analysis Center, 1983.

Mandelker, G. "Risk and Return: The Case of Merging Firms." *Journal of Financial Economy,* Dec. 1974, pp. 303–335.

Mangum, W. T. "In the Merger Hurricane, Keep an Eye on the Human Side of Change." *Data Management,* Summer 1984, pp. 26–29.

Manne, H. "Mergers and the Market for Corporate Control." *Journal of Political Economy,* 1975, *73* (2), 110–120.

Manzini, A. O., and Gridley, J. D. "Human Resource Planning for Mergers and Acquisitions: Preparing for the 'People Issues' That Can Prevent Merger Synergies." *Human Resource Planning,* 1986, *9* (2), 51–57.

Marks, M. L. "Merging Human Resources: A Review of the Literature." *Mergers & Acquisitions,* Summer 1982, pp. 38-44.

Marks, M. L., and Mirvis, P. "Merger Syndrome: Stress and Uncertainty." *Mergers & Acquisitions,* Summer 1985, pp. 50-55.

Marks, M. L., and Mirvis, P. "The Merger Syndrome." *Psychology Today,* Oct. 1986, pp. 36-42.

Marshall, J. "Trends: Wave of Mergers Doesn't Impress Investors." *American Banker,* Nov. 4, 1985, p. 11.

Martin, J. "Relative Deprivation: A Theory of Distributive Injustice for an Era of Shrinking Resources." In L. L. Cummings and B. M. Staw (eds.), *Research in Organizational Behavior.* Vol. 3. Greenwich, Conn.: JAI Press, 1981.

Martin, J., and Siehl, C. "Organizational Culture and Counterculture: An Uneasy Symbiosis." *Organizational Dynamics,* 1983, *12* (2), 52-64.

Matteson, M. T., and Ivancevich, J. M. *Managing Job Stress and Health.* New York: Free Press, 1982.

Mayers, J. "Living with the Done Deal: How to Withstand a Merger." *Management Review,* Oct. 1986a, pp. 39-42.

Mayers, J. "Living with the Done Deal: How to Withstand a Merger, Part II." *Management Review,* Nov. 1986b, pp. 54-58.

Metz, R. "Share Prices Don't Always Improve with Mergers, Study Finds." *Boston Globe,* May 28, 1985, p. 42.

Michel, A., and Shaked, I. "Evaluating Merger Performance." *California Management Review,* 1985, *27* (3), 109-118.

Michel, A., and Shaked, I. *Takeover Madness: Corporate America Fights Back.* New York: Wiley, 1986.

Miles, R. H. "Role Requirements as Sources of Organizational Stress." *Journal of Applied Psychology,* 1976, *61,* 172-179.

Miles, R. H. *Macro Organizational Behavior.* Santa Monica, Calif.: Goodyear, 1980.

Milliken, F. J. "Three Types of Perceived Uncertainty About the Environment: State, Effect, and Response Uncertainty." *Academy of Management Review,* 1987, *12* (1), 133-143.

Mills, C. W. "The Professional Ideology of Social Pathologists." In B. Rosenberg and others (eds.), *Mass Society in Crisis: Social Problems and Social Pathology.* New York: Macmillan, 1964.

Mintzberg, H. *The Nature of Managerial Work.* Englewood Cliffs, N.J.: Prentice-Hall, 1980.

Mirvis, P. H. "Negotiations After the Sale: The Roots and Ramifications of Conflict in an Acquisition." *Journal of Occupational Behavior,* 1985, *6,* 65–84.

Mirvis, P. H., and Lawler, E. E. "Measuring the Financial Impact of Employee Attitudes." *Journal of Applied Psychology,* 1977, *62* (1), 1–8.

Mirvis, P. H., and Lawler, E. E. "Systems Are Not Solutions: Issues in Creating Information Systems That Account for the Human Organization." *Accounting, Organizations and Society,* 1983, *8,* 175–190.

Mirvis, P. H., and Marks, M. L. "Merger Syndrome: Management by Crisis." *Mergers & Acquisitions,* 1985, *20* (3), 70–76.

Mirvis, P. H., and Marks, M. L. "The Creation of UNISYS: Strategy and Tactics in the Mega-Merger of Burroughs and Sperry Corporation." Paper presented at the 47th annual meeting of the Academy of Management, New Orleans, La., Aug. 1987.

Mitchell, G. D. (ed.). *A Dictionary of Sociology.* London: Routledge & Kegan Paul, 1973.

Mitroff, I. I. *Stakeholders of the Organizational Mind: Toward a New View of Organizational Policy Making.* San Francisco: Jossey-Bass, 1983.

Mobley, W. H. *Employee Turnover: Causes, Consequences and Control.* Reading, Mass.: Addison-Wesley, 1982.

Mobley, W. H., Griffith, R. W., Hand, H. H., and Meglino, B. M. "Review and Conceptual Analysis of the Employee Turnover Process." *Psychological Bulletin,* 1979, *80,* 151–176.

Montgomery, C. A., and Wilson, V. A. "Mergers That Last: A Predictable Pattern?" *Strategic Management Journal,* 1986, *7,* 91–96.

Moore, M. L. "Designing Parallel Organizations to Support Organizational Productivity Programs." In J. J. Famularo (ed.), *Handbook of Human Resources Administration.* New York: McGraw-Hill, 1986.

Morey, N. C., and Luthans, F. "Refining the Displacement of Culture and the Use of Scenes and Themes in Organizational

Studies." *Academy of Management Review*, 1985, *10* (2), 219–229.

Morris, B., and Johnson, R. "Case of Indigestion: How Beatrice Adjusts to Latest Takeover, This Time of Itself." *Wall Street Journal*, Dec. 1985, p. 1.

Mueller, D. C. "Mergers and Market Share." *Review of Economics and Statistics*, 1985, *67*, 259–267.

Mueller, R. K. *The Incompleat Board: The Unfolding of Corporate Governance.* Lexington, Mass.: Lexington Books, 1981.

Mullins, D. W. "Does the Capital Asset Pricing Model Work?" *Harvard Business Review*, 1981, *60* (1), 105–114.

Nadler, D. A. "Managing Transitions to Uncertain Future States." *Organizational Dynamics*, Summer 1982, pp. 37–45.

Nahavandi, A., and Malekzadeh, A. "The Role of Acculturation in the Implementation of Mergers." In J. A. Pearce and R. B. Robinson (eds.), *Academy of Management Best Paper Proceedings 1986.* Academy of Management, 1986.

Nahavandi, A., and Malekzadeh, A. R. "Acculturation in Mergers and Acquisitions." *Academy of Management Review*, 1988, *13* (1), 79–90.

Nurick, A. J. "Participation in Organizational Change: A Longitudinal Field Study." *Human Relations*, 1982, *35* (5), 413–430.

Nurick, A. J. *Participation in Organizational Change: The TVA Experiment.* New York: Praeger, 1985.

Nystrom, P. C., and Starbuck, W. H. "Managing Beliefs in Organizations." *Journal of Applied Behavioral Science*, 1984, *20* (3), 277–287.

O'Boyle, T. F. "Loyalty Ebbs at Many Companies as Employees Grow Disillusioned." *Wall Street Journal*, July 11, 1985, p. 27.

O'Boyle, T. F., and Russell, M. "Troubled Marriage: Steel Giants' Merger Brings Headaches, J&L and Republic Find." *Wall Street Journal*, Nov. 30, 1984, pp. 1, 20.

Ogburn, W. F. *Social Change with Respect to Culture and Original Nature.* New York: B. W. Heubsch, 1922.

Ouchi, W. G. *Theory Z: How American Business Can Meet the Japanese Challenge.* Reading, Mass.: Addison-Wesley, 1981.

Ouchi, W. G., and Wilkins, A. L. "Organizational Culture." *Annual Review of Sociology*, 1985, *11*, 457–483.

Paine, L. S. "Management Buyouts and Managerial Ethics." Paper presented at the 7th national conference on business ethics, Center for Business Ethics, Bentley College, Waltham, Mass., Oct. 1987.

Pappanastos, J. S., Hillman, L. T., and Cole, P. A. "The Human Resource Side of Mergers." *Business,* July–Sept. 1987, pp. 3–11.

Parsons, T. *The Social System.* New York: Free Press, 1951.

Parsons, T. *Structure and Process in Modern Societies.* New York: Free Press, 1960.

Pascale, R. T. "The Paradox of 'Corporate Culture': Reconciling Ourselves to Socialization." *California Management Review,* 1985, *27* (2), 26–41.

Patterson, G. A. "Two Top VPs Fired in Jordan Marsh Restructuring." *Boston Globe,* Jan. 13, 1988, p. 25.

Pear, R. "Clarifying Some Mixed Signals on Antitrust." *New York Times,* July 19, 1981, p. E4.

Pearce, J. L. "Bringing Some Clarity to Role Ambiguity Research." *Academy of Management Review,* 1981, *6,* 665–674.

Pelster, W. C. "Basic Antitrust Guidelines in Federal and State Laws." In S. J. Lee and R. D. Colman (eds.), *Handbook of Mergers, Acquisitions and Buyouts.* Englewood Cliffs, N.J.: Prentice-Hall, 1981.

Perrow, C. *Organizational Analysis: A Sociological View.* Monterey, Calif.: Brooks/Cole, 1970.

Perry, L. T. "Key Human Resource Strategies in an Organizational Downturn." *Human Resource Management,* 1984, *23* (1), 61–75.

Perry, L. T. "Merging Successfully: Sending the Right Signals." *Sloan Management Review,* Spring 1986, pp. 47–57.

Peters, T. J. "Symbols, Patterns, and Settings: An Optimistic Case for Getting Things Done." *Organizational Dynamics,* 1978, *7* (2), 3–23.

Peters, T. J. "Management Systems: The Language of Organizational Character and Competence." *Organizational Dynamics,* Summer 1980, pp. 3–27.

Peters, T. J., and Waterman, R. H. *In Search of Excellence: Lessons from America's Best-Run Companies.* New York: Harper & Row, 1982.

Pettigrew, A. M. "On Studying Organizational Culture." *Administrative Science Quarterly,* 1979, *24* (4), 570–581.

Pettigrew, A. M. "Is Corporate Culture Manageable?" Keynote address, 6th annual Strategic Management Society Conference, Singapore, Oct. 1986.

Pfeffer, J. "Merger as a Response to Organizational Interdependence." *Administrative Science Quarterly,* 1972, *17,* 382–394.

Pfeffer, J., and Jones, J. "OD Readiness." In W. W. Burke (ed.), *The Cutting Edge: Current Theory and Practice in Organization Development.* La Jolla, Calif.: University Associates, 1978.

Pickens, T. B. *Boone.* New York: Houghton Mifflin, 1987.

Pitts, R. A. "Diversification Strategies and Organizational Policies of Large Diversified Firms." *Journal of Economics and Business,* 1976, *28,* 181–188.

Plovnick, M. S., Fry, R. E., and Burke, W. W. *Organization Development: Exercises, Readings and Cases.* Boston: Little, Brown, 1982.

Pond, S. B., Armenakis, A. A., and Green, S. B. "The Importance of Employee Expectations in Organizational Diagnosis." *Journal of Applied Behavioral Science,* 1984, *20* (2), 167–180.

Pondy, L. R. "Organizational Conflict: Concepts and Models." *Administrative Science Quarterly,* 1967, *12,* 296–320.

Porras, J. I., and others. "Modeling-Based Organization Development: A Longitudinal Assessment." *Journal of Applied Behavioral Science,* 1982, *18,* 433–446.

Porter, L. W., and Steers, R. M. "Organization, Work, and Personal Factors in Employee Turnover and Absenteeism." *Psychological Bulletin,* 1973, *80,* 151–176.

Porter, M. E. *Competitive Advantage: Creating and Sustaining Superior Performance.* New York: Free Press, 1985.

Premack, S. L., and Wanous, J. P. "A Meta-Analysis of Realistic Job Preview Experiments." *Journal of Applied Psychology,* 1985, *70,* 706–719.

Pritchett, P. *After the Merger: Managing the Shockwaves.* Homewood, Ill.: Dow Jones–Irwin, 1985.

Pritchett, P. *The Employee Survival Guide to Mergers and Acquisitions.* Dallas, Tex.: Pritchett and Associates, 1987a.

Pritchett, P. *Making Mergers Work: A Guide to Managing Mergers and Acquisitions.* Homewood, Ill.: Dow Jones–Irwin, 1987b.

"Quarterly Profile." *Mergers & Acquisitions,* 1987a, *21* (4), 71.

"Quarterly Profile." *Mergers & Acquisitions,* 1987b, *22* (1), 95.

Quinn, J. B. *Strategies for Change: Logical Incrementalism.* Homewood, Ill.: Irwin, 1980.

Radcliffe-Brown, A. R. *A Natural Science of Society.* New York: Free Press, 1957.

Rappaport, A. "Corporate Performance Standards and Stockholder Value." *Journal of Business Strategy,* 1983, *3* (4), 28–38.

Reimer, B. "Corporate Identity of Dana Corporation: Implications for Acquisitions." In V. J. Sathe, *Culture and Related Corporate Realities.* Homewood, Ill.: Irwin, 1985.

Rennert, V. P. "The Raiders." *Across the Board,* July 1979, pp. 12–22.

Reynolds, P. C. "Imposing a Corporate Culture." *Psychology Today,* March 1987, pp. 33–38.

Rich, D. W. "Testimony of Dennis W. Rich." *Oversight Hearing on Mergers and Acquisitions: Hearing Before the Subcommittee on Economic Stabilization of the Committee on Banking, Finance and Urban Affairs, House of Representatives.* Washington, D.C.: U.S. Government Printing Office, 1987.

Richman, J. D. "Merger Decision Making: An Ethical Analysis and Recommendations." *California Management Review,* 1984, *27* (1), 177–184.

Rizzo, J. R., House, R. J., and Lirtzman, S. I. "Role Conflict and Role Ambiguity in Complex Organizations." *Administrative Science Quarterly,* 1970, *15,* 150–163.

Robino, D., and DeMeuse, K. "Corporate Mergers and Acquisitions: Their Impact on HRM." *Personnel Administrator,* 1985, *30* (11), 33–44.

Robinson, R. A. "Bank Mergers: Valuation Strategies." *Bankers Monthly Magazine,* Sept. 15, 1983, pp. 20–23.

Rosenberg, R. "Computervision Corp. Adopts 'Poison Pill' Merger Defense." *Boston Globe,* Feb. 12, 1987, p. 45.

Roszak, T. *The Making of a Counterculture.* Garden City, N.Y.: Anchor, 1969.

Rumelt, R. *Strategy, Structure, and Performance.* Cambridge, Mass.: Harvard University Press, 1974.

Runciman, W. G. *Relative Deprivation and Social Justice: A Study of Attitudes to Social Inequality in Twentieth-Century England.* Berkeley: University of California Press, 1966.

Ryan, W. *Blaming the Victim.* New York: Harper & Row, 1972.

Sales, A. L., and Mirvis, P. H. "When Cultures Collide: Issues in Acquisition." In J. R. Kimberly and R. E. Quinn (eds.), *Managing Organizational Transitions.* Homewood, Ill.: Irwin, 1984.

Salter, M., and Weinhold, W. *Diversification Through Acquisition.* New York: Free Press, 1979.

Sanders, P. "Phenomenology: A New Way of Viewing Organizational Research." *Academy of Management Review,* 1982, 7 (2), 353-360.

Sansweet, S. J. "Major Oil Firms Are Slashing Jobs as Takeovers Rise, Demand Sags: Uncertainty Racks Getty Workers." *Wall Street Journal,* Apr. 19, 1983, p. 33.

Sashkin, M. "Participative Management Is an Ethical Imperative." *Organizational Dynamics,* Spring 1984, pp. 5-22.

Sashkin, M., Burke, R. J., Lawrence, P. R., and Pasmore, W. "OD Approaches: Analysis and Application." *Training and Development Journal,* 1985, *39* (2), 44-50.

Sathe, V. "Implications of Corporate Culture: A Manager's Guide to Action." *Organizational Dynamics,* Autumn 1983, pp. 5-23.

Sathe, V. *Culture and Related Corporate Realities.* Homewood, Ill.: Irwin, 1985.

Schein, E. H. "Personal Change Through Interpersonal Relations." In W. G. Bennis and others (eds.), *Interpersonal Dynamics.* Homewood, Ill.: Dorsey Press, 1973.

Schein, E. H. *Organizational Psychology.* (3rd ed.) Englewood Cliffs, N.J.: Prentice-Hall, 1980.

Schein, E. H. "The Role of the Founder in Creating Organizational Culture." *Organizational Dynamics,* Summer 1983, pp. 13-28.

Schein, E. H. *Organizational Culture and Leadership: A Dynamic View.* San Francisco: Jossey-Bass, 1985.

Schneider, B. "Employee and Customer Perceptions of Service in Banks." *Administrative Science Quarterly,* 1980, *25* (2), 252-267.

"Schwab to Buy Back Brokerage." *Boston Globe,* Feb. 3, 1987, p. 34.

Schwartz, H., and Davis, S. M. "Matching Corporate Culture and Business Strategy." *Organizational Dynamics,* Summer 1981, pp. 30–48.

Schweiger, D. L., and DeNisi, A. S. "The Effects of a Realistic Merger Preview on Employees: A Longitudinal Field Experiment." Paper presented at the 47th annual meeting of the Academy of Management, New Orleans, La., Aug. 1987.

Schweiger, D. L., and Ivancevich, J. M. "Human Resources: The Forgotten Factor in Mergers and Acquisitions." *Personnel Administrator,* 1985, *30* (11), 47–54, 58–61.

Schweiger, D. L., and Ivancevich, J. M. "The Effects of Mergers and Acquisitions on Organizations and Human Resources: A Contingency View." Paper presented at the 7th annual Strategic Management Society Conference, Boston, Oct. 1987.

Schweiger, D. L., Ivancevich, J. M., and Power, F. R. "Executive Actions for Managing Human Resources Before and After Acquisition." *Academy of Mangement Executive,* 1987, *1* (2), 127–138.

"Shearson Offers $1B for E. F. Hutton." *Boston Globe,* Dec. 3, 1987, p. 63.

Shortell, S. M., and Wickizer, T. M. "New Program Development: Issues in Managing Vertical Integration." In J. R. Kimberly and R. E. Quinn (eds.), *Managing Organizational Transitions.* Homewood, Ill.: Irwin, 1984.

Shrallow, D. A. "Managing the Integration of Acquired Operations." *Journal of Business Strategy,* 1985, *6,* 30–36.

Shrivastava, P. "Integrating Strategy Formulation with Organizational Culture." *Journal of Business Strategy,* 1985, *5,* 103–111.

Shrivastava, P. "Postmerger Integration." *Journal of Business Strategy,* 1986, *7,* 65–76.

Shuman, J. C., and Buono, A. F. "Dynamics of Post-Acquisition Integration: A View from an Acquired Firm's Management." Paper presented at the 48th annual meeting of the Academy of Management, Anaheim, Calif., Aug. 1988.

Siehl, C. "Management or Culture: The Need for Consistency and Redundance Among Organizational Components."

Paper presented at the 42nd annual meeting of the Academy of Management, New York, Aug. 1982.

Siehl, C., Ledford, G., and Siehl, J. "Strategies for Managing Post-Merger Integration." Paper presented at the 46th annual meeting of the Academy of Management, Chicago, Aug. 1986.

Siehl, C., Ledford, G., Silverman, R., and Fay, P. *Managing Cultural Differences in Mergers and Acquisitions: The Role of the Human Resource Function.* Los Angeles: Center for Effective Organizations, University of Southern California, 1987.

Sinetar, M. "Mergers, Morale and Productivity." *Personnel Journal,* Nov. 1981, pp. 863–867.

Smircich, L. "Concepts of Culture and Organizational Analysis." *Administrative Science Quarterly,* 1983, *28* (3), 339–358.

Smith, F. J. "Work Attitudes as Predictors of Attendance on a Specific Day." *Journal of Applied Psychology,* 1977, *62* (1), 16–19.

Smith, W. K. *Handbook of Strategic Growth Through Mergers and Acquisitions.* Englewood Cliffs, N.J.: Prentice-Hall, 1985.

Stein, C. "A Day to Remember in Boston." *Boston Globe,* Mar. 1, 1988, pp. 25, 30.

Steiner, P. O. *Mergers: Motives, Effects, Policies.* Ann Arbor: University of Michigan Press, 1975.

Stouffer, S. A., and others. *The American Soldier: Adjustment During Army Life.* Vol. 1. Princeton, N.J.: Princeton University Press, 1949.

Stybel, L. "After the Merger the Human Element." *New England Business,* Nov. 2, 1986, pp. 67–68.

"Successful Mergers Require a Mesh of Corporate Cultures." *Savings & Loan News,* Mar. 1983, pp. 94–95.

Taft, R. W. "Public Relations Aspects of Mergers and Acquisitions." In S. J. Lee and R. D. Colman (eds.), *Handbook of Mergers, Acquisitions and Buyouts.* Englewood Cliffs, N.J.: Prentice-Hall, 1981.

Thompson, D. B. "Surviving a Merger." *Industry Week,* Sept. 6, 1982, pp. 41–44.

Thurow, L. C. "Rape of the Sabines." *Boston Globe,* Feb. 9, 1988, p. 30.

Tichy, N., and Ulrich, B. "The Leadership Challenge—A Call for the Transformational Leader." *Sloan Management Review,* 1984a, *24* (1), 59–68.

Tichy, N., and Ulrich, B. "Revitalizing Organizations: The Leadership Role." In J. R. Kimberly and R. E. Quinn (eds.), *Managing Organizational Transitions.* Homewood, Ill.: Irwin, 1984b.

Triandis, H. D. "Cross-Cultural Social and Personality Psychology." *Personality and Social Psychology Bulletin,* 1977, *3,* 143–158.

Triandis, H. D., and others. *The Analysis of Subjective Culture.* New York: Wiley-Interscience, 1972.

Trice, H., and Beyer, J. "The Routinization of Charisma in Two Social Movement Organizations." In B. M. Staw and L. L. Cummings (eds.), *Research in Organizational Behavior.* Vol. 7. Greenwich, Conn.: JAI Press, 1985.

Tuchman, B. "Developmental Sequence in Small Groups." *Psychological Bulletin,* 1965, *63,* 384–399.

Tylor, E. B. *Primitive Culture: Researches into the Development of Mythology, Philosophy, Religion, Language, Art, and Custom.* Vol. 1. New York: Holt, Rinehart & Winston, 1871.

Van de Ven, A. "An Attempt to Institutionalize an Organization's Culture." Paper presented at the 43rd annual meeting of the Academy of Management, Dallas, Tex., Aug. 1983.

Wallner, N., and Greve, J. T. *How To Do a Leveraged Buyout or Acquisition: For Yourself, Your Corporation or Your Client.* San Diego, Calif.: Buyout Publications, 1982.

Wallum, P. "Personnel's Role in Company Mergers." *Personnel Management,* Oct. 1980, pp. 58–61.

Walsh, J. P. "Top Management Turnover Following Mergers and Acquisitions." *Strategic Management Journal,* 1988, *9,* 173–183.

Walter, G. A. "Organization Development and Individual Rights." *Journal of Applied Behavioral Science,* 1984, *20* (4), 423–439.

Walter, G. A. "Culture Collisions in Mergers and Acquisitions." In P. Frost and others (eds.), *Organizational Culture.* Beverly Hills, Calif.: Sage, 1985a.

Walter, G. A. "Key Acquisition Integration Processes for Four Strategic Orientations." Paper presented at the 45th annual meeting of the Academy of Management, San Diego, Calif., Aug. 1985b.

Wanous, J. P. *Organizational Entry: Recruitment, Selection and Socialization of Newcomers*. Reading, Mass.: Addison-Wesley, 1980.

Warren, D. L. "Managing in Crisis: Nine Principles for Successful Transition." In J. R. Kimberly and R. E. Quinn (eds.), *Managing Organizational Transitions*. Homewood, Ill.: Irwin, 1984.

Wells, K., and Hymowitz, C. "Takeover Trauma: Gulf's Managers Find Merger into Chevron Forces Many Changes." *Wall Street Journal*, Dec. 5, 1984, pp. 1, 24.

Westhues, K. *Society's Shadow*. Toronto: McGraw-Hill Ryerson, 1972.

Wilkins, A. L. "The Culture Audit: A Tool for Understanding Organizations." *Organizational Dynamics*, Autumn 1983, pp. 24-38.

Wilkins, A. L. "The Creation of Company Cultures: The Role of Stories and Human Resource Systems." *Human Resources Management*, 1984, *23* (1), 41-60.

Wilkins, A. L., and Bristow, N. J. "For Successful Organizational Culture, Honor Your Past." *Academy of Management Executive*, 1987, *1* (3), 221-228.

Wilkins, A. L., and Ouchi, W. G. "Efficient Cultures: Exploring the Relationship Between Culture and Organizational Performance." *Administrative Science Quarterly*, 1983, *28* (3), 468-481.

Wishard, B. "In Mergers, Remember That the Human Element Is Vital." *American Banker*, 1983, *148*, 4, 15-16.

Wishard, B. "Merger—The Human Dimension." *Magazine of Bank Administration*, 1985, *61* (6), 74-79.

Wright, M., and Coyne, J. *Management Buy-Outs*. London: Croom Helm, 1985.

Yinger, J. M. "Contraculture and Subculture." *American Sociological Review*, 1960, *25*, 625-635.

Yinger, J. M. *Countercultures*. New York: Free Press, 1982.

Young, J. B. "A Conclusive Investigation in the Causative Elements of Failure in Acquisitions." In S. J. Lee and R. D. Colman (eds.), *Handbook of Mergers, Acquisitions and Buyouts.* Englewood Cliffs, N.J.: Prentice-Hall, 1981.

Yunker, J. A. *Integrating Acquisitions: Making Corporate Marriages Work.* New York: Praeger, 1983.

Zimbardo, P. G., Ebbesen, E. B., and Maslach, C. *Influencing Attitudes and Changing Behavior.* (2nd ed.) Reading, Mass.: Addison-Wesley, 1977.

Zonana, V. F. "The Porches and Saabs at Schwab Aggravate Some at BankAmerica." *Wall Street Journal,* Jan. 20, 1983, p. 27.

Name Index

Smith, F. J., 233
Smith, W. K., 4, 15, 21, 62
Starbuck, W. H., 169, 223
Steers, R. M., 233
Stein, C., 4
Steiner, P. O., 78
Stouffer, S. A., 126
Strauss, A. L., 267
Stybel, L., 12, 15, 101, 194, 233, 258
Sundar, S., 8

T

Taft, R. W., 198
Thompson, D. B., 22
Thurow, L. C., 264
Tichy, N., 221, 223, 228
Triandis, H. D., 136, 137
Trice, H. M., 165, 221
Trullinger, J., 228
Tuchman, B., 88
Tylor, E. B., 135

U

Ulrich, B., 221, 223

V

Van de Ven, A., 165
Van der Woerd, T. G., 60–61
Van Schaick, J., 181, 262
Vise, D. A., 6, 77

W

Wade, M. R., 92
Wallner, N., 21
Wallum, P., 72
Walsh, J. P., 64, 65, 114, 232
Walter, G. A., 22, 78, 88, 135, 173, 217
Wanous, J. P., 132, 205
Warren, D. L., 90
Waterman, R. H., 135, 138
Weinhold, W., 21, 87
Wells, K., 15, 19, 141
Westhues, K., 176
Whetten, D. A., 8
Wickizer, T. M., 90
Wiener, W. K., 194
Wilkins, A. L., 17, 135, 137, 141, 148,
   150, 151, 156, 165, 175, 192
Wilson, V. A., 9, 85, 87
Wishard, B., 5, 112, 117, 197
Wouterse, J. J., 60–61
Wright, M., 255

Y

Yinger, J. M., 175, 176, 177, 179, 181
Young, J. B., 238
Yunker, J. A., 7, 9, 10, 11, 15, 229

Z

Zimbardo, P. G., 166
Zonana, V. F., 138

Subject Index

A

Acculturation: and cultural change, 172-175; and cultural pluralism, 221

Acme, Inc., and symbolic communication, 222-223

Acquisitions. *See* Mergers and acquisitions

Aero Corporation: in acquisition and divestiture, 39-46, 264; coercion or participation in, 260; and competing claims, 252-253; and costs of merger, 241; and laissez-faire merger, 75; and product extension, 63, 65; research methods on, 269; and respect for employees, 263; and secrecy or deception, 257; and stress, 125, 130. *See also* Conglomerate

Allegheny International, and white knight rescue, 67

Ambiguity: acceptance of, 104-105; in announced combination stage, 89, 93-95; aspects of, 87-107; background on, 87-88; benefits of, 105; in combination aftermath, 89, 99-100; in combination planning stage, 89, 91-93; in combination stages, 88-102; conclusion on, 106-107; cultural, 96-97, 104-105; effects of, 104-106; environmental, 90, 103, 104-105; at formal combination stage, 89, 97-99; and information, 91-92, 100, 102-103; in initial combination process, 89, 96-97; in organizational combinations, 102-106; at precombination stage, 88-91; in psychological combination stage, 89, 100-102; role, 104-105; and stress, 115; structural, 104-105; types of, 103-104

American Bankers Association, 7, 13, 16, 71, 72, 82-83, 84, 94, 135, 143, 144, 146, 147, 150, 151, 173, 197, 198, 254

American Express Corporation, structure of, 158

American Motors Corporation (AMC): in megamerger, 4; and product extension, 63

Announced combination stage, ambiguity in, 89, 93-95

Anxiety, and stress, 115

Arm-wrestling stage: in bank merger, 32, and stress, 119

Assimilation, and cultural change, 173

Assumptions, shared, and acculturation, 172

Printed in the United States
89632LV00007B/44/A